A History of Progress

Chronicle of the AUDI AG

Audi UW (1934)

DKW Front (1931)

Horch 853 (1937)

Wanderer W21 (1933)

Foreword

"A History of Progress" first appeared as an AUDI publication (the German title is "Rad der Zeit") in 1973. Since then it has been updated at frequent intervals, to include the latest company facts and figures. "A History of Progress" has built up a loyal readership among AUDI owners and other enthusiasts for the marque.

This edition of "A History of Progress" has been completely revised and redesigned. The text has been rewritten to take into account recent research findings and to include data and statistics from the archives. Among the illustrations are many which have not been previously published.

Once again, the focus of attention is not so much current events as the background and development of the company which now bears the name AUDI AG. This record makes clear the extent to which its traditions extend right back into the nineteenth century and today form a fundamental element in a modern marque's conception of itself.

AUDI AG
PR/Public Affairs

Contents

*WANDERER W25 K
(1936)*

HORCH 853 (1937)

AUTO UNION
1000 Sp (1958)

Audi A8
(1994)

The corporate "family tree"

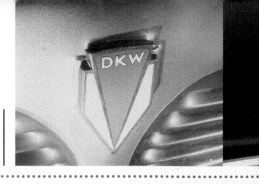

1909 AUDI

1899 HORCH

1907 DKW

1885 WANDERER

1873 NSU

*1960 NSU
Motorenwerke AG*

1932
AUTO UNION AG

1949
AUTO UNION GmbH

1969
AUDI NSU
AUTO UNION GmbH

1985
AUDI AG

The early years

How humanity acquired the automobile

The motor vehicle wasn't built in a day, so to speak. Nor in a year, or for many years in the eras which preceded our own. The desire for mobility, to voyage as effortlessly as the birds fly has always been within us – certainly for many thousands of years. Yet somehow the dream began to come true, though generations would be born before the initial sensation transformed itself into the everyday routine of motorised travel so familiar to us now, with all its joys and problems.

Famous names line the route: Aristotle, Archimedes, Hero of Alexandria, Leonardo da Vinci, Roger Bacon. None of them created an automobile, but they were convinced that people would one day be able to multiply their natural strength by means of machinery, or use it as a substitute to enhance mobility. Were these visions, or merely the rational conclusions of sages who had absorbed the teachings of natural science and understood its laws?

As the Middle Ages gave way to enlightenment, many fascinating toys, including mechanically driven vehicles, were built for the amusement of princes. They remained exceptions, like the hand-propelled wheelchair tricycle built by the paralysed Nuremberg watchmaker Stefan Farffler. They were neither faster nor more efficient than the horse, man's favoured mode of transport at the time.

The move forward from such contraptions to a mechanised means of transport had to wait until engines were available to perform the work. Historically speaking, the steam engine is the ancestor of all the heat engines invented since. It was not, of course, originally developed by its inventors with a view to propelling any form of vehicle, not even a ship. On the contrary, it was needed to pump the

Goldsworthy's steam-driven vehicle (1827 England) with a separate of lightly-loaded steered wheels at the front

The Nuremberg compass-maker Johann Hautzsch designed this spring-driven vehicle about 1650

Church's steam omnibus, operated between London and Birmingham (1832)

Propelled by pedal power: a vehicle built by Elias Richard in Paris (1674)

ground water out of Great Britain's coalmines. Not until it had proved its worth as motive power for mills, spinning machines and the like, did it occur to a clever man to harness the steam engine to a vehicle. That man was Nicolas Joseph Cugnot, a French artillery officer, who in 1769 built a steam tractor to pull cannon. This was the first road vehicle to be driven by a heat engine, and it marks the very beginning of the motor vehicle's history.

The first road accident

Cugnot's first run ended abruptly against a garden wall – not because he had failed to see it, but because his monstrous, clumsy vehicle simply could not be manoeuvred with sufficient accuracy to avoid it. The first motor vehicle – the first road accident! And the first problem to solve: how to steer a vehicle from inside it. Teams of horses were harnessed to long shafts, but was there any similarly effective way of keeping a steam engine under control? Small wonder that this form of propulsion established itself far more quickly and comprehensively on the railway, where the problem of steering was neatly avoided.

Be that as it may, steam-driven vehicles were to be encountered surprisingly often on the nineteenth-century roads, particularly in Great Britain: we are told that by 1830 a hundred of them were in use, including 26 in London alone. Nevertheless, this form of road-vehicle propulsion was not destined to succeed: it was too heavy, too complex and suffered from a monumental thirst for water.

Cugnot's steam-driven vehicle (1769)

Its most important service to mankind was to open our eyes to the problems facing a powered road vehicle: the need for compact dimensions, for some form of non-solid fuel and for a more versatile means of transmitting the power, which proved initially to be the chain.

As the face of Europe was changed by the industrial revolution in the 18th and 19th centuries, the steam engine became its symbol. But other power sources were desperately being sought: small ones in particular, suitable for immediate, short-term operation.

When what we know as coal gas was developed at the beginning of the 19th century, the turn of the internal combustion engine had come. Up to a dozen English, French and Italian inventors designed, built and tested gas engines, but it was 1860 before the Belgian Lenoir succeeded in Paris in demonstrating the first stationary gas engine which used piston movement to draw in a fuel-air mixture, and which promised to be economically viable in operation.

Adding movement to an idea

Only four years later, there were 130 such engines at work in the French capital city, and reports of their success reached the ears of a German businessman named Nikolaus August Otto. He was not technically skilled, and it took him many years, all his savings and the loss of his profession before, with the help of

Eugen Langen, he achieved a sensational breakthrough: the direct-acting four-stroke engine. Otto and Langen set up the Gasmotorenfabrik Deutz AG, and for ten years employed a certain Gottlieb Daimler as their production manager, who

later joined forces with Wilhelm Maybach to develop the small, high-speed motor-vehicle engine, using petrol (gasoline) as a fuel. At the same time, a few hundred kilometres up the Rhine, Carl Benz was building a vehicle powered by an internal combustion engine. The patent granted to him on January 29th, 1886 is generally regarded as the motor vehicle's birth certificate. This is where its pre-history ends and its history begins.

Before long, this automobile was being manufactured on a scale greater than craft methods would have allowed. By

As this century began, so did mobility: cyclists and pedestrians but also buses and cars were to be seen in our city centres (this is the Friedrichstrasse in Berlin))

midway through the 1890s, Benz was urgently looking for someone capable of running his motor-vehicle assembly operations. August Horch proved to be that man. Between 1896 and 1899, he occupied a senior position in Mannheim and could be said to have supervised the introduction of the motor vehicle. In his last year with Benz, the factory produced 572 vehicles; no other manufacturer in the world matched this figure.

Since the eighteen-sixties and seventies, Germany's industry had enjoyed an unparalleled boom. Immense strides in metallurgy and mechanical engineering had given rise to the term "The Age of Steel", and the pace of life accelerated at an incredible rate. Romantic idylls were abandoned, vast cities were built. Progress in science and technology was marked by events and personages whose names were soon to be household words. In 1872 Ernst Abbe developed the first

Richard Trevithick's steam-driven vehicle (1801) was steered by a single front wheel

microscope for the Zeiss workshops. Three years later Carl von Linde produced the first ammonia-cooled refrigerating system and ushered in the era of low-temperature engineering. His lectures were later attended by a certain Rudolf Diesel, who was obsessed by the urge to build the perfect engine. In 1879 Werner von Siemens exhibited the world's first electric locomotive in Berlin. Before the century was out, Schott had developed high-temperature glass, Mannesmann was manufacturing seamless tubes, Hertz had formulated the principle of electrical frequencies, Röntgen had discovered X-rays – and Diesel's engine was a runner! Otto, Benz and Daimler made equally outstanding contributions to this magnificent mosaic of scientific and technical mastery. A belief in the powers of technology grew up in Germany, strengthened by confidence in the engineers' skills and the abundance of technical innovation that was there for all to see. Between 1877 and 1907, no less than 195,000 patents were granted in the German Reich.

A new day dawns

These were the years in which technical progress flowed unceasingly from laboratories and academics' studies, from workshops and universities, and caught the fancy of the "man in the street". Inside factories, the nature of the work began to change; at home, life itself was different, and in the streets, on the rail-

Cycles with two, three or four wheels, high and low frames, either sporting or with the emphasis on comfort, flooded the streets at the end of the 19th century

The HORCH automobile's "birth certificate" (1901)

ways and on the water, the pattern of modern mobility was emerging. All of society was caught up in these epoch-making changes, of which the development of the automobile was one.

From the very outset the automobile had something rather special to offer its users: a means of multiplying their effective mobility. What could have been more in accord with the country's pioneering spirit ? The railway had provided a foretaste of what travel could mean, and the bicycle too had started on its all-conquering way by the end of the 19th century. The freedom that mobility offered was for the first time sensed as a personal desire, and tens of thousands of people were prepared to spend their money to satisfy it. Early traffic surveys tell us that by 1899 there were more bicycles on the roads than any other form of passenger vehicle. Germany's municipalities had begun to electrify their tramlines by 1891, and within 20 years every German town with a population of more than 100,000 was operating its own tram system. Passenger levels went up unceasingly – a sure sign of the still-unsatisfied demand for greater mobility. What was therefore more logical than the next step: to create an increasingly reliable form of motorised transport at reasonable cost, without recourse to a fixed transport infrastructure? This was the demand which the automobile industry was created to satisfy.

Horch

Before the turn of the century, more than three dozen companies were already building automobiles in Germany. One of them was August Horch & Cie, established on November 14th, 1899 with head offices in Cologne. Its founder was one of the pioneering engineers in the motor-vehicle field. Even while still an apprentice and journeyman, Horch had frequently demonstrated his practical skills when there were complex problems to be solved. By the mid-1890s, as a graduate in engine construction, he had become increasingly interested in the motor vehicle. In 1896 he succeeded in obtaining a post with Benz & Cie in Mannheim, where he was soon promoted to be manager of the motor vehicle construction department. He held this key position at the epicentre of the still-young automobile industry for three years, obtaining an excellent picture of the motor vehicle's growing pains and development problems. With this knowledge and experience at his disposal, Horch set up in business on his own account in 1899, initially repairing motor vehicles which were already in use and replacing the Bosch contact-breaker ignition system by a linkage which he had himself developed and patented.

The start of a legend

Horch was soon hard at work designing his first automobile, which he was able to test-drive at the beginning of January 1901. Its engine was at the front, a concept for which Horch had fought in vain while working for Benz. To eliminate the drawbacks of the hammer-blow caused by a horizontal cylinder located along the vehicle's direction of travel, but also the unsatisfactory opposed engine, the two cylinders of Horch's new engine had a common combustion chamber. Horch referred to this as his "impact-free" engine. The gearbox was mounted on the frame, behind the rear axle, and was in unit with the differential. From there, power was transmitted to internally toothed gear rings bolted to the rear wheels.

A HORCH sightsee-ing bus (17 passen-gers) with the seats ascending towards the back (1912)

The first HORCH car from Saxony, a two-cylinder model (1902/03)

Ludwig Kathe in a HORCH for the Prince Heinrich Run, for which he built the body (1908)

Delivery van on 10/30 chassis (1913)

The gearbox contained constant-mesh wheels with double helical teeth, shifts being made by small intermediate clutches. A particularly interesting decision on Horch's part was to cast the crankcase from light alloy.

Early in 1902 Horch moved his factory to Reichenbach in Saxony, where a local businessman had offered him the capital needed to establish an automobile manufacturing operation. Once again, Horch was busy at the drawing board with plans for a new car. In the period which followed, he put many an innovative idea into practice, for instance shaft drive to the wheels and the use of chrome-nickel steel for heavily stressed gearwheels. Convinced of the importance of reducing mass by the use of light alloys, he was now using them for the gearbox and differential housings as well as for the crankcase.

In 1904, Horch transferred his head offices to the town of Zwickau and converted the firm into a share-issuing company. Production expanded relatively rapidly, from 18 cars in 1903 to 94 in 1907; a year later the magic figure of 100 was exceeded. Whereas only two-cylinder cars were built in Reichenbach, the HORCH factory in Zwickau produced only four-cylinder vehicles. After moving to the new premises, a further significant technical decision was made: as one of the first automobile engine designers to do so, Horch adopted overhead inlet valves. Driving a car with this latest type of OHV engine, the Zwickau lawyer Dr. Stöss won the Herkomer Run in 1906, one of the most arduous international motoring competitions of the time.

Horch formulated his company's philosophy in quite unequivocal terms: "I was determined in all circumstances to build only strong, good-quality cars!" This was the approach which the HORCH marque pursued throughout its existence.

The four-cylinder models from Zwickau had 22 horsepower engines initially, increasing later to 40 hp. These power outputs were obtained from swept volumes of 2.2 and 5.8 litres respectively. The cars were lavishly equipped, with technical features of great strength.

Horch's experiments with a six-cylinder engine were a failure, nor did his cars quite live up to the reputation gained from further sensational competition successes. Try as he might, Horch could not repeat his victory in the Herkomer Run. His board of directors and supervisory board were riddled with squabbling and intrigue. When these disputes reached their peak, Horch had had enough, and left the company on June 16th, 1909 with the shamefully small sum of 20,000 Marks in his pocket by way of compensation.

Luxury in the style of the times

Starting afresh

Less than a month elapsed before this pioneering engineer had set up a new HORCH company: it was entered in the trade register as a limited partnership on July 16th, 1909. Horch had needed only 72 hours to obtain the necessary capital of 200,000 Marks.

Following Horch's departure, Fritz Seidel took over as chief designer and Heinrich Paulmann as technical director, and were able for a long time to utilise the legacy left to them by the company's founder.

One of their very first moves was to protect the HORCH name after the sudden departure of its owner, by means of no fewer than 13 trade-mark applications. By January 10th, 1910 these had risen to 26, covering every possible combination of the name which could have been applied to a technical product of some

kind. Even the actual name "A. Horch" was protected as a final precaution! This was precisely what the bearer of the name, August Horch himself, had failed to do, thus ruining his chances of running another company under his own name. Horch's fundamental development principles remained valid for Seidel and Paulmann: good quality and strength. They launched a new 28 hp car, with an engine that was later uprated to 35 and finally 40 horsepower. With Horch's views on engine valve gear from just after the turn of the century as their guide, it was not surprising that their products were still among the best the German automobile industry had to offer even in 1913. In the 10 hp tax category at the time, only six makes used an engine with overhead inlet valves; MERCEDES, HORCH and WINDHOFF operated these valves from the piston, whereas AUDI, KOMNICK and NACKE did so via the exhaust valves.

Economic strategy

The two new men in control of HORCH were fully aware that even with the order books full, economic production methods were essential. This in turn called for various design changes, notably the change from cylinders cast in pairs to a single engine block. The new designs had side valves. Smaller cars for newcomers to motoring also took shape on the drawing boards. In 1911, 6/18 hp and 8/24 hp models were introduced. They were obviously modern in design, with a smooth engine block and extremely good road behaviour. For the Summer of 1914 the introduction of an even smaller car was planned, to be called the Pony and to have a 1.3-litre, four-cylinder engine developing 14 horsepower. The HORCH company also intended to launch a series of sleeve-valve engines. These were considered to be particularly smooth-running, but were of course more complex to manufacture and needed very careful attention to detail design features. To avoid any commercial risk, HORCH planned to import Daimler engines from Great Britain for these cars, with sleeve valve gear manufactured in accordance with the American engineer Knight's patents.

Then came the outbreak of the First World War, and both plans – small car and sleeve valve engines – had to be postponed indefinitely.

For the 1914 model year, the HORCH product programme consisted of four

basic types, powered by 30, 40, 50 and 60 horsepower four-cylinder single-block engines. There were also obsolescent models still in production and even intermediate types, obtained in the modern style by varying the engines' bore and stroke. Vehicles for commercial purposes were also becoming increasingly important. HORCH built its first trucks before the outbreak of hostilities: the first-ever HORCH commercial vehicle was an ambulance dating from 1910. The company also supplied automobile chassis designed to carry various items of machinery, for instance silage choppers. The 8/24 chassis was used for a variety of delivery van bodies, which proved to be extremely popular. With the 40 and 50 hp engines, light omnibusses and small truck bodies were also feasible, and the 55 hp engine proved capable of powering a 3-tonner complete on occasion with trailer. Just before war was declared, a 33/80 hp car was announced; in this case its four-cylinder engine had the cylinders cast in pairs and boasted the impressive displacement of 8 litres.

This 18/50 hp HORCH was evidently in use as a demonstrator (1913)

Dates in the history of HORCH

1899 August Horch & Cie established on November 14th in Cologne

1902 August Horch & Cie Motor- und Motorwagenbau set up in Reichenbach on March 3rd

1904 August Horch Motorwagenwerke AG established on May 10th in Zwickau

1918 Change of name to Horchwerke AG Zwickau on February 16th; capital 3 million Marks

The principal HORCH models, 1901–1918

Designation	Number/layout of cylinders	Bore x stroke in mm	Displacement in cm³	Horsepower	Years of manufacture
Model 1	2			4-5	1901
Model 2	2 inline		2500	10-12	1902–1904
Model 3	4 inline	85 x 105	2383	18-21	1903–1905
Model 4	4 inline	85 x 100	2270	14-17	1903–1905
- for competition:	4 inline	85 x 120	2725	22-25	1903–1905
Model 5	4 inline	115 x 140	5810	35-40	1903–1905
Z	4 inline	84 x 120	2660	11/22	1906–1909
ZD	4 inline	115 x 140	5810	23/40	1906–1910
6-cylinder	6 inline	115 x 140	8725	31/60	1907–1908
S	4 inlinc	115 x 155	6440	25/55	1908–1922
K	4 inline	83 x 120	2600	10/25	1910–1911
H	4 inline	100 x 135	4240	17/42	1910–1919
C	4 inline	74,5 x 120	2090	8/24	1911–1922
N	4 inline	80 x 130	2600	10/30	1911–1921
P	4 inline	100 x 150	4710	18/50	1914–1922

The first HORCH took to the road in January 1901. By December 31st, 1918 about 9,100 HORCH vehicles had been produced. Only chassis were supplied: the bodies had to be obtained from coachbuilders. Between 1901 and 1910 a HORCH chassis cost between 9,400 and 16,300 Marks, depending on engine size.

In 1904, its first year of business, the company employed about 100 people; by 1918 the total was 1,800. Turnover rose to 5.8 million Marks by 1914, and had reached 30 million Marks by 1918.

August Horch

1868	Born in Winningen (Moselle) on October 12th, 1868 Apprentice and journeyman smith Technical studies in Mittweida Plant engineer for an engine manufacturer
1896	Joined Benz in Mannheim as manager of the motor-vehicle assembly department until 1899
1899	Opened his own workshop in Cologne
1902	Business transferred to Reichenbach, in the Vogtland region
1904	Establishment of A. HORCH Motorwagenwerke AG in Zwickau
1909	Dispute and departure; AUDI factory set up in Zwickau
1912–1914	Triumphant successes for AUDI cars in the world's toughest competition events
1920	Horch moved to Berlin and acted as an expert and consultant on technical motor-vehicle matters
1922	Honorary doctorate from Brunswick College of Advanced Technology on February 20th
1932	On the supervisory board of Auto Union AG in Chemnitz
1944	Bombed out several times in Berlin; moved to Langenhessen in Saxony
1945	Fled to the Upper Palatinate and took up residence in Münchberg.
1949–1950	Helped to set up the new Auto Union in Ingolstadt
1951	August Horch died on February 3rd in Münchberg at the age of 83

August Horch was one of the pioneers of motor-vehicle engineering. Before the turn of the century he was working on the initial problems facing the automobile, and made many significant contributions towards solving them in practice, notably the very first applications of aluminium for the engine block, the introduction of shaft drive and the use of high-strength steels in the transmission. Horch's activities as an engineer were concentrated above all on taking the automobile as a still-new invention and improving it consistently until it became practical for day-to-day use.

After 1909, Horch had no further connection with the automobiles bearing his name. He left the HORCH company which he had previously established, and devoted his energies in later years to the AUDI marque.

The HORCH 33/80 hp Phaeton (1914) already had electric lights

*August Horch
(1868 - 1951)*

August Horch speaks about his motoring experiences in the very first years of the automobile:

"Below the ring on the steering column there were two handles, used to transfer the drive belt from the engine to the layshaft. Below the steering tiller, on the left, was a lever to vary the strength of the fuel-air mixture, and another lever connected to a rod which led to the throttle butterfly. This rod was used to open and close the throttle and thus vary the speed of the engine. Also to the driver's left was the handbrake, which acted on the rear tyre. To start the engine, the flywheel had to be turned; in those days, even the starting handle was a thing of the future. The flywheel was turned until the mixture ignited; this was not only an exciting moment but a strenuous one too. If ignition failed to take place, the next step was to hurry round to the front of the vehicle and turn the mixture control lever. But even if one was fortunate and the mixture did ignite, one still had to rush back to the controls and adjust the throttle lever until the engine ran regularly. Then, with God's blessing, the journey could begin.

"One climbed on to the driver's seat and selected low gear at the lever under the steering tiller. This moved the belt, which was running on the smallest diameter of the stepped pulley, slowly on to the fixed layshaft pulley. The vehicle then began to move at its lowest speed of three to five kilometres an hour. On reaching a speed of eight kilometres an hour, the belt had to be shifted to the second, larger pulley, after which the vehicle could be driven up to its maximum speed of eighteen kilometres an hour."

Poster on the mutation from HORCH to AUDI (1910)

The birth of AUDI

The new company bearing the name August Horch Automobilwerke GmbH was entered in the Zwickau trade register on July 16th, 1909. This led to an immediate protest from the existing HORCH company, which took action before the Imperial courts and won its case. Horch was forbidden to use his name for another automobile company. His next move was recorded by the trade register in Zwickau on April 25th, 1910 as follows: the new company's name was changed to AUDI Automobilwerke GmbH.

Horch's first aim was to publicise the new name without sacrificing the company's existing identity. Work began in much the same way as Horch's initial business venture: with maintenance work and repairs. The reputable name of August Horch proved to have a powerful publicity effect. Work began even before the company was officially registered, and provided it with a solid financial basis in these early days. Although Horch began to design a new car without delay, aided by Hermann Lange, who had moved with him from the old company as chief engineer, more than a year none the less elapsed before the first car was delivered from the factory in Zwickau, in July 1910. August Horch's name was to be found on every advertisement in these early years, and was used to maximum effect on every AUDI poster as well. Furthermore, Horch pursued a policy of entering his vehicles for motor sport events, having long since realised that the general public responded positively to such successes. His participation in the International Austrian Alpine Run in May 1911 proved to be a most fortunate decision. The event had been held only for small cars since 1906, but touring-car entries were invited for the first time in 1910. In subsequent years this event effectively took over from the famous Prince Henry runs, with conditions becoming increasingly severe. In the 1911 Alpine run, for example, only ten of the 75 vehicles which left the starting line reached their destination without penalty points. August Horch took the wheel of his new AUDI personally, and

The first AUDI, seen in July 1910 in front of the shop in Munich run by Zeidler, its owner

won the driver's trophy after negotiating 2,250 kilometres of exceptionally tough mountain passes and Alpine roads successfully. A year later, in June 1912, a complete AUDI team was entered for the Alpine Run: three AUDI cars secured the team prize, a triumph which they promptly repeated in 1913. However, it was in the 1914 event that the AUDI entries demonstrated their superiority over the competition to maximum effect. Five cars went to the starting line, driven by Horch, Graumüller, Lange, Obruba and Muri. All of them completed the course without penalty. The leading German-language motoring journal of the time, the "Motorwagen", commented on AUDI's victory in the following terms: "Above all, the result is a major triumph for the German AUDI marque, which entered five cars for this event and brought them all home across the finishing line without incurring a single penalty. This victory on AUDI's part need come as no surprise: on previous Alpine Runs, AUDI cars have always achieved the best results ..."

The Alpine Trophy

From Sport to market success

The cars with which AUDI pulled off this triumphant success bore the unmistakable marks of the school of design headed by August Horch. The engines had a familiar feature: valve gear with overhead inlet and side exhaust valves, the one positioned directly above the other. The exceptionally wide crankcase was another such trade-mark: it provided additional protection underneath the car and also had a load-bearing function to perform. Horch's spur-gear differential was also to be found on the new cars; it enabled the final drive to the rear wheels to be enclosed within a very compact housing.

As had been the usual practice at the first HORCH company, AUDI designated its models by capital letters. A start was made logically enough with A in 1910, and by the outbreak of the First World War the letter E had been reached. In all cases, these models had four-cylinder engines, with

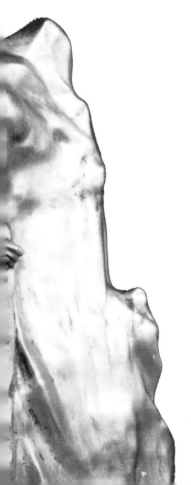

A smile from a multiple winner: August Horch in his AUDI at the end of the International Austrian Alpine Run (1914)

the Type C gaining lasting fame as the winner of the Alpine Run, a title also bestowed on succeeding models. Its 14/35 horsepower engine had a crankshaft of entirely new design, offset by 14 millimetres from the engine's centreline and running in three gunmetal main bearings with a cast white-metal surface layer. The exhaust valves in these engines were angled, to reduce the length of the gas flow path and enable the shape of the combustion chamber to be improved.

After his first spectacular successes, Horch had aimed this, his third new model, more and more specifically at motor sport. Experience had shown that the cars' main weakness lay in the engine's cooling system. A sturdy design capable of surviving long distances reliably was needed.

HORCH therefore provided extremely generous cooling water jacketing round the ignition points, the exhaust valves and the internal exhaust ports. Together with a large-area radiator, this solved any thermal problems so effectively that the vehicles were able to tackle a succession of Alpine passes without their cooling systems needing the assistance of a water pump. Gaining the Alpine Trophy outright after successive wins from 1912 to 1914 was of immense importance for AUDI's subsequent development. It helped to establish the company and consolidate its reputation within a remarkably short time. This reputation was based on the company founder's two overriding ambitions: on the sporting side, to be faster and better than all the others, but also to build vehicles that were reliable in severe conditions and entirely suitable for practical use. Instead of producing highly-tuned individual cars in order to secure success in competition, the aim was to make every AUDI equally efficient and practical for its user. The competition successes extending over several years were evidence that this objective had been achieved.

August Horch's hopes of being able to increase production and sales came to fruition rapidly as a result of his vehicles' competition successes. If 1911 is taken as the first full year of production, output of motor vehicles doubled by 1914 – the same rate of growth as was enjoyed by the rival company HORCH in the same town.

Last but not least, it is only fair to state that with his series of motor sport triumphs Horch was able to justify his own methods in the most convincing way possible. The design of the Type B and C cars, the Alpine Run champions, was undoubtedly one of the climaxes in his creative technical career.

Although the competition successes referred to above most definitely established the reputation of AUDI as a manufacturer of automobiles, output in numerical terms none the less remained modest. By the time war broke out, the plant in Zwickau had built precisely 754 cars, equivalent to an annual output of under 200. Growth could certainly have been more rapid, had it not been for a lack of capital within the new company. For this reason Horch had begun to prepare the way, during the last few days and months of peace, to convert AUDI into a share-issuing company.

On 21st December 1914 and on 14th and 20th May 1915, with effect from 1st January 1915, the new AUDI Werke AG company was established in Zwickau with a capital of one and a half million Marks. Its directors were August Horch (sales), Hermann Lange (technical) and Werner Wilm (general administration).

An AUDI engine with cylinders cast in pairs, non-detachable cylinder head and light alloy cross-member (1913)

A new chapter

The designated duties of the new board of directors were a sign that August Horch intended to withdraw from the technical and design side of the work. This was to be taken on by Hermann Lange, assisted as chief designer by the graduate engineer Erich Horn, who had been with the company since 1910.

Success multiplied by three

In the five years of the AUDI company's existence before the First World War, the three-man team of Horch, Lange and Horn had created no less than five passenger-car and two truck models. All of these designs exhibited quite astonishing creativity and powers of engineering design. For a small company, admittedly, such a large and varied range of models is normally regarded as a recipe for disaster rather than for successful growth. With this model policy, however, Horch was able to supply evidence of his skill in combining unity with variety and achieving highly practical results. The engine castings used for Type B to E models, for instance, differed only in stroke and bore, but were of identical external dimensions. The crankcases, with their box-pattern extensions, were identical in size and could therefore be installed in the same frame side mem-

Praise and fame for the "Alpine" victors

bers. Track and wheelbase of Types B and C were also identical. Horch and his technical colleagues were able to demonstrate the logical steps leading to efficiency in production and systematic standardisation. It was quite possibly for this reason that he was honoured with membership of the German automobile industry's standardisation committee.

AUDI taxicab on Type B chassis (1913)

Dates in the history of AUDI

1909	Establishment of August Horch Automobilewerke GmbH in Zwickau on 16th July, after Horch himself has parted from the original Horch Werke AG
1910	On 10th April, change in the new company's name to AUDI Werke GmbH, with head offices in Zwickau, after defeat in a legal dispute
1915	From 21st January on, re-organisation of AUDI in Zwickau as a share-issuing company (AG) with a capital of 1,500,000 Marks

The principal AUDI models, 1910–1918

Designation	Number/layout of cylinders	Bore x stroke in mm	Swept volume in cc	Output in hp	Years of manufacture	Notes
A	4 inline	80 x 130	2600	10/22	1910–1912	
B	4 inline	80 x 130	2600	11/28	1911–1917	
C	4 inline	90 x 140	3560	14/35	1911–1925	
Ct	4 inline	90 x 140	3560	14/35	1912–1928	Truck
D	4 inline	100 x 150	4710	18/45	1911–1920	
E	4 inline	110 x 150	5700	22/50	1911–1924	
G	4 inline	75 x 118	2071	8/22	1914–1926	

The company employed 33 people in 1909, its first business year, and 543 by 1918. The first AUDI was built in July 1910, another 753 by 1914. Total AUDI output up to December 31st, 1918 was 2,130. Only chassis were supplied; the bodies had to be constructed by selected coachbuilding companies. The first AUDI chassis, dating from 1910, was listed at a price of 8,500 Marks.

August Hermann Lange

*August Hermann Lange
(1867–1922)*

1867	Born on 7th November 1867 in Strehla near Torgau as the son of landowner August Lange and his wife Amalie (née Kopsch)
1874–1884	Attended school in Leipzig
1884	On 1st April, started a three-year training period as a lathe operator at Bleichert & Co, mechanical engineers, in Leipzig, where he was taken on as an apprentice and worked until 2nd November, 1888
1892–1894	Studied engineering at the technical college in Mittweida
1894–1895	Designer for the engine manufacturer Grob & Co in Leipzig
1895	From 1st November, designer at the engine manufacturer Leipziger Dampfmaschinen- und Motorenfabrik
1897	From 1st January, designer and later manager of the experimental engine installation at Rheinischen Gasmotoren- fabrik Benz & Co in Mannheim
1904	From 1st April on, works manager and independent designer for the engine manufacturer Osers & Bauer in Vienna
	From 1st September on, Technical Director of the Horchwerke AG in Zwickau (appointed engineer-in-charge in 1905)
1909	From July on: Technical Director, later Plant Director of AUDI
1915	Member of the Board of Directors
1922	Died of cardiac asthma on 19th February 1922 in Zwickau; his grave can be seen in the town's main cemetery

August Horch describes how the AUDI brand name was created

"We weren't allowed to trade as August Horch, although this was my own name! We held a meeting without delay in Franz Fikentscher's apartment, and spent some time thinking about an alternative name. We were all aware that we couldn't leave the meeting without having come up with a different name for our company. I can't convey to you just how many strange and improbable names we dreamed up that day.

"One of Franz's sons sat quietly in a corner of the room and learned his home-work – or at least pretended to do so. In actual fact he was listening to our high-ly interesting and heated discussion with all the passion that lurks within a young man's breast. He seemed to be on the brink of saying something on sever-al occasions, but swallowed his words and went back to work. Then suddenly it burst out of him like an active volcano: he turned to his father and exclaimed: 'Father – audiatur et altera pars ... wouldn't it be a good idea to call it AUDI instead of HORCH?' This gem of an idea had us all speechless with amazement and enthusiasm."

Luxurious interior equipment and trim for the demanding customer

An AUDI ambulance (1913)

And then a WANDERER came along

On 15th February 1885 two mechanics, J. B. Winklhofer and R. A. Jaenicke, set up a repair business for bicycles in Chemnitz. Shortly afterwards they began to make bicycles of their own, since demand at the time was consistently high. These were sold under the WANDERER name, and in 1896 the company itself began to trade as the WANDERER Fahrradwerke AG, formerly Winklhofer and Jaenicke.

Six years before that date, Winklhofer had started to manufacture the milling machines needed for the production of bicycles; in due course, this became a separate production division of the company. From 1904 onwards, there were also WANDERER typewriters, sold under the name "Continental", and in 1909 adding and subtracting machines were introduced to the office machinery range.

The first WANDERER motorcycle, however, predated these events by some years: it was of 1.5 hp, with a single-cylinder air-cooled engine, with an inlet valve in the cylinder head of the snifting type, operated by pressure in the cylinder. Only the exhaust valve was positively actuated by a camshaft. This motorcycle weighed 45 kilograms and was able to reach a top speed of 50 km/h. It was distinctly arduous to ride at that speed, no doubt, since it had no form of suspension whatsoever until 1905, when a sprung front fork was introduced. By that time, engine power had gone up threefold, permitting speeds of up to 80 km/h. In 1910, an even more powerful twin-cylinder motorcycle appeared; from this time on WANDERER motorcycles boasted rear suspension, a centre stand and a rear-wheel brake. As an option at extra charge, a kick-starter could be ordered as well.

The idea of branching out into automobile production was clearly in the air. A prototype had in fact been constructed in conditions of some secrecy in 1905: a small two-seater powered by a twin-cylinder engine. It had no particularly note-

This WANDERER prototype (1905) had no successor

A WANDERER motorcycle with 500 cc twin-cylinder engine (1914)

The "Puppchen" had two seats in tandem

worthy features, and its driveline and body were in line with what competitors were already offering at the time. Those in charge at WANDERER evidently felt little enthusiasm for this first prototype, and so another design was prepared, this time with a four-cylinder engine, and built in 1907 or thereabouts. This too was clearly not regarded as sufficiently promising, and in any case the German automobile industry had just passed through a period of crisis which had seen the demise of a number of seemingly successful marques. Clearly this was reason enough to be extra-cautious. Furthermore, fiscal legislation in 1906 had imposed a considerable financial burden on large cars, leading to something of a flood of smaller models on the market in the years which followed. The lower price group evidently offered the best sales prospects for a new car. Nor was WANDERER prepared to risk launching an immature or largely unproven design, only to have to eliminate its teething troubles after series production had commenced. It was this desire to introduce a high-quality product which explained the experimental period lasting a number of years which culminated in the appearance of the WANDERER "Puppchen" (which could perhaps be translated in modern terms as "Baby Doll").

On 27th August 1912, two members of the WANDERER company's staff undertook a trial run through the Northern and Southern Tyrol. Eleven days later, they and the car arrived back in Chemnitz in the best of spirits, having mastered the high mountain passes en route and their seemingly endless series of hairpin bends with absolute ease. The 12 horsepower, four-cylinder engine and the light, delicately styled car which it drove had proved to satisfy all their creators' hopes in terms of performance and economy. WANDERER's basic concept was thus justified. Indeed, the company was so convinced that it was on the right path that an engineer who offered it his own plans for a small car was shown the door forthwith: his name was Ettore Bugatti.

There can be no reproaching the company for its self-confident attitude, as events subsequently proved: for 15 years, this small car with its affectionate nickname not only earned good money for the WANDERER automobile division but was in fact one of the best small-car designs on the German market.

Dates in the history of WANDERER

1885	On 26th February, establishment of the "Chemnitzer-Velociped-Depot Winklhofer & Jaenicke"
1887	On 4th January, adoption of the WANDERER name for the company's bicycles
1896	Change of company name to WANDERER Fahrradwerke AG (formerly Winklhofer & Jaenicke, Schönau/Chemnitz) on 5th May
1900	Start of machine tool production
1902	Start of motorcycle production
1904	Start of typewriter production ("Continental" brand)
1905	First experiments in automobile design
1908	From 15th January on: WANDERER Werke, prev. Winklhofer & Jaenicke AG; capital: 1,600,000 Marks, increased in 1915 to 5,250,000 Marks
1913	Start of WANDERER automobile production
1918	By this year, well over 10,000 motorcycles and over 2,000 automobiles had been built. The price of the 1.5 hp motorcycle was some 750 Marks; the WANDERER Puppchen automobile cost 4,000 Marks

The principal WANDERER automobile types up to 1918

Designation	Number/layout of cylinders	Bore x stroke in mm	Displacement in cc	Output in hp	Years of manufacture	Notes
W 3	4 inline	64 x 95	1222	5/12	1913–1914	"Pupp
W 3/II	4 inline	64 x 100	1280	5/15	1914–1919	

The principal WANDERER motorcycle types up to 1918

Designation	Number/layout of cylinders	Bore x stroke in mm	Displacement in cc	Output in hp	Years of manufacture
	1			1.5	1902
	1			2.5	1904
	2			3	1910
	1	60 x 70	198	1.5	1912
	2	60 x 72	408	2.5	1914

Johann Baptist Winklhofer (1859–1949)

Johann Baptist Winklhofer

1859	Born on 23rd June 1859 in Munich; son of a brewer
1875	After apprenticeship in the Imperial Laboratories in Munich, began work as a lathe operator
1880	Moved to the Josef Hofer mechanical engineering company in Ingolstadt, remaining there until 1883
1883	From 1883 on, Winklhofer was a travelling salesman for the British high-wheel bicycle manufacturer Rudge; in this job, he made the acquaintance of his later partner Jaenicke
1885	Set up a bicycle repair shop in Chemnitz with Jaenicke, converting it into a share-issuing company in 1896
1897	From 1st October on, sole chairman of the board of directors of the WANDERER Fahrradwerke AG bicycle company
1902	Retired as chairman of the board on 4th October 1902 and joined the supervisory board, on which he remained until 1929
1911	Granted Commercial Counsellor's title by the government
1916	Established a company in Munich to make munitions and later chains. These became well-known under the IWIS brand name, an abbreviation for "Johann Winklhofer Söhne"
1949	Winklhofer dies in Landsberg am Lech on 28th March 1949

10 commandments for the ambitious, as set down by J. B. Winklhofer, the founder of WANDERER

1. A thorough understanding of one's own profession is a basic prerequisite. 2. The urge to do everything better than anyone else can. 3. Adherence to the principle that the customer must be supplied with the best possible value for money. 4. The work must always remain a source of pleasure. 5. The factory should always use the latest working methods and the finest equipment. 6. The bulk of the money which is earned must be devoted to the acquisition of these business improvements. 7. The right man must be allocated to the right job. 8. Live a simple, sound life, so that the work can be tackled from an early hour with a clear head. 9. Be aware of the fact that not every transaction can or must be undertaken. 10. Finally, a large portion of patience is needed when waiting for one's endeavours to be crowned with success, even if the prospects sometimes look black.

DKW gets up steam

Jörgen Skafte Rasmussen was born in Denmark in 1878 but came to Germany while still young. He studied engineering in Mittweida and Zwickau before settling in Chemnitz in 1904 and, with a partner, establishing the "Rasmussen & Ernst" company. On 14th October 1906, Rasmussen purchased a textile mill in Zschopau together with a plot of land in the Dischau valley nearby, and transferred the company there in the following year. The trade register entry dated 13th April 1907 only shows Rasmussen as the proprietor. The company's business activities were described as the manufacture of machinery, metal goods and fittings. It concentrated in particular on valves for steam boilers, but also made firelighters and vegetable cleaning and peeling machines.

An indirect route to the automobile

By 1909 the company was offering waste-steam recovery systems, equipment for the cleaning of rags, centrifugal oil separators, mechanical stokers, and grids and firing systems for steam-raising plant. This indicates a certain degree of specialisation in steam technology, but this aspect of the small company's activities was not to remain dominant for long.

By the nineteen-twenties, accessories for motor vehicles were gaining steadily in importance. In 1912, the company's sales prospectus included passenger-car mudguards, motor-vehicle lighting systems, anti-slip chains and vulcanising equipment. It also sold oxy-acetylene welding gear. Since 1909 the full company designation had been Rasmussen & Ernst, Zschopau and Chemnitz, Manufacturers of

The steam-driven DKW (1917)

Machinery and Fittings and Mechanical Equipment Suppliers, but by 1912 this had been simplified to Zschopauer Maschinenfabrik I.S. Rasmussen.

Plenty of steam – meagre results

Rasmussen began to experiment with a steam-driven motor vehicle in 1916. With this in mind he recruited an engineer and fellow-Dane, Mathiessen, who had acquired much experience in the design of successful steam-driven vehicles in the USA before the First World War. The project was extremely topical, in that it was inspired by the shortage of conventional fuel from which the German Reich suffered increasingly as the war continued.

Mathiessen first built a truck with a vertical-tube boiler heated with diesel oil, which he positioned behind the driver's seat. He constructed a passenger car at the same time, in this case with a flame-tube boiler behind a sheet-metal cover at the front. After having reached a pressure of 100 bar, the steam passed through a condenser direct to the twin-cylinder engine, which in turn drove the rear wheels with no intermediate gears. Steam pressure and volume could be varied according to the amount of power required.

As we have said, these experiments were stimulated by the shortage of conventional liquid fuels, and subsidised generously by the Reich's war ministry. Their eventual failure was due to technical shortcomings. The amount of water that could be carried on the vehicle was consumed too rapidly, despite the installation of a tank holding no less than 500 litres. The time-consuming task of refilling the tank would have called for water columns to be set up along the route. Nor was the available volume of steam sufficient to maintain full load on an uphill gradient. The steam-driven vehicle had a theoretical action radius of 90 kilometres, but its unladen weight was so high that six horses were needed to drag it back to the Zschopau factory in the far from infrequent eventuality of it having broken down. After the war, the experiments were halted.

Should the vehicle have proved a success and entered production, Rasmussen would have needed a name for it, and he therefore had one registered as a precautionary measure. His choice derived directly from the German words for "steam-driven vehicle": DKW ("Dampfkraftwagen"). The three letters were arranged around a volcano emitting a column of smoke.

J. S. Rasmussen's
first factory building
in Zschopau (1907)

Dates in the history of DKW

1904	The Rasmussen & Ernst company was established in Chemnitz to make exhaust steam fittings
1907	On 13th April, transfer of the company to Zschopau, where Rasmussen had purchased land in 1906. Rasmussen was registered as sole proprietor; the sales office remained in Chemnitz
1909	Rasmussen & Ernst, Zschopau-Chemnitz, Maschinen- und Armaturenfabrik, Apparatebauanstalt
1912	Zschopauer Maschinenfabrik J. S. Rasmussen

*Jörgen Skafte Rasmussen
(1878–1964)*

Jörgen Skafte Rasmussen

1878	Born on 30th July 1878 in Nakskov (Denmark) Apprenticed to a forge in Copenhagen after leaving school
1898–1900	Studied engineering in Mittweida, concluding his studies in Zwickau.
1904	Left the Rheinische Maschinenfabrik in Düsseldorf, where he had been employed as an engineer
1904	Set up in business, initially as a manufacturer of boiler fittings. Rasmussen remained in Chemnitz for the duration of the war, then moved to Zschopau
	During the 1920s, the DKW Group expanded considerably, with much support from the State Bank of Saxony. Its main lines of business were DKW engines and motorcycles
1928	Start of automobile production
	Rasmussen was one of the first businessmen to start manufacturing electrical domestic appliances and commercial refrigerators (in Scharfenstein; from 1932 on, the company was known as Deutsche Kühl- und Kraftmaschinengesellschaft mbH, Scharfenstein).
	Rasmussen actively pursued the AUTO UNION concept as an industrial group to be owned by the State Bank (though he assumed that this would be followed by reprivatisation)
1932–1934	Board member of AUTO UNION AG for technical matters
1935	Irrevocable differences of opinion regarding the management of the AUTO UNION led to Rasmussen being obliged to leave and to a subsequent court case in which he received compensation
1937	Rasmussen moved to Sacrow, near Berlin
1938	Honorary engineering doctorate from the Dresden college of advanced technology for services to motor transport on the occasion of Rasmussen's 60th birthday. At this time he was engaged in propagating the Imbert wood-gas system, which was initially manufactured by Framo
1945	At the end of the war, fled to Flensburg
1948	Return to Denmark, where he again initiated and financed the design of automobiles and motorcycles together with a Danish industrial syndicate, which built and sold three models under the DISA name
1964	Rasmussen died on 12th August 1964 in Copenhagen.

HORCH – an overview

Chassis with twin-cylinder engine (1903)

Type 23/45 hp saloon (1908)

31/60 hp six-cylinder model (1908)

Special 3-seater body for 6/18 hp chassis

August Horch during the Prince Heinrich Run (1908)

8/24 hp phaeton (1911)

Delivery van (1912)

Saloon body with detachable roof (1913)

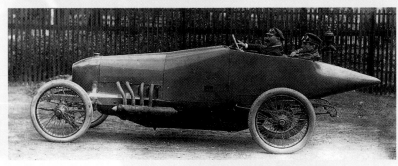

10/30 hp car for ice racing in Sweden (winner of 1st prize)

Phaeton on 14/40 hp chassis (1913)

AUDI – an overview

Type B chassis (1911)

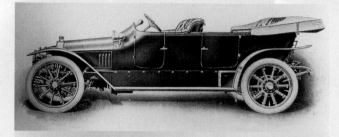

Sport Phaeton,
type A (1910)

Type A and B
phaeton (1911)

Type B delivery van
(1912)

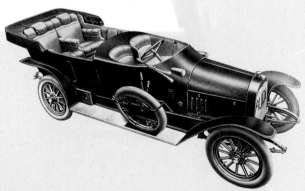

Type B phaeton
(1911)

Saloon body,
type C (1913)

Type C landaulet
(1913)

AUDI Type G 8/22 hp
sport two-seater
(1914)

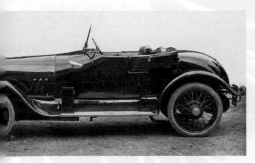

AUDI Type D
18/45 hp (1914) –
property of the King
of Saxony

WANDERER – an overview

The first WANDERER motorcycle, 1.5 hp (1902)

WANDERER 2 hp single-cylinder motorcycle (1914)

WANDERER 4 hp twin-cylinder motorcycle (1914)

The first WANDERER car, with twin-cylinder engine (1905)

WANDERER W 3 Puppchen, 5/12 hp, during a trial run in the Alps (1912)

*WANDERER
Puppchen, 5/12 hp,
with tandem seating
(1913)*

*WANDERER W 3,
5/15 hp,
side-by-side seating
(1914)*

*WANDERER Pupp-
chen, 5/15 hp, at the
starting line for the
Katschberg Trial (1914)*

*WANDERER
Puppchen, 5/15 hp,
three-seater (1914)*

*WANDERER W 3
Puppchen (1913)*

Growth between inflation and economic crisis

Parking lot in front of the Dresden Employment Office (1931)

The First World War having been brought to an end by virtue of the armistice and the Treaty of Versailles, the automobile industry began to manufacture products for the civilian population once again. Models dating from before the war were restored to the assembly lines almost unchanged, with only the electric lighting to distinguish them from those which had been sold "when the Kaiser was on the throne". Then, in the early nineteen-twenties, the German currency collapsed; although this aided exports as never before, inflation led to a total collapse of the economy by the end of 1923: the spurious boom came to an abrupt end. There was no further market for obsolete cars produced on elderly machinery.

Recovery

Various aspects of modern motor-vehicle engineering, for instance the one-piece cylinder block, left-hand drive or four-wheel brakes, and other improved technologies – the changeover from craft to volume-production methods in the assembly shop, the introduction of conveyor belts – had been neglected in the economic chaos which prevailed in the immediate post-war years. International competitors too were active on the German market, and from the mid-1920s onwards forced the domestic manufacturers to modernise their plants and adopt mass-production methods.

Automobiles were becoming more powerful and more in accordance with contemporary requirements; this in turn meant that new and more expensive manufacturing methods had to be introduced. To reduce weight, new light metals and alloys were developed with names such as Dural, Lautal, Silumin and Elektron (magnesium). They had to be machined on specially made equipment with higher cutting speeds and separate drive motors. Completely new processing methods revolutionised the equipment of the production plant. For the first time, gigantic presses and similar machines began to appear, to supply pressed-steel body elements, fittings, linkages, levers and gear wheels. With the introduction of honing, grinding technology made a step forward to surfaces of previously unattainable quality, but once again totally new machines had to be installed. Even methods of painting the cars changed: conventional stove enamelling gave way to air-drying nitro paints. Automobile manufacturers found themselves in a pioneering rôle for the whole of industry. Most of their factories, including those operated by HORCH, DKW und WANDERER, switched to assembly-line methods between 1925 and 1929; during that period, German automobile production doubled in volume.

Growth

None of the companies within the German automobile industry was in a position to finance these developments from its own resources. Nothing would have been possible without the commitment of the major banks. This was not only in view of the need for investment in new and expensive machinery, but also because financial support was needed to build up the companies' sales operations. In 1928, for instance, no fewer than 70 percent of all automobiles sold in Germany were being paid for in instalments.

The market remained in any case a restricted one. War and inflation had destroyed the financial basis previously contributed by the middle classes. The Treaty of Versailles obliged Germany to grant most-favoured-nation conditions to all the victorious powers, so that there was effectively no protection in the form of customs barriers, and competitors from various countries flocked to Germany, eager to secure their share of the market.

The streets changed their appearance once and for all as the motor vehicle took over. From 420,000 of them in Germany by 1924, the figure had risen sharply to 1,200,000 only four years later. Such growth rates were not equalled again until recent times, when German re-unification opened up an unsatisfied market in the new Eastern states. Motor vehicles were still largely restricted to the towns and cities during the 1920s. Right up to the war, the horse had been the most important source of motive power. In Berlin alone, 5,500 of them were needed to operate the bus fleet! Every year, the Berlin bus company earned itself 100,000 gold Marks simply from the sale of horse manure. The true burden on the environment can be judged from the lamentations of a contemporary writer: "The horses made their presence felt everywhere in the form of dung, and this despite the efforts of a horde of youths in red jackets, who mingled with the hooves and wheels of the traffic, armed with buckets and brooms. The buckets were dis-

Major events with tens of thousands of visitors have always stretched road transport systems to the limit

An illusion instead of an idyll: conditions in many vauable and historic town and city centres became disastrous as motorised traffic increased

charged at the kerbside, but the mess still overflowed everywhere into the roads ... or coated them with a greasy deposit, to the great delight of the pedestrians, no doubt. Not to mention the noise of passing horsedrawn vehicles, like a mighty heartbeat in every inner city area."

The remedy came in the form of the electric railway and the bus, but they could not entirely satisfy the individual's desire for personal mobility. The bicycle, of course, had long since been the "poor man's horse" which enabled him to reach certain desirable goals not accessible by rail or bus. But only motorisation as a private commodity brought true mobility to the average citizen, and even then, the motorcycle easily outnumbered the car until many years after the Second World War.

The passenger car spread through society from the top down. Luxury travel and competition came first, but in the 1920s, small cars aimed at the proverbial "man in the street" appeared, and many new technical concepts were dreamed up and put into practice.

HORCH – quality and quantity

In 1920, the majority of the shares in HORCH Werke AG was acquired by Dr. Moritz Strauss, who was already the major shareholder in the Berlin aircraft engine company Argus Flugmotorenwerke GmbH. The contacts between these two companies extended back before the First World War, when HORCH had experimented with aircraft engines to be built under licence from Argus. Nothing came of this, but the two companies remained aware of each other's activities.

After the war, the production of aircraft engines was prohibited, and therefore Dr. Strauss's contacts with HORCH acquired a more urgent character. He wasted no time in commissioning the Swiss designer Arnold Zoller to design a passenger car which would then be built at the HORCH plant in Zwickau and would, as a single model, take the place of the variety of cars which HORCH had previously offered for sale.

Zoller suggested several engines; Strauss settled for the cheapest of these. His design work took place at the Argus plant in Berlin-Reinickendorf, where he developed various experimental engines of considerable interest, all of which were rejected as too complex and too expensive. In due course Strauss and Zoller parted company, and on July 1st 1922 Paul Daimler, the son of Gottlieb Daimler, began work as the new Argus chief designer. In a consultant's agreement concluded at the same time, he undertook to update the design of the HORCH models.

In the second half of the nineteen-twenties, production capacity rose from four cars (1925) to 12 cars a day (1928), and reached the dizzy heights of 15 cars a day in the following year. Since 1927, only eight-cylinder models had been built. Paul Daimler retired in 1930, and was succeeded as HORCH's chief designer by Fritz Fiedler.

William Werner had been technical director of the HORCH Werke since the summer of 1926, and was appointed a deputy member of the board of directors a

A HORCH 10/35 in front of the Hagia Sophia (1923)

year later. He was reputedly one of the leading experts of his time in German company management.

Six months after William Werner, Fritz Zerbst joined the HORCH Werke, becoming plant manager in Zwickau a short time afterwards, a position he retained for the next fifteen years.

Within a very short space of time at the end of the 1920s, the HORCH 8 became a symbol of quality representative of the entire German automobile industry. Its exceptionally quiet, smooth running and its high standard of workmanship were among the deciding factors. The Zwickau company had amassed a unique concentration of know-how, in particular with regard to the prodcution of large

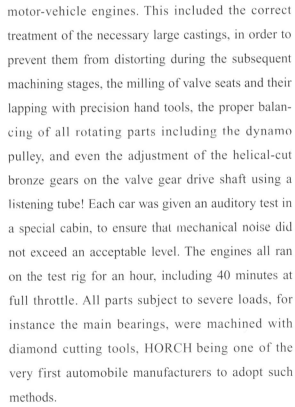

motor-vehicle engines. This included the correct treatment of the necessary large castings, in order to prevent them from distorting during the subsequent machining stages, the milling of valve seats and their lapping with precision hand tools, the proper balancing of all rotating parts including the dynamo pulley, and even the adjustment of the helical-cut bronze gears on the valve gear drive shaft using a listening tube! Each car was given an auditory test in a special cabin, to ensure that mechanical noise did not exceed an acceptable level. The engines all ran on the test rig for an hour, including 40 minutes at full throttle. All parts subject to severe loads, for instance the main bearings, were machined with diamond cutting tools, HORCH being one of the very first automobile manufacturers to adopt such methods.

The funds at the disposal of Dr. Strauss were far from sufficient to finance the purchase of all the necessary production machinery and equipment. In due course the banks – the Allgemeine Deutsche Credit Anstalt (ADCA) and the Commerzbank of Berlin – took a financial stake in the Zwickau plant. These banks were also members of the consortium which set up the AUTO UNION in 1932, into which the HORCH Werke were absorbed.

The products

By 1920 the post-war HORCH model programme was in production, and comprised six passenger cars and three types of truck. All of these had been designed and developed before the war, including the top model with an 80 horsepower, four-cylinder engine and the immense displacement of 8.5 litres.

In 1923 this varied assortment of models was deleted, to be replaced by the 10/35 hp car designed by Zoller, which had joined the production programme a year previously. This had a four-cylinder side-valve engine developing, as the designation implied, 35 horsepower. The chassis was also new, and incorporated no fewer than seven patents and eight registered designs. These related to the rear axle casing and also to the engine, which was combined with the steering and the front bulkhead to form a single ready-to-install unit.

When Paul Daimler joined the company, he revised the design of this model, adopting an OHC version of the engine also designed by Zoller, which developed 50 hp with no increase in displacement. The car was given four-wheel brakes and a flat radiator of more conventional appearance then the fashionable pointed one which embellished the 10/35 hp model. The new company badge also appeared for the first time: an H surmounted by the word HORCH so as to resemble a crown. It was designed by Professor Fritz Böhm, lecturer in industrial design at the Berlin College of Advanced Free and Applied Art.

However, the climax of Paul Daimler's period of activity for HORCH was most definitely the eight-cylinder inline engine which he designed subsequently.

In order to keep the length of his engine within practical limits, Daimler cast the cylinders in siamesed pairs, so that the coolant only flowed between each second pair. The engine had a displacement of approximately 3 litres and developed

The HORCH radiator mascot: a winged globe (1929)

60 horsepower. Its valves were operated by double overhead camshafts driven by a vertical shaft with Gleason-pattern spiral bevel gears. The distributor was also mounted at the top of this shaft, and its lower bevel gear drove the gear-type engine lubrication pump. Since the worm drive to the coolant pump and dynamo were also driven from the same shaft, no less than eight gearwheels were in mesh at this point. The exhaust manifold was ribbed externally and extended forwards along the side of the engine. Many of the car's design details were not only impressively executed but also well ahead of the standards generally

HORCH 10/50 with changeover body

The HORCH off-road vehicle designed by Paul Daimler(1928)

HORCH Type 375 sedan-cabriolet

applied at the time. The four-wheel brakes, for instance, had vacuum servo assistance using the manifold depression created inside the engine (a principle developed by the Belgian engineer Dewandre). This reduced the effort needed at the brake pedal. The cooling system was maintained at an optimum temperature by a thermostat, which opened the flow to the radiator only when the coolant had reached 72 degrees Centigrade.

The new car was shown to the public for the first time towards the end of 1926, at the Automobile Exhibition in Berlin. The type designation for the first of the HORCH eight-cylinder models was 303. The asking price made it quite clear where its creators wished it to sell: among the top-class luxury models. The most basic version of this HORCH, an open tourer, was listed at 11,900 Marks. Few of its competitors were more expensive, and indeed many of them undercut this price significantly, notably the Mercedes Mannheim and the 3.3-litre Röhr.

The new car was offered from the outset in short- and long-wheelbase versions; bodies were initially made by the coachbuilder Gottfried Lindner in Ammendorf, near Halle, a company previously active in the construction of trailers and rail

wagons. Convertible bodies were obtained from Gläser in Dresden or Dietsch in Glauchau. Two years later, a successor was announced: the HORCH 350, with bodywork styled by Professor Hadank from the same Berlin Art College as Böhm, the

designer of the company's badge. Instead of the customary angular outline and flat roof, the new model had more rounded-off outlines and a curved roof form, which gave it a lower, more elongated appearance. A half-dozen of the new models was on display at the Berlin show in December 1928, including a Pullman limousine and convertible, an open tourer, a saloon and a sports convertible. The main attraction on the HORCH stand, however, was the so-called sedan-cabriolet, a feast of harmoniously matching colours with a grey body, scarlet leather upholstery and a sand-coloured folding top. HORCH was the first German automobile manufacturer to offer its cars from that time on with safety glass windows. The front end of the new model was dominated by large headlights produced by the Zeiss company of Jena. They were linked by a cross-bar, in the centre of which an 8 in a circle drew attention to the HORCH eight-cylinder engine. The radiator, previously exposed, was now panelled in the same colour as the body, and had a thermostat-controlled shutter with a chromium-plated border. A new mascot appeared on the radiator cap: a winged arrow, once again the work of Professor Böhm.

Elegance in the style of the late nineteen-twenties: the HORCH

The engine was increased in displacement to 4 litres, and in power output to 80 hp. Starting in 1928, HORCH drivers no longer had to attend to all of the car's 32 lubrication points with a grease gun, but were able to depress a pedal which operated a central lubrication system.

Two years later, HORCH introduced a special version of its eight-cylinder engined car, bearing the anonymous-sounding type code 375. The body was once again styled by Hadank, and in the mechanical engineering area the careful hand of Paul Daimler was again evident. The frame was sharply cranked over the rear axle, and the springs repositioned to permit a wider track and more stable axle location. The rear springs were no less than 1.45 metres long, with 18 chrome vanadium steel leaves. This HORCH was the first to have hydraulic shock absorbers. The mascot on the radiator cap changed once again – though still the work of Fritz Böhm – and now consisted of a winged globe.

This car represented the culmination of Paul Daimler's creative efforts. Initial difficulties with the eight-cylinder engine were long since overcome, and it ran

HORCH automobiles were regularly among the winners of "concours d'élégance" competitions

with impressive smoothness. The chassis and body design were fully its equal, and indeed set new standards within the German automobile industry. The quality of workmanship and the air of restrained luxury were unsurpassed. When Paul Daimler retired at the end of 1929, more than seven thousand HORCH eight-cylinder cars had already been built, a figure of which other German competitors could only dream.

The first task facing Daimler's successor Fritz Fiedler, however, was to reduce both the car's weight and its production cost. He also revised the range as offered for sale. The eight-cylinder inline engine, now in single OHC guise, was available in three sizes: 4 litres with an output of 80 horsepower, 4.5 litres with 90 hp or 5 litres with 100 hp. In each case, a short- or long-wheelbase chassis could be ordered. The factory itself offered eight body styles, though every HORCH customer was of course able to purchase a chassis only and have the body attached to it by such renowned coachbuilders as Gläser, Erdmann & Rossi or various others.

Stars of the show

At the 1931 Paris Salon de l'Automobile it was the HORCH Werke once again who created the major sensation. Their stand featured a yellow-painted convertible with a brown soft top and green kid leather upholstery; flanked on one side by a Type 500 in steel blue with a grey soft top and on the other by a 470 sedan-cabriolet painted grey, with a lighter grey soft top and blue leather upholstery. The bonnet of the main attraction, the yellow sports convertible, was open to reveal the latest and most dramatic HORCH development: a 6-litre V 12 engine! Fritz Fiedler had spared no effort or expense to achieve the very highest levels of refinement. To prevent any troublesome vibration from the crankshaft, despite its seven main bearings, he had given it twelve balance-weights and a vibration damper at the front end. He had installed a special system of oil lines to lubricate the pistons and ensure the presence of a protective film of oil as soon as the engine started. On each revolution of the engine the gudgeon pins were supplied

The first version of the HORCH straight-eight engine had double overhead camshafts

with oil through the crankshaft and drillways in the connecting rods; the valves had hydraulic clearance adjusters. For this impressively quiet car, only the ZF "Aphon" transmission was considered good enough; it was one of the first in Germany to have a low-noise second gear as well as the higher ratios.

Fiedler installed his magnificent new engine in an electrically welded box-section chassis frame which also supported the steel and timber body framework. To provide additional strength in the composite frame and body structure, the front bulkhead was hollow and acted as a torsionally rigid cross-member directly above the engine's flywheel.

The new flagship of the HORCH fleet was available as the Type 670 two- or four-seater convertible, and as the Type 600, a Pullman sedan or convertible.

A striking feature of the HORCH 670 was its three-piece windscreen, the centre section of which could be opened. The fascia, with its fine wood trim, included a map reading lamp and various telltale and warning lights. The interior equipment and trim was highly luxurious, and included front seats with fully reclining mechanisms.

The new top model reached the market early in 1932, and cost between 24,000 and 26,000 Reichsmarks, depending on the verison ordered. Only the supercharged Mercedes models and the Maybach Zeppelin were more expensive. It is therefore hardly surprising that it failed to sell in great numbers. By the time it was deleted in 1934, only 27 Type 600 and 53 Type 670 cars had been produced.

The luxury car market in Germany was the scene of tougher competition than in scarcely any other country, with up to 17 eight-cylinder cars in 47 versions contending for the well-off customer's business. Though the absolute sales figures may seem modest, they fail to reveal the fact that HORCH was distinctly more successful than many of its rivals: the market share enjoyed by the high-quality automobiles from Zwickau in the class above 4.2 litres' displacement, for instance, was no less than 44 percent.

Motor sport was of only secondary interest to the HORCH Werke in the nineteen-twenties. Cars powered by an overhead-valve four-cylinder engine were

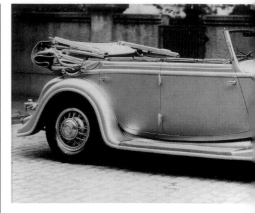

Surely one of the finest-looking of all classic cars: the HORCH 780

The man behind the Nürburg Ring racing circuit, Regional Administrative Director Dr. Creutz, was one of many enthusiasts for HORCH automobiles

tried out in events on the Avus racing circuit in Berlin, but with only moderate success. The factory decided not to pursue this side of its activities any further. Private entrants, however, achieved some quite remarkable results on occasion: Prince Schaumburg-Lippe, for example, the Cologne driver A. Broschek or Marion v. d. Heydt. Furthermore, HORCH cars were among the most regular winners of the beauty competitions or "concours d'élégance" which became popular at the end of the 1920s and in the early 1930s.

Dates in the history of HORCH

From 1920 until their liquidation on June 29, 1932 the HORCH Werke AG were owned by the Berlin-based aircraft engine company Argus. The HORCH board of directors also met in Berlin, at the registered offices of the company in No. 15, Mittelstrasse. The equity was 5 million Reichsmarks (RM).

Production figures

About 15,000 HORCH cars were produced between 1922 and 1932, some 12,000 of them powered by an eight-cylinder engine from 1927 onwards. Average annual output was accordingly about 1,300 cars. Between 1925 and 1930, annual turnover averaged 23 million RM. The workforce varied between 2,200 and 2,400. In 1932 the HORCH marque accounted for 44 percent of all German new-car registrations in the over-4.2-litre engine-size category.

The principal HORCH models, 1919–1932

Designation	Number/layout of cylinders	Bore x stroke in mm	Displacement in cc	Output in hp	Years of manufacture	Notes
10 M 200	4 inline	80 x 130	2600	10/35	1922–1924	
10 M 201	4 inline	80 x 130	2600	10/50	1924–1926	
303	8 inline	65 x 118	3132	12/60	1927	DOHC
305	8 inline	67,5 x 118	3378	13/65	1927–1928	
350	8 inline	73 x 118	3950	16/80	1928–1930	
400	8 inline	73 x 118	3950	16/80	1930–1931	
420	8 inline	87 x 95	4517	18/90	1931–1932	SOHC
500	8 inline	87 x 104	4944	20/100	1930–1932	
600	8 inline	80 x 100	6021	120	1932–1934	
750	8 inline	87 x 95	4517	90	1932–1934	

Prices

The 10/50 hp tourer cost 12,876 Reichsmarks in 1926. The eight-cylinder models were in some cases more expensive than their competitors. In 1927, 11,900 RM were asked for the 303 tourer. A similar version of the Type 350 cost 14,000 RM, whereas the twelve-cylinder model cost 24,500 RM as a Pullman sedan.

The twelve-cylinder HORCH was not only available as a Pullman sedan but also as a neatly styled four-seater sports convertible

Just in time – HORCH production methods in 1928

The starting point when calculating the time for delivering raw materials is when the finished car leaves the assembly line. Working backwards from this point, a precise "manufacturing timetable" has to be compiled, showing every work stage and the time which is needed to complete it. Specially appointed "progress chasers" must supervise this timetable in the central office and ensure that it is complied with.

The engine and rear axle must leave the "listening rooms" (the final stage in their production cycle) and reach the chassis assembly line at precisely the moment when their installation is due to take place. Each engine and rear axle should only be completed in sufficient time to reach the designated installation point as needed.

The body should have been fully painted just before it is installed on the completed chassis; this process should continue until the car has been thoroughly inspected under powerful spotlights and leaves the factory.

P. Friedmann writing in the magazine "Deutsche Motor-Zeitschrift" 1928, No. 6

Ernest Friedländer: Auto Test Book (1931)

"The car has exceptionally flowing lines. Although it is clearly styled with more of an eye to current fashion than the standard products from Daimler-Benz, it is superior to them in elegance and sublimity of expression. HORCH today gives precedence to formal matters, with even design factors rendered subservient to this overriding principle. Not surprisingly, the results of this concept are of a scarcely to be surpassed delicacy. Despite their size, the current large HORCH convertibles and saloons are among the most inspired, striking creations that automobile engineering has to offer."

Paul Daimler

Paul Daimler (1869–1945)

1869	Born on 13th September 1869
1897	Following school and engineering studies at the Stuttgart College of Advanced Technology: designer for the Daimler-Motoren-Gesellschaft engine company
1902–1905	Managing director of the Austrian Daimler-Motoren-Gesellschaft in Vienna
1907–1922	Chief designer and director of the Daimler-Motoren-Gesellschaft in Stuttgart
1915	Appointed Building Planning and Control Officer – this was the period in which Daimler served the national cause well by developing aircraft engine superchargers; after the war he pursued the same line of research for road vehicles
	Paul Daimler designed the Mercedes racing cars which secured the legendary 1-2-3 victory in the 1914 French Grand Prix
1922	After serious disputes with the Board, Daimler left the company in Untertürkheim and on July 1st became chief designer at Argus-Motoren-Gesellschaft mbH in Berlin-Reinickendorf. His consultancy agreement called for him to develop engines for the HORCH Werke, in which Argus held a majority holding
1926	In December the HORCH Type 303 straight-eight designed by Paul Daimler was shown at the Berlin Automobile Exhibition. This engine established the Zwickau company's reputation as Germany's leading manufacturer of eight-cylinder cars .
1929	Paul Daimler retired, but was still active in various honorary capacities.
1945	Died in Berlin on 15th December 1945

AUDI – noblesse oblige

Like many national competitors, the AUDI Werke AG emerged from the war years with considerable profits at their disposal, and reverted to the production of civilian vehicles. These included light trucks, an attractive market area in the immediate post-war years, when there was a shortage of transport capacity.

Technical Director Hermann Lange realised very soon that a change in the company's model policy would be necessary. In October 1919 he visited the first post-war automobile exhibition, held in Copenhagen, where he became aware that manufacturers would have to limit their production programmes to fewer but more elaborate designs in the future. He returned to the factory and drew up the design principles for a new AUDI model on this basis.

Inflation caused AUDI no problems at first, and under the influence of paper money which tended to lose its value almost overnight, the company even took on additional workers. Its cars became more complex, and by 1923 more than 1,300 man-hours were needed to produce a Type C chassis (basically the pre-war Alpine Run winner). For the new Type K, the figure was 4,000 man-hours, which was considered acceptable because labour was so cheap.

Compared with its rivals, AUDI was only a medium-sized company at this time. In terms of its capital resources too, AUDI had to be regarded as one of the smaller market contenders, and as far as the technical ambitions of its cars were concerned, its motto seemed to be "small but good". Unfortunately, the first half of this slogan tended to outweigh the second. An average output of fewer than 190 cars could scarcely generate a turnover of more than 5 million Reichsmarks. In 1928 the AUDI Werke AG was acquired by the head of the DKW empire, J. S. Rasmussen. He had bought the production facilities of an American manufacturer of six- and eight-cylinder engines and had them shipped to Scharfenstein, a town in Germany's Erz Mountains region. His next move was to look for automobile manufacturers prepared to install the engines he planned to manufacture

In 1923 AUDI adopted the "1" on a globe, designed by Professor Drescher, as its emblem

62

AUDI was Germany's first manufacturer to offer left-hand drive and a central gear shift as standard features, from 1921 on

there. His acquisition of AUDI was decided on with this in mind – but proved to be a disaster, since as economic crisis loomed in Germany, the demand for expensive cars flagged more and more.

Following the death of Hermann Lange in 1922, Dipl.-Ing. Erich Horn became chief designer. His plans were used for AUDI's first six-cylinder car (1923). He was followed in 1926 by Heinrich Schuh, who had been factory manager since 1920, and who not only developed the first eight-cylinder AUDI but was also responsible for re-organising the company's entire production routine.

Before the war, the AUDI logo had consisted only of the name. In 1922 the company therefore announced a competition for a new symbol to act as an emblem for its products and be registered as a trade mark.

150 entries were received, and the Board of Directors chose a proposal from Professor Arnold Drescher: a figure 1 placed in front of a globe. AUDI registered this new trade mark in 1923, and applied it to the radiators of four-, six- and eight-cylinder cars. In 1931 Rasmussen decided to use the Zwickau plant to build his front-wheel-drive DKW small cars.

The products

The first new post-war AUDI, developed by Hermann Lange, was clearly a direct successor to the triumphant "Alpine Run" model. It was given the designation "K" and had the same engine bore and stroke dimensions. Lange, however, discarded the cylinders cast in pairs in favour of an aluminium block with a cast-iron head. The combustion chambers were of unusual shape: instead of the usual elongated form with the valves vertical, Lange chose a hemispherical combustion chamber with angled valves operated from the camshaft at one side of the block by means of pushrods and rockers. The camshaft was driven by helical-cut gears. Engine lubrication was taken care of by no fewer than three oil pumps; the cooling system still retained the traditional thermosyphon principle, with no water pump, but was aided by a four-bladed fan which could be driven at various speeds. The steering was of considerable significance, for a reason which deserves closer attention at this juncture: for the first time on any German passenger car, this AUDI exhibit at the 1921 Berlin Automobile Exhibition had left-hand drive. Today, this is so commonplace as to need no particular explanati-

on, but in those days the steering wheel position was the subject of extensive testing and analyses in the trade press and elsewhere by highly reputed experts. Since they unanimously declared the correct position to be on the left (for countries practising the right-hand rule of the road), AUDI came to a quick decision which it justified with the following concise remarks in the new car's sales brochure: "We have now abandoned the previous practice of installing the steering wheel on the right-hand side of the car, having come

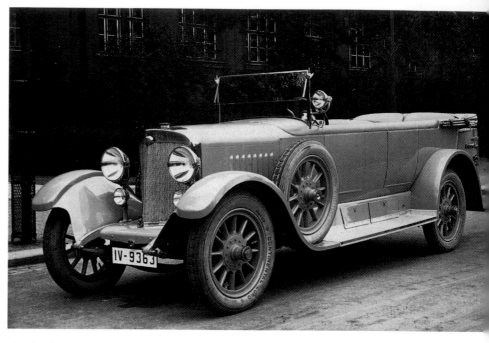

AUDI Type K,
10/50 hp
(1921)

to accept the advantages of left-hand drive for driving on the right."

If we recall that in 1922 about 90 percent of all new passenger cars in Germany still had right-hand drive, and that even in 1923 the figure was about 75 %, we can well understand why AUDI considered itself to be something of a technical pioneer in this respect.

There were various other interesting details on the car exhibited at the show. The steering wheel could be folded, as on many sports cars of the time, and in much the same spirit, a revolution counter was standard equipment. The AUDI K's fuel tank held a remarkable 125 litres, with 15 liters in reserve. The changeover lever for the reserve fuel supply was still outside, mounted on the fuel tank itself, so that the driver was obliged to stop, climb down and make the necessary adjustment. The new AUDI model, however, had a most ingenious reserve fuel supply lever which prevented the fuel filler cap from being removed to add fuel unless the lever was first reset to the normal fuel-supply position. This helped to aid a far from infrequent occurrence that always enraged the driver who was incautious enough to provoke it: continuing the journey on reserve until no fuel remained at all in either tank. The AUDI K also boasted a tyre inflating pump driven from the engine.

The first six-cylinder engine

Another two years elapsed, and the Berlin Motor Show was again the venue chosen to launch a successor model, developed by Erich Horn. This was the first six-cylinder AUDI. Its crankshaft ran in eight white-metal bearings and had very large balance weights. Later, a torsional vibration damper was attached, with AUDI once again being able to claim a place among the few pioneering manufacturers who appreciated the need for such a device and its practical benefits.

The six-cylinder engine's valves were operated by a single overhead camshaft, itself driven by a vertical shaft and gears from the crankshaft. The engine was constructed entirely from light alloy, with cast iron cylinder liners inserted into the block. Its power output was quoted as 70 hp at 2500 rpm. The intake air cleaner was another most ingenious design detail: contemporary engines usually permitted the air to reach the cylinders either entirely unfiltered or after passing through only a very primitive form of air cleaner or mesh filter. In this case the dirt particles were deposited on the cylinder walls or the piston crowns, with undesirable effects which involved time-consuming repair and decarbonisation work.

AUDI's first six-cylinder model appeared in 1923, with an all-alloy engine

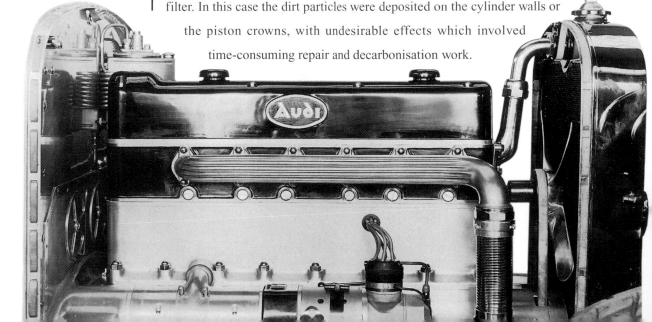

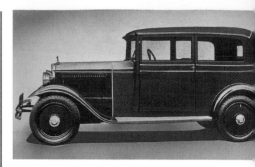

The AUDI M drew in its intake air through circular apertures in the frame on the carburettor side of the engine, whence it passed to an oil-wetted filter in the lower part of the crankcase. The airflow was then pre-heated by the exhaust system, settled to eliminate turbulence and supplied to the carburettor. This elaborate system was another pioneering technical development on AUDI's part.

The six-cylinder model was equipped with hydraulic brakes; they were designed and built by AUDI and represented one of the first hydraulic brake systems to appear on a German motor vehicle.

In 1927, the first-ever AUDI with an 8-cylinder engine was announced.

It was given the model letter R within the AUDI alphabet. The technical description was expressed as 19/100 PS (hp), and the Type reference quoting the number of cylinders and horsepower was Type 819. The new engine had an output of 100 horsepower at 3000 rpm; with it, the car was good for a top speed of 110 km/h. The engine proved to be quite remarkably flexible, with the excellent torque of 28 mkg at 1100 rpm. Not surprisingly, the car was claimed to accelerate smoothly and powerfully from only 8 km/h in top gear right up to its maximum speed.

Weighing 340 kilograms, the engine was no longer made entirely from light alloy as had been the case with the Type M, but had instead a grey cast-iron cylinder block on a light alloy crankcase. The straight-eight engine posed the usual manufacturing problems on account of its considerable length. For the first time in AUDI's history, the gearbox had only three forward ratios.

This was in accordance with Heinrich Schuh's declared intention of simplifying the company's car designs and eliminating over-ambitious constructional features. Although the new car was larger than before and created a distinctly luxurious impression, it was actually very much cheaper to build. Based on the

The first AUDI with eight-cylinder engine appeared in 1927

The small AUDI with Peugeot engine (1931)

same production volume as for the M, it was intended to cut production costs to only 47 percent of the previous figure. The car was named "Imperator" as a sign of AUDI's intention to play a dominant market rôle and to set new standards.

New approaches

Despite all the optimism which manifested itself in the creation of new and larger engines, the market itself remained obstinately limited in volume. In July 1930, for instance, only 541 new cars with a power output of more than 75 hp were registered in Germany. The individual makes provide a remarkably clear picture of market shares at the time: HORCH 170, Daimler-Benz 75, Maybach 12, Packard 15, Buick 76, AUDI 20 etc.

In view of this, Rasmussen insisted that AUDI produce a small car. He wished to make more effective use of the production capacity at his DKW factory in Berlin-Spandau, and offer the DKW cars produced there with a four-stroke engine as an alternative. The actual engine he was planning to install came from Peugeot, was of 1000 cc displacement and developed 30 hp. This car in fact acquired the "1" badge on its radiator and was sold as the AUDI P model.

By the autumn of 1930, however, Rasmussen had created an entirely new AUDI model line. Accompanied by Heinrich Schuh, he appeared one day in the AUDI design office and instructed the surprised staff to develop a small car with a DKW motorcycle engine, swing-axle suspension, front-wheel drive and a wooden body. For this he graciously allowed them a period of six weeks. In fact the two designers confronted with this thankless task not only kept within the deadline but produced a car of which more than a quarter of a million were to be sold in the years to come, making it Germany's most popular small car of all.

AUDI was among the leaders in streamlined bodywork. This aluminium body is on an AUDI Type K chassis (1923)

Rasmussen was concentrating at that time on gaining public acceptance for front-wheel drive in the medi-umsize automobile category as well. Other makes' experiments in this direction had not shown much promise, but Rasmussen felt that what was such a success in the DKW "driving machine" ought to work equally well in a larger car too.

After taking control at AUDI in 1928 he instructed the factory in Zwickau to use the Rickenbacker engines he was producing in Scharfenstein. These two straight eights, of 4.3 and 5.1 litres' displace-ment, acquired by Rasmussen in the USA, meant that AUDI had three weight-cylinder models in its pro-gramme! This was flying in the face of any wor-thwhile company rationalisation, in other words precisely the policy which Rasmussen had pursued with his other, much more cheaply produced engines. The Imperator was deleted in 1929, and with it the small eight-cylinder engine. The next AUDI, the Type S, inherited the remaining engine, which also develo-ped 100 hp. It had a grey cast-iron cylinder block but an aluminium crankcase. It was also rated for exceptional flexibility, fourth gear being an overdrive ratio. The name chosen for this car was "Zwickau". A year later this series of German city names was continued with the "Dresden", which had a six-cylinder Ricken-backer engine.

AUDI bus chassis with eight-cylinder Rickenbacker engine, produced for export (1929)

Dates in the history of AUDI

1928	On 20th /21st August 1928, J. S. Rasmussen acquired a majority share in AUDI Werke AG
1929	He purchased the remaining shares. The equity value was 2.6 mil. RM
1932	On 29th June the company was liquidated and integrated into AUTO UNION AG

The principal AUDI models, 1919–1932

Designation	Number/layout of cylinders	Bore x stroke in mm	Displacement in cm³	Output in hp	Years of manufacture	Notes
	4 inline	90 x 140	3560	10/50	1921–1926	First production car with left-hand drive
	6 inline	90 x 122	4655	18/70	1924–1928	
	8 inline	80 x 122	4900	19/100	1927–1929	"Imperator"
	8 inline	82.5 x 121	5130	19/100	1929–1932	Rickenbacker engine
	6 inline	82.5 x 121	3838	15/75	1930–1932	Rickenbacker engine
	4 inline	63 x 90	1122	5/30	1931	Peugeot engine

Production figures

Some 2,500 AUDIs were built between 1921 und 1932, equivalent to an average of about 200 a year.

The number of employees went down, for instance from 370 in 1925 to only 169 in 1930.

The company's share of the German market can at best be described as marginal, being usually in the region of 3.7 percent.

The prices charged for AUDI automobiles were based on the levels prevailing in the large luxury class, The six-cylinder Type M was offered at 22,300 RM in 1925; a Maybach with the same specification cost 25,000 RM. Thanks to design changes and more efficient methods of construction, the eight-cylinder AUDI Imperator had come down in price by 1927 to only 16,575 RM, and the Type S with Rickenbacker eight-cylinder engine was actually listed at only 12,950 RM.

From a 1919 AUDI owner's handbook

"When driving in city traffic, always select the gear ratio which matches your road speed, and never attempt to control the car's speed by slipping the clutch … the leather clutch facing needs to be treated with special care.

AUDI "Dresden" with 75 hp six-cylinder engine (1929)

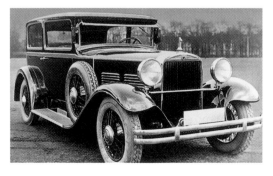

If it becomes dry and hard, a squeaking noise will be heard when it is engaged. The leather must then be washed thoroughly with gasoline or petroleum spirit and coated with liver or fish oil, castor oil or the finest quality Vaseline.

This will render it supple again, so that it conforms smoothly to the shape of the flywheel cone. To ensure that the leather facing absorbs the oil effectively, you are recommended to leave the clutch disengaged overnight by wedging a piece of wood between the pedal and the gearbox."

Heinrich Schuh

1886	Born on 28th February 1886 in Edingen (Baden), son of a farmer
1901–1909	Apprentice metalworker and journeyman
1910–1911	Designer of trucks for Benz in Gaggenau
1911–1918	Zeppelin on-board engineer for the Deutschen Luftschiffahrts AG (DELAG); factory manager at the Zeppelin airship factory in Potsdam
1919–1920	Factory manager at the Maybach engine plant in Potsdam
1920	Appointed AUDI plant director in Zwickau
1923	Study trip to the USA, financed by AUDI
1926	From 1st April on, Technical Director of AUDI Werke AG; also Chief Designer as the successor to Erich Horn
1927	Introduction of the Type R 19/100 hp, designed by Schuh; this was the first eight-cylinder AUDI
	A talent for production engineering A reference granted to Schuh confirms that he possessed immense practical experience in automobile engineering and the machine tool area, in test gear and in precision mass production: "He is a complete master of tool and fixture making. Several thousand fixtures have been built to his designs and have proved admirably successful"
1931	In the following years, he supervised production of the DKW Front and shared in the task of converting the AUDI plants in Zwickau to produce small front-wheel-drive cars in large numbers
	Schuh persisted with a competent and humane approach to plant management during the Third Reich
1945	In October 1945 he was denounced to the Red Army, arrested and taken to Mühlberg Camp
1950	Schuh died at an unknown place in Russia

*Heinrich Schuh
(1886–1950)*

This panoramic windscreen was a special option on the AUDI Type C (1921)

Police van on AUDI E 55 hp chassis (1925)

From the introduction to the AUDI K Owner's Handbook (1924)

"To own such a noble vehicle is to have one's good taste and culture in some way legitimised – in the same sense as an upper-class Englishman might regard membership of a select club as evidence of his character as a gentleman. To possess an AUDI automobile, therefore, is to respect the laws of "noblesse oblige" … .

WANDERER – from tradition to innovation

The WANDERER Werke in Chemnitz were among Germany's leading vehicle manufacturers in the widest sense of the term. The bulk of their production was of course bicycles, but motorcycles of this make were also extremely popular. During the First World War, WANDERER had supplied almost half of all the motorcycles purchased by the Army. In the medium-size category, WANDERER cars competed against models from all the main German makes. Among them, it was regarded as a company firmly rooted in tradition, with a conservative approach to design and a loyal group of customers who did not wish to be offered any epoch-making innovations. For the manufacturer, these customers were worth their weight in gold: even in years of crisis, sales seldom dropped unduly.

Since the mid-1920s, every area of WANDERER's production facilities had been thoroughly streamlined. Significantly, the bicycles led the way, with the automobile division being attended to last of all. The whole process was linked with a change of location: from the company's headquarters in Schönau, the machine tool production department was the first to move to new buildings in Siegmar. From 1927 onwards, this was also the home of the WANDERER automobile. The initial production volume at the new plant was 25 cars a day.

Since 1928 a young man by the name of Baron Klaus-Detlof von Oertzen had been a member of the Board of Directors, which was headed by the two managing directors Daut and Stuhlmacher. It was the young Baron who arranged in 1929 for the motorcycle division to be sold. The 500 cc shaft-drive model which had just been developed went to Janecek in Prague, the remaining designs were disposed of to NSU. At the same time, von Oertzen pleaded for further modernisation of the automobile departments, and in fact more than 11 million Reichsmarks were invested in them between 1929 and 1931.

It was also Baron von Oertzen who established the link with Ferdinand Porsche which was to prove of such importance for the future. Thanks to his initiative,

WANDERER 10/50 hp with open tourer body

Porsche's recently established design office was awarded a development contract for several new projects. The first climax in this most fruitful relationship was an agreement commissioning Porsche to develop a racing car for WANDERER.

The products

Immediately after the First World War, and based directly on a pre-war design, a twin-cylinder motorcycle with gearbox in unit, kick-starter and chain drive was produced, and remained on sale until 1924. A year later, the legendary WANDERER twin with four valves per cylinder followed. There was also a smaller version of this model with a 200 cc horizontal single-cylinder engine, again with four-valve head. However, the last of the large WANDERER models with 500 cc single-cylinder engine, pressed-steel frame and shaft drive was not a sales success, and midway through 1929 WANDERER withdrew from motorcycle production altogether.

In the automobile area, the Puppchen had become highly popular after only a short production period, and was to remain on sale for a long time. After the war, the engine was given overhead valves and a slightly larger bore, yielding a displacement of 1.3 litres. Although the model was still referred to as the 5/15, its maximum power output was now 20 horsepower. The three-quarter elliptic rear leaf springs proved unable to cope with this additional power, and were replaced by a most carefully designed cantilever-arm suspension layout. First launched before the outbreak of war, this basic model remained in production for over 14 years. It was not until 1926 that this highly successful WANDERER automobile was superseded by a more powerful design, powered by a 1.5-litre four-cylinder engine rated at 30 hp. This was known as the W 10 in the WANDERER model hierarchy. It was endowed with all the latest features of modern automobile engineering practice: left-hand drive, a central gear lever, a multiple dry-plate clutch, a unitary engine block and gearbox and four-wheel brakes.

Further modernisation of this 6/30 model took place a few years later, when the chassis was given hydraulic shock absorbers and central lubrication. WAN-

DERER also sold a six-cylinder car now, the 10/50 hp. Bodies came from various leading companies, including Daimler-Benz in Sindelfingen, Reutter in Stuttgart and Gläser in Dresden. This, then, was the WANDERER: a slightly dull but immensely sound piece of car design. The technical and commercial staff in Siegmar and Schönau could well have persisted much longer in their idyllic

pursuit of quality, but a rough awakening was in store for them: the world economic crisis. They were forced to admit that even modern engineering could, indeed should, be-

nefit from being clothed attractively. A complete change of heart set in. The most distinguished designer on the market was commissioned to work for WANDERER: Ferdinand Porsche. For the Saxony-based company he drafted out newsix-cylinder OHV engines with a light-alloy cylinder block and wet cylinder liners, either of 1.7- or 2.0-litres' capacity and developing 35 and 40 horsepower respectively. They differed only in respect of the cylinder bore, and were installed in the existing W 10's almost unmodified chassis, together with a four-speed gearbox. These cars were known as the W 15 (7/35 hp) and W 17 (8/40 hp).

This was by no means all: on November 29th, 1930 WANDERER concluded a further agreement with the gifted automobile designer for three further models. One was to have a six-cylinder engine, the other two eight-cylinder engines, with one of the latter in turn equipped with a supercharger.

The WANDERER name was also familiar in the motor sport arena. These small cars were so amazingly lively that enthusiasts very soon began to prepare them for competition use. In the early 1920s, private entrants were highly successful in hillclimb events and short-distance races in particular. They became exceptionally popular in Italy following a number of successes on local circuits by the

Contemporary elegance in the WANDERER six-cylinder sports cabriolet with dickey seat

Although now equipped with a Porsche-designed engine, the new WANDERER looked very much the same as its predecessor

The six-cylinder 10/50 hp WANDERER at the Berlin Motor Show

racing driver Cercignani, often at average speeds not far below ninety kilometres an hour. In view of this surge of popularity on the Italian market, WANDERER resolved to enter two cars with 1.5-litre OHC engines in the 1922 Targa Florio race. The cars did in fact reach the starting line, but unfortunately, both of them failed to complete the distance.

In the second half of the nineteen-twenties, WANDERER cars were often entered for reliability trials. They achieved considerable success in the international Alpine rallies, for instance an overall team prize in 1931 and, a year later, the Glacier Trophy: this was awarded to WANDERER drivers Bernet and Kappler for completing the course without penalty points. The Alpine trophy itself went to the WANDERER team.

Dates in the history of WANDERER

From 1st January, 1932 WANDERER leased its automobile division in Siegmar, near Chemnitz, to the AUTO UNION for a period of ten years.

By 30th June, 1932 the WANDERER company was already producing automobiles for AUTO UNION's account.

Initially, however, production volume seldom exceeded 500 cars a year.

In the early nineteen-twenties, production was running at about 1,500 cars a year, rising later to 3,500.

In the engine-size category from 1.2 to 2.1 litres, WANDERER's share of new registrations in, for instance, 1932 was just over 10 percent. The prices were in accordance with WANDERER's perceived status in the midsize automobile category. The W 4 open tourer cost 7000 gold Marks, and for the W 10 with the same body style, 6000 gold Marks had to be paid in 1929. By 1931 the price charged for a four-door saloon version of the W 10 was only 4,850 RM.

Klaus-Detlof von Oertzen

1894	Born on 13th April 1894 in Inowrazlav (Hohensalza), Poznan province
	On leaving schol, trained as an officer with the Imperial Flying Corps, but was invalidated out in 1916 after suffering severe injuries.
1919–1924	Commenced a commercial career with the Harburg-Vienna tyre company (which later became Phönix)
1925–1928	Managed the Phönix subsidiary in Dresden and was sales manager for Central Germany
1928	Joined the Board of Directors of the WANDERER Werke in Siegmar near Chemnitz, with responsibility for sales
1932	Played a major part in establishing the AUTO UNION AG and is regarded as the originator of its four-ring badge
1935	Retired from the position of AUTO UNION Sales Director
1935–1939	General Manager (Exports) for AUTO UNION in South Africa, Asia and Australia
1940–1946	Interned in India during the Second World War
1946–1948	Managing Director of the China Diesel Motors Corporation in Shanghai, a General Motors company
1949	Moved to Johannesburg (South Africa) and acted as an independent adviser to the VW and Büssing companies
1950	Appointed Head of VW Exports for Africa, Australia and Asia
1963	Retired on 31st December
1991	Died in Switzerland on 25th July 1991

Klaus-Detlof von Oertzen
(1894–1991)

Fast food and grocery delivery trucks were a WANDERER speciality

WANDERER was one of the first German companies to produce what we would now call an estate car

WANDERER director von Oertzen on the commercial and technical developments with which he was associated:

"I visited Mercedes in Sindelfingen and said to them: 'Look, my good people, you make such attractive bodies, why don't you make a few for us?' And in due course we came to an agreement. Thyssen never forgot how I summoned up all my courage and gave him an order on the spot for a thousand bodies. Not that they weren't pleased about it in Sindelfingen too! I never had any trouble about this within WANDERER. I wasn't that easy to dislodge from my seat, and the Supervisory Board was on my side. In 1929 and 1930 we built no bodies of our own at all at WANDERER. They all came either from the Rhineland, or the convertibles from Gläser in Dresden and the saloons from Reutter in Stuttgart. I persuaded Ferdinand Porsche to develop the engines – six-cylinder units with either 1.7 or 2 litres. WANDERER used them first, then the AUTO UNION. Porsche sent his son-in-law Dr. Piëch, to me in Chemnitz so that we could sign the two contracts."

Source: tape-recorded archives

DKW – forging the AUTO UNION

At the end of the First World War Rasmussen encountered Hugo Ruppe in Zschopau. Ruppe had already gained a reputation as an engine designer, and in particular for developing and building small air-cooled twin- and four-cylinder engines. Before the end of 1918 he had designed for Rasmussen a ported two-stroke engine with a swept volume of 25 cc; Rasmussen exhibited it at the 1919 Leipzig Spring Fair. Sales were sufficient for this miniature engine to qualify as a definite success. Having already coined the DKW name for his experimental steam-driven vehicles, the Dane chose the same initials for the latest development, naming it 'Des Knaben Wunsch' (literally: 'The Boy's Wish'). An auxiliary engine for bicycles based on this unit ('Das kleine Wunder' – 'The Small Miracle') was a considerable commercial success. Rasmussen now had a clear picture of what form production should take. His firm was renamed "Zschopauer Motorenwerke J. S. Rasmussen" in 1921, and expanded in parallel with the success of the product.

Businesses established or bought by Rasmussen

1920	Rota Magnet Apparatebau GmbH, Zschopau (flywheel magnetos)
1922	Zöblitzer Metallwarenfabrik (metal fittings)
1922	Frankenberger Motorenwerke (saddles, carburettors, after 1926 three-wheeled delivery vehicles); moved to Hainichen in 1934
1924	Slaby-Werke Berlin (electric vehicles, later wooden bodies)
1926	The Scharfenstein plant of the Moll-Werke (engines, refrigerating-equipment, after 1930 Junkers opposed-piston diesel engines) and the Schüttoff-Werke in Chemnitz (motorcycles)
1928	AUDI Werke, Zwickau
1928	An iron foundry in Wittigsthal
1930	Luma Werke in Stuttgart (dynastarters)

Three-wheeled delivery vehicles with DKW engines were also built in Zschopau

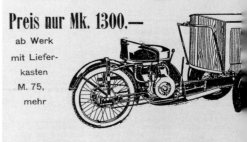

The DKW auxiliary bicycle engine

Rasmussen also purchased companies, mainly metallurgical undertakings, in the Erzgebirge region, for instance in Marienberg and Annaberg, and a major share in the Prometheus Gearbox Company of Berlin-Reinickendorf.

DKW motorcycles were flourishing. The company's advertising triumphed with such encouraging claims as "DKW – the Small Miracle – goes up hills like the others go down!".

By 1928 DKW was the largest motorcycle manufacturer in the world. In a country that had seen its middle classes severely mauled by war and inflation, access to personal mobility was to a far greater extent than elsewhere concentrated on the motorcycle.

The DKW's popularity owed a lot to company management that was extremely well-informed on technical matters and able to combine this with plenty of commercial talent. It was to Rasmussen's credit that he was able to find the right people to put his ambitions into practice. Hugo Ruppe from Leipzig introduced him to the two-stroke engine; Friedrich Münz from Stuttgart offered him the "dynastarter", a unique combination of dynamo and starter motor that has a firm place in automobile history; Dr. Herbert Venediger was the first person in the company to scrutinise the two-stroke engine systematically, and immediately discovered the work of Schnürle, which was of immense importance in the construction of small engines in particular; Hermann Weber, when chief designer in Zschopau, created motorcycles which were among the best obtainable anywhere, including such landmarks as the RT 125, which earned the ultimate accolade of quality by being slavishly copied by any number of competitors. Nor should one forget the Austrian Dr. Carl Hahn, who was Rasmussen's personal assistant and whose dedicated work helped to enhance the DKW brand image.

Rasmussen was only too well aware that success was a question of technical capability, but that organisation and management had to satisfy equally high standards. DKW built up a widespread network of factory-authorised dealers. They attended annual conferences and sent their mechanics to regular training courses; this encouraged loyalty and maintained communication on both technical and commercial levels.

DKW was a pioneer of credit purchase for motorcycles; starting in 1924, a DKW could be bought on weekly instalments of 10 Reichsmarks. This aspect of management owed much to a man whose talents had been recruited by Rasmussen at an early stage; Dr. Carl Hahn, known within and beyond the automobile trade as "DKW Hahn". He possessed a rare combination of technical comprehension, commercial skill and dynamic initiative, and created for DKW one of the industry's most advanced sales organisations.

Rasmussen's own financial assets were clearly insufficient to finance all this expansion. The main source of funds was the State Bank of Saxony, with which increasingly close links were built up from the mid-1920s onwards. The bank had held 25 percent of DKW's shares since 1929 – easily its largest commitment in the State of Saxony at the time.

The first bicycle with DKW auxiliary engine, in Nuremberg (1921)

There was clearly much to be said for amalgamating the remaining automobile companies in the region, in view of the potential they still possessed. The HORCH Werke, also borrowers on a considerable scale from the State Bank, were an obvious candidate, and the Dresdner Bank was trying hard to find a purchaser for the WANDERER automobile division. AUDI had already been bought out by DKW, but there were no plans to include commercial vehicle manufacturers in the scheme.

The concept took shape in Rasmussen's mind, with support from a personal friend and director of the State Bank, Dr. Herbert Müller, until in due course the idea of an 'Auto Union' based in Saxony began to approach reality.

*The DKW
'Reichsfahrt' model
with 1.5 hp engine
and belt drive*

Motorcycles

In view of the success of Ruppe's engines, Rasmussen decided to pin his faith entirely on the two-stroke engine. Although this operating principle, using the crankcase to deliver the mixture to the cylinder through ports, had been known since the end of the 19th century, and was valued for its simplicity, it presented a number of problems in practice which had caused both manufacturers and vehicle buyers to view it with caution. Such problems centred round the need to ensure good heat dissipation from the two-stroke engine, which had twice the firing rate of the four-stroke, to seal the pressurised crankcase effectively, to reduce its high fuel and lubricating oil consumption, to control its speed over a broad operating range – and of course to do most things better than the mature, thoroughly familiar four-stroke engine. The two-stroke soldiered on for many years with a reputation for mediocrity, unreliability and poor operating economy. Undeniable drawbacks of the two-stroke when in operaton were its loud, staccato noise pattern, its high fuel consumption, the engine's poor braking effect and its tendency to oil up its spark plugs.

Advantages which it could claim over the four-stroke engine were higher power output from a unit of equivalent size, considerably lower weight, the sheer simplicity of 'petroil' lubrication, the need for far fewer moving parts and the flexible power flow.

Ruppe and Rasmussen regarded these as decisive advantages. The motorised bicycle unit which they developed from the original miniature engine, the "Small Miracle" as it was rightly called, was an indication of the path they intended to take. Lubricated by oil added to the fuel, a flywheel magneto with the contact breaker mounted externally for easy access, an output shaft driven at a 3:1 reduction ratio and above all precision in manufacture – these were the secrets of the DKW auxiliary engine's success despite the presence of 20 other two- and four-stroke rivals on the German market. Sold initially with a power output of 1 horsepower and later with 1.75 hp, the engine had forced-air fan cooling. The airflow, produced with brilliant simplicity by blades on the rotor of the flywheel magneto and supplied to the cylinder barrel and head by a sheet-metal shroud, was an essential feature and continued to ensure good temperature control when later applied to increasingly larger, more powerful DKW engines.

The DKW bicycle engine was supplied to about 70 other manufacturers for installation in the frame triangle of lightweight motorcycles. By November 1922 about 30,000 of these DKW engines were in use. They were delivered complete, including a bolted-on fuel tank holding 1.5 litres and all the necessary wire cables, control levers, V-belt and belt pulley for the bicycle wheel. A support fork with clamp was also provided for the engine. This miniature power-pack could propel the average bicycle up to a road speed of almost 40 km/h, a situation which obliged Rasmussen to produce his own uprated bicycles for use with the auxiliary engine.

In due course a dispute broke out between Rasmussen and Ruppe, which led to the latter departing in anger. Ruppe's successor in Zschopau as chief engineer was the young Hermann Weber. Weber's handwriting, so to speak, can be seen on all the remaining DKW models produced under his aegis until the outbreak of the Second World War. Without Weber occupying the chief designer's chair, it is impossible to conceive of DKW's technical development having made such unparalleled progress during those years.

Weber was also successful as a competition and racing rider for DKW; his first design task for the company was the "Reichsfahrt" model, weighing 40 kg and capable of 65 km/h. It was a major step forward from the motorised bicycle to the genuine motorcycle.

The Lomos "armchair motorcycle" was developed at the same time. An ambitious design, particularly in the suspension area, the final version boasted a cast magnesium frame and a rear swinging arm with spring suspension strut. The back of the shaped sheet-steel seat acted as a fuel tank. The following years were also notable for a series of advanced ideas from DKW's engineers. An initial highlight was the E 206, which also became a sales hit. It cost only 750 Reichsmarks, whereas most of its competitors were between 100 and 200 RM more ex-

The Lomos "armchair motorcycle" with DKW engine (1922) was an early precursor of the modern motor scooter.

pensive. It had a genuine dry-plate clutch, the flywheel magneto was given additional coils to supply the lights and the carburettor was equipped with an intake air cleaner – a feature not seen before on a motorcycle. In 1928, when all motorcycles in Germany up to 200 cc were exempted from road tax and could be ridden without a driving licence, the Zschopau-based company seized the opportunity immediately. This already successful model's cylinder bore was reduced by one millimetre to bring its displacement down from 206 to 198 cubic centimetres. The previous grey cast-iron piston was replaced by an aluminium one, and for the up to 35,000 motorcycles already delivered, a conversion kit was offered. The DKW E 200, to give it its new name, was for some months the only bike to take full advantage of the new tax category, so that demand for it rose very steeply.

A DKW motorcycle for the more demanding rider: the 500 Sport De Luxe with twin cylinder engine

This led to a new production record being set up: instead of the usual 100 to 150 motorcycles a day, no less than 450 were produced on one occasion.

1926 was the first year in Germany in which more two-stroke than four-stroke motorcycles had been produced; between 60 and 65 percent of all German motorcycles were either DKWs or were powered by a DKW engine.

Examination of contemporary documents confirms that more than 60 German motorcycle manufacturers installed engines from DKW.

Starting in 1929, a pressed-steel frame was gradually introduced for all models larger than 200 cc. At the same time, the transition to the modern saddle tank took place, and the motorcycle began to acquire a quite different, modern appearance. In the same year DKW became the first manufacturer in Germany to chromium plate various nickel-plated surfaces. The company also pioneered the unitary engine and gearbox, obtained by bolting together the otherwise separate engine and gearbox; this had many advantages and was a characteristic visual feature of the DKW motorcycle for a whole decade.

In 1931 Dr. Herbert Venediger was called upon to defend the theories he had advanced in a dissertation written at the Munich College of Advanced Technology, entitled "Increasing the Performance and Economy of Two-stroke Carburettor Engines for Motor Vehicles". In it, he analysed the reverse-flow scavenging principle put forward by Schnürle. Rasmussen was immediately aware of the promise which more intensive research into the two-stroke motorcycle engine had to offer. He hired Dr. Venediger to manage the experimental department in Zschopau, and instructed him to look closely into the Schnürle scavenging principle, which had already been patented in 1924. The astonishing advantages of this operating method were soon revealed: reduced thermal loads on the engine, so that the blower or radiator could be dispensed with; lower fuel consumption, increased power output and more simple piston design were only the main ones. The flat piston crown, for instance, was clearly far more efficient than the existing type with high baffle to deflect the incoming mixture, which was highly unfavourable in its weight distribution. On behalf of his Zschopau plant, Rasmussen immediately purchased the sole rights to the Schnürle patent for spark-ignition engines from the owner, Klöckner-Humboldt-Deutz AG, which was Schnürle's employer. In this way he once again prepared the ground for a technical breakthrough in two-stroke engine construction; thanks to the ingenious formulation and definition of the patent application, only DKW engines were able to benefit initially from this development. Competitors had no choice but to pay a considerable sum of money to DKW for a licence. It was not until 1950 that this two-stroke principle became freely accessible to all users.

Automobiles

In parallel with the production of motorcycles, Rasmussen had never lost sight of his intention to become an automobile manufacturer. Shortly after the end of the war he examined a baby car built in Berlin by one Dr. Ing. Rudolf Slaby; this

In Berlin in the 1920s Slaby and Beringer developed a load-bearing plywood body structure which they used for a small electric vehicle. Rasmussen experimented with it when adapting his two-stroke engines for automobile use

A DKW dealer always had plenty to offer: this was the DKW product range at a special display in Zwickau (1929)

was powered by an electric motor located under the seat, and built according to very much the same principles as Rasmussen felt to be correct. He contacted the designer at once, and with him set up the Slaby-Beringer Automobilgesellschaft mbH in Berlin-Charlottenburg, in which he held a one-third stake. By June 1924, 2005 of these electric vehicles had been produced.

At the Berlin Motor Show in the autumn of 1923, the same vehicle was exhibited with a 170 cc, 2.5 hp single-cylinder DKW engine.

In due course, Slaby & Beringer went bankrupt, whereupon Rasmussen took over the company and made Slaby the director of what was now the Berlin plant of DKW. It moved to Spandau in 1927 and joined forces with the AEG company to develop electric taxi-cabs and delivery vans for city use. The energy source was a standard lead-acid battery with 40 cells, located under the bonnet and supplying a 3.5 kW electric motor. The vehicle had a load-bearing bodyshell made of copper-covered plywood. The main control switch was centrally located. The designer was Dr. Klingenberg, with DKW contributing the load-bearing plywood superstructure and the transverse-spring suspension. As an echo of the already familiar initials DKW, these electric vehicles were sold as the DEW, and in 1926/27 up to 500 were allegedly in use in the city of Berlin.

The first DKW small car with two-stroke engine was exhibited at the Leipzig Spring Fair in 1928; its inline twin-cylinder engine had a displacement of 600 cc and was rated at 15 horsepower. Using Slaby's principle, vertical plywood panels and a wooden frame supported the body, and there were transverse springs for the front and rear suspension. This principle dispensed with a separate chassis frame. The rear wheels were driven. This was the start of the two-stroke engine's highly successful career as an automobile power unit, and also of the load-bearing plywood body structure covered in imitation leather.

Although both principles were used by other companies, none of these came close to matching the hundreds of thousands of sales achieved by the originators.

A new power unit

At about this time the designers Gehle und Paffrath developed an engine which they offered for sale to Rasmussen. It was a V4 with a 90-degree included angle between the cylinder blocks. Each block had a double-acting charge pump which filled one cylinder on the upward and one on the downward stroke. This avoided the principle of mixture pre-compression in the crankcase, and also the addition of lubricating oil to the fuel. A major advantage was that the crankcase itself was no longer pressurised. Other positive features were the increase in mixture intake time, which improved cylinder filling, the lower scavenging losses and the resulting higher efficiency. The first car to use this principle had an engine of just under 800 cc capacity developing 22 hp, and was delivered early in 1930. It was advertised ambitiously as the 4 = 8, that is to say the "four-cylinder engine with the same effect as an eight-cylinder". From 1932 on, it was known as the "Sonderklasse" (literally: "Special Class") or the "Sonderklasse De Luxe", the latter having a raked windscreen, more lavish equipment, more chromium plate applied to the body and additional lighting and electrical equipment. For this car, the customer was asked to pay 3,175 Reichsmarks – a large sum in view of conditions at the time, but representing good value for money when compared with what competitors had to offer. The profit from each car had been only 57 RM from the previous two-cylinder model, but climbed steeply now to 95 RM.

Rasmussen systematically developed his small-car programme. He had by now acquired the AUDI plant in Zwickau and was searching for a worthwhile product

The DKW Front was designed in Zwickau at the end of 1930, a small car which pioneered the use of front-wheel drive

to manufacture there. Large cars had lost most of their market potential in view of dwindling public purchasing power, and above all because prices had dropped by half since 1925.

One day in September 1930, Rasmussen and AUDI plant director Heinrich Schuh paid a surprise visit to the AUDI design office. The company showed every sign of being in deep crisis. The yard was full of unsold cars, and of the 24 designers employed in better times, only two remained: Oskar Arlt and Walter Haustein.

Oskar Arlt (1889-1945) had trained as a mechanical fitter, worked for machinery manufacturers in Berlin and signed up for the engineering college in Zwickau in 1910. He graduated from there three years later with an "excellent" grade. He then worked initially for Protos and later for Hansa Lloyd before joining AUDI in 1920 and becoming one of its leading designers.

Walter Haustein (1903-1988) learned the technical draughtsman's trade at HORCH, before joining AUDI in 1925. He was self-taught, but possessed considerable talent. He worked as a designer for AUDI from 1926 onwards, remaining with the company as one of its chief designers until 1956; he retired from the company only in 1968.

As we have already mentioned, Rasmussen horrified these two remaining designers by calling for a complete small car to be sketched out within six weeks. In point of fact, the idea reached the driveable prototype stage in only 36 days, an almost unbelievably short time. This was the kind of hectic activity that Rasmussen loved: development work completed by January, finished car ready for sale at the Berlin Motor Show in February 1931.

This vehicle from the AUDI design office, which was not so much a new development as a most ingenious combination of familiar and well-proven components, not only set the Zwickau plant on the road to a new and extremely active future but also stimulated the development and introduction of front-wheel drive for automobiles for the first time on a worthwhile scale.

The first DKW automobile with two-stroke spark-ignition engine, rear-wheel drive – and of course a plywood body – appeared in 1928

Motor sport

Even the company's first auxiliary bicycle engines, the "racing" versions of which were capable of 65 km/h, were used in sporting events. DKW's first victory in this category was obtained on 20th September 1920 in The Hague.

A DKW racing department was formed in 1925, with the task of designing its own competition vehicles. From that time on, the rapid DKW two-strokes featured water cooling and forced aspiration by charge pump. The first 175 cc bike was followed in 1928 by a 250 cc single-cylinder version developing 18 hp and capable of reaching 130 km/h. In the same year the PRe 500 twin-cylinder bike appeared, initially rated at 26 and later at 32 hp. These were extremely successful motorcycles, enabling DKW's advertising to refer to no less than a thousand race victories in only two years.

DKW automobiles took part in reliability trials. A newspaper report dating from 1928 tells us just how standard the competing cars were: "Miss Hildegard Kallweit of Danzig entered her DKW on the very day she took delivery of it for the ADAC Overnight Rally from Danzig to Königsberg and back (400 km), and won a silver trophy and a plaque." In 1929, Rasmussen formed a competition department for DKW automobiles, appointing Gerhard Macher, a very well-known BMW/Dixi competition driver, to manage it.

The first sports car was based on the two-cylinder engine with charge pump, and among the successful drivers were Simons, Oestreicher, Macher himself and Bauhofer.

In 1930, racing driver F. C. Meyer set up 12 international class records on the track in Montlhéry, near Paris, at the wheel of a car specially developed by aerodynamics expert Koenig-Fachsenfeld. The DKW was driven for 24 hours at an average speed of 91.5 km/h. In 1931 the new DKW Front was entered for races with a single-seater body, and achieved considerable success in the small-car class.

DKW's mascot in the nineteen-twenties

Numerous DKW P 15 cars took part in this concours d'élégance in Berlin. The friction-type front shock absorbers can easily be seen

Dates in the history of DKW

1916	Experiments with steam-driven vehicles continued until 1918
1919	The 25 ccm miniature two-stroke engine ("Des Knaben Wunsch")
1921	Zschopauer Motorenwerke J. S. Rasmussen; the first auxiliary bicycle engine ("Das kleine Wunder")
1922	DKW trade mark registered for engines and motorcycles
1923	Zschopauer Motorenwerke J. S. Rasmussen AG established on 22nd December. Capital in 1924: 1 million RM, increased in 1929 to 10 million RM
1928	World's largest motorcycle manufacturer; start of car production
1932	On 29th June, amalgamation of HORCH Werke AG, AUDI Werke AG and the car division of WANDERER Werke AG to create the AUTO UNION AG with headquarters in Chemnitz.

The principal DKW car models up to 1932

Designation	Number/layout of cylinders	Bore x stroke in mm	Displacement in cc	Output in hp	Years of production
With rear-wheel drive					
P 15	2 inline	74 x 68	584	15	1928–1929
4=8, V 800	4 V	60 x 65.5	780	22	1930–1931
4=8, V 1000	4 V	68 x 68.5	980	25	1931–1932
With front-wheel drive					
F	2 inline	68 x 68	494	15	1931–1932
F	2 inline	74 x 68	584	18	1931–1932

A standard DKW P 15 being raced in 1929

In 1928, motorcycle output rose from 5,000 to more than 65,000. 375 motorcycles and 500 engines were being built every day. The company's share of new registrations in Germany was 30 percent in 1930. The prices reflected the low manufacturing costs: the cheapest DKW was available for only 485 RM.

DKW automobiles with rear-wheel drive were made at the Spandau plant from 1928 onwards. Starting in 1931, DKW cars with front-wheel drive began to leave the AUDI plant in Zwickau, which had been acquired by the DKW group three years previously. Both models used the leatherette-covered wooden body principle. By 1932, Spandau's output of small rear-wheel-drive DKW cars had reached approximately 10,000 units, an average of 2,500 annually. Before the AUTO UNION came into being, almost 5,000 front-wheel-drive DKWs had also been built. DKW's share of the small-car market was only a modest one at first, but soared when the "Front" was introduced. Prices were very low, as befitted the character of this small car. The DKW 4=8 sold for 3,300 RM in 1930, whereas in 1931 it was possible to become the owner of a DKW Front for only 1,685 RM.

The principal DKW motorcycle models up to 1932

Designation	Number of cylinders	Bore x stroke in mm	Displacement in cc	Output in hp	Years produced
Auxiliary engine	1	50 x 60	118	1	1919–1923
Golem chair-bike	1	50 x 60	118	1	1921–1922
Lomes chair-bike	1	55 x 60	143	2.5	1922–1925
Reichsfahrt model	1	55 x 60	143	2.5	1922–1924
ZM	1	59 x 64	175	2.5	1924–1925
E 206	1	64 x 64	206	4	1925–1928
Z 500	2	68 x 68	494	12	1926–1929
200 De Luxe	1	63 x 64	198	4.5	1929–1932
KM 175	1	59 x 64	172	4	1930–1933
Block 300	1	74 x 68	294	9	1931–1933
Super Sport 500	2	68 x 68	494	18	1929–1933
ZIS 200	1	63 x 64	198	4	1929–1931

DKW Super-Sport 500 with water-cooled twin-cylinder engine

*Hugo Ruppe
(1879–1949)*

*Entrance to the DKW
plant in Spandau,
where the assembly
of rear-wheel-
drive DKW cars
commenced in 1928*

Hugo Ruppe

1879	Born on 15th August 1879 in Apolda. Apprenticeship as a mechanic followed by engineering studies at Ilmenau Technical College
1904	Design and construction of the Apoldania motorcycle, with four-stroke engine
1907	Established own automobile factory in Markranstädt, near Leipzig
1910	Name changed to Markranstädter Automobilfabrik (MAF) GmbH
1912–1914	Trials with two-stroke engines and flywheel magneto
1914–1918	Military service
1918	Moved to Zschopau, two-stroke engine offered to Rasmussen
1920	Left Rasmussen, moved to Berlin and set up the Bekamo company (Berliner Kleinmotoren Fabrik) to make two-stroke engines with a piston charging pump, light alloy pistons and cylinders with grey cast-iron liners, detachable aluminium cylinder heads and a most ingenious scavenge-air control principle. These were elaborate engines, but easily the most powerful two-strokes of their time. After a short period with Framo in Frankenberg, Ruppe moved to Festenberg (Silesia) and set up a mechanical engineering factory. At the end of the war, he fled to Zschopau and attempted to start production of small stand-by electric generators, but this project failed
1949	Immediately after the death of his wife, Hugo Ruppe died destitute and almost completely forgotten on 23rd January 1949

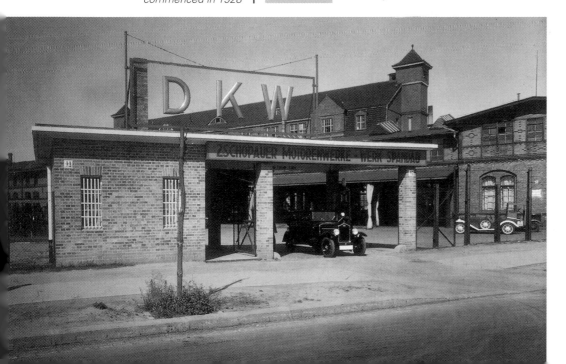

Carl Hahn

1894	Born on 4th March 1894 in Nove Hrady (Gratzen, Bohemia). After the First World War, studied agronomy at the Vienna College of Advanced Agriculture, taking his doctorate in 1922
1922	Joined the Zschopauer Motorenwerke J.S.Rasmussen in Zschopau, Saxony, on 20th April 1922. Hahn worked closely together with Rasmussen. He created an efficient sales organisation. His enthusiasm and dedication to the interests of the brand acquired him the respectful nickname "DKW-Hahn"
1932	When the AUTO UNION AG was set up in Chemnitz, Hahn was appointed to the board of directors with responsibility for sales
1945	After fleeing to the West, Hahn was one of the founders of the central depot for AUTO UNION spare parts in Ingolstadt, from which today's AUDI AG has grown
1949	Hahn was appointed deputy chairman of the board of management of AUTO UNION GmbH.
1957	On 30th June 1957 he resigned from the company for health reasons.
1961	Dr. Carl Hahn died on 5th June, 1961.

Dr. Carl Hahn
(1894–1961)

Dr. Ove Rasmussen speaking about his father, DKW founder J. S. Rasmussen:

"My father was much loved in his companies. He knew almost all the workers' names. Every day he would walk through the factory smoking a big cigar and followed by his dog. Sometimes the dog would wander off and lose him, then panic when an engine was started up. The workers would then bring the dog back to my father, where it would slink along close behind him for a while. They liked my father although he certainly wasn't a particularly generous person. He didn't donate a complete hospital like Robert Bosch did in Stuttgart. He did set up quite a few useful institutions, but he never managed a complete hospital! Incidentally, the wages he paid in Zschopau were a problem during the Third Reich and also during the war: they were altogether too high!"

Ready for despatch

HORCH – an overview

10/35 hp Phaeton
(1923)

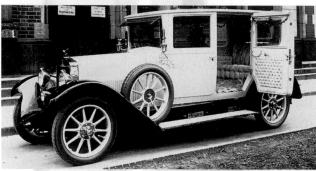

10/45 hp sports car
(1924)

10/50 hp saloon
(1924)

10/50 hp Phaeton
(1925)

306 Roadster (1928)

420 Sports convertible (1930)

350 personnel carrier (1929)

480 Sports convertible (1929)

375 Pullman cabriolet (1930)

670 Sports convertible (1932)

*C 14/35 hp phaeton
(1921)*

*E 22/55 hp phaeton
(1922)*

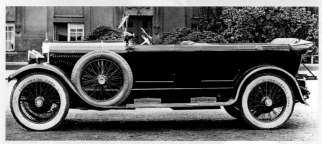

*K 14/50 hp phaeton
(1924)*

*M 18/70 hp chassis
(1924)*

*R 19/100 hp
sports convertible
(1927)*

*The 100 hp
"Zwickau" (1929)*

*A 100 hp "Zwickau"
convertible (1930)*

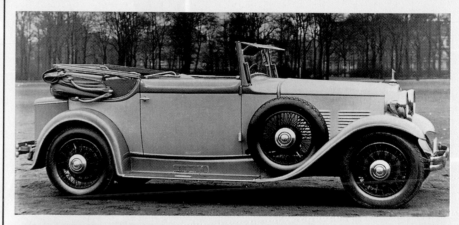

*The 75 hp "Dresden"
convertible (1932)*

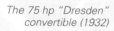

*P 5/30 hp saloon
(1931)*

WANDERER – an overview

*WANDERER W 10/IV
four-cylinder as an
open tourer (1930-31)*

*WANDERER W 11
six-cylinder (1931)*

*WANDERER W 11
two-seater sports
convertible (1931)*

*WANDERER W 11
Pullman saloon and
WANDERER
W 10/IV convertible
(1931)*

*The distinguished
WANDERER W 11
four-door "sedan-
cabriolet"(1931)*

The black-and-white stripes identify this WANDERER W 10/IV as a taxicab (1930-31)

Various convertible versions of the WANDERER W 11 (1929-30)

The WANDERER W 11 with a spacious six-light saloon body

WANDERER W 17 convertible with two-litre, six-cylinder engine developed by Ferdinand Porsche (1932)

DKW – an overview

DKW sports cars were highly successful in small-car events (1929)

A standard DKW P 15 took part in the 1929 Monte Carlo Rally

DKW 4=8 800 cc four-cylinder, two-stroke engine, developing 22 hp (1930)

For many Germans, the DKW Front (F 1) was the first step towards serious motoring (1931)

The DKW Front was introduced at the Berlin Motor Show in February 1931

DKW auxiliary engine for bicycles, 1919-23

Many other manufacturers installed the small DKW engine in their own products (1920)

The DKW E 206, a successful model from Zschopau (1925-28)

The DKW Lomos chair-bike was a forerunner of the motor scooter (1922)

The DKW Golem with horizontal single-cylinder two-stroke engine (1921)

The popular DKW 200 De Luxe, known disrespectfully as the "Blood Blister" on account of its red-painted fuel tank (1929)

The sign of the Four Rings

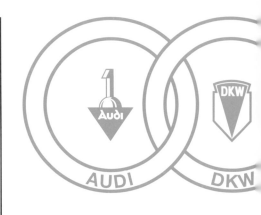

In the technical development area, the nineteen-twenties proved to be a period in which knowledge was acquired, much pleasure and benefit were derived from experimental work and an abundance of technical novelties appeared everywhere. Then came the Thirties, which were a time for implementing these technical achievements in volume production. The fruits of this pioneering technical groundwork could be seen in radio and television and in aviation as well as in motor-vehicle engineering.

As the economy grew rapidly, it gave rise to an equally strong and increasingly diversified demand for communication. For this, suitable and above all well-proven technical facilities had yet to be developed. One can only admire an era which was evidently accustomed to thinking well ahead into the future, and which produced technical solutions to problems which had, strictly speaking, not yet arisen! The aircraft and the motor vehicle could be said to fall into this category, with the result that by the time they had become indispensable, they were not only available but also technically mature.

By the 1920s, this lead in technical knowledge over actual practice had ceased to exist in the motor vehicle industry. The last fundamental engineering invention for the automobile is generally regarded as Porsche's torsion-bar suspension, dating from 1930. This was also the period in which conveyor-belt assembly took over increasingly, and in which extensive standardisation of parts made it possible to build large numbers of vehicles to a consistent quality standard. In those days, the motor-vehicle industry came to be regarded as an outstanding example of production efficiency. Demand was growing, latent at first and only modest in its extent, for everything associated with mobility. This was the almost magical attraction of the "automobile", as implied in its name:

the Americans had demonstrated to the rest of the world what could be done to open up a vast country by means of the motor vehicle. When the Chamber of the US National Automobile Industray asked 40,000 farmers' wives which consumer goods they regarded as most essential to their living standard, almost all of them put the automobile at the top of the list. Only then followed such alleged luxuries as tap water in the kitchen, telephone or radio.

Germany pounds the pedals

In the Germany of the 1930s, however, the most significant form of personal transport was also the cheapest: the bicycle. There were more than 20 million of them in use by 1939, and their owners covered a greater total distance than even the Reichsbahn, the German railway system, could claim. A census of working-day transport conducted in the Halle and Merseburg region in 1937 revealed for example that 29 percent of those in paid employment used the train to reach their place of work, but no less than 54 percent went by bicycle. In the same survey, incidentally, passenger-car journeys were lost in the heading "Miscellaneous", which accounted for little more than 3 percent of the total.

Despite this, the number of motor vehicles was growing rapidly all over the world. More than 80 percent of them were used for private transport – individual mobility was on its way up at last. In Germany, this was the area in which the motorcycle was enjoying a continued boom. It could be turned into a three-wheeler if the need arose, by fitting a sidecar. Its purchase and upkeep costs were then lower than any other form of family conveyance. The motorcycle acted as the lowest step on the motoring ladder, attracting all those whose financial resources would not extend to an automobile. Motorcycles also played an increasing part in trade and commerce: the Post Office used them, and they were even pressed into service as a cheaper alternative to the taxicab. Logically enough, the first motoring boom came at the cheapest end of the mar-

A typical city street scene from the Germany of the Thirties: the small car is already strongly in evidence

ket. It is surely justified to speak to some extent of "mass motorisation" in such circumstances, even if only half a million motorcycles were being used by a population of more than 60 million.

Sales of small cars also prospered, and in due course the medium-sized and large-car categories also exhibited a modest degree of growth.

One of the stimulating factors in Germany was undeniably the fact that the National Socialists encouraged mass motoring in their propaganda campaigns. This began with a speech by Hitler when opening the Berlin Motor Show in 1933, in which he announced a programme of tax exemptions for all new motor vehicles and the immediate start of construction work on a main road ("autobahn") network. This was of course Hitler at his demagogic best; the Nazis had little chance of achieving their bombastic aims in the short term because of increasing raw-material supply problems. Starting in 1936/37, vital raw materials such as rubber and iron had been rationed, and companies were receiving far smaller quantities than they could actually have processed on the basis of their order books. By 1937, delivery times for vehicles had lengthened to a year or more, and production plant was not running at full potential capacity. In contrast to this, orders for the military authorities were given top priority. It is an unfortunate fact that despite the trumpetings of the leading Nazis, the German motor vehicle industry's task was already at that time to supply the armed forces and not to promote public motorisation. It is a tragic element in the history of the automobile in Germany that the products of large, respected companies, who had gained their reputations as a result of hard and dedicated work on the part of whole generations of employees, technical and commercial staff,

Germany's first dedicated vehicle highway was opened from Cologne to Bonn in 1932

Rush-hour traffic on the Pariser Platz in Berlin

were so sadly degraded to instruments of war, death and destruction. For some of these celebrated marques the war itself marked the end of their long history, since they were unable to find their feet again when peace was eventually restored.

AUTO UNION AG, Chemnitz

This company was established on the initiative of the State Bank of Saxony, which held the majority of the shares from the start (culminating in a 97 % holding). On 29th June 1932 the AUDI and HORCH companies and the Zschopauer Motorenwerke J. S. Rasmussen joined forces to create the AUTO UNION. A purchase and leasing agreement was concluded at the same time with the WANDERER company, for the take-over of its automobile division. The new board of directors consisted of Dr. Richard Bruhn, Jörgen Skafte Rasmussen und Klaus Detlof von Oertzen. Dr. Carl Hahn was appointed as deputy director.

The climb to the number-two position

The founder-companies retained their presence in the form of the familiar brand designations.

AUTO UNION AG of Chemnitz soon became Germany's second-largest motor-vehicle manufacturing group. Its own emblem, with four intersecting rings, symbolised the inseparable character of the new undertaking according to the will of the four founder-companies. In view of the variegated product ranges which they were selling at the time, it took about three years before the desired concentration process got under way and a clear AUTO UNION profile emerged. This can be seen from the model brochures dating from 1935 onwards: the bodies became more standardised and various assemblies were shared between models, for example rear axles. This marked the end of decentral model strategies. AUTO UNION's technical policy was quite openly based on its member-companies' traditions, but was certainly not averse to fundamental changes when the occasion arose. The day-to-day emphasis, however, was on cutting costs, primarily by standardising chassis frames, the four-, six- and eight-cylinder engines and the transmissions. Improved operating economy was another priority, and in this connection the aerodynamics came in for much attention, in particular by utilising the patents granted to Paul Jaray and also extensive wind-tunnel tests, culminating in the DKW F 9 and HORCH 930 S production

AUTO UNION cars during the procession when the "Reichsautobahn" highway was opened between Frankfurt and Darmstadt (1935)

models. By 1935 all technical development had been transferred to the new Central Design Office and Central Experimental Department in Chemnitz, where the AUDI 920, DKW F 9, WANDERER Types 23 and 24 and the HORCH 930 S were developed. Two-stroke engine research went ahead enthusiastically, particularly on scavenging air blowers, injection pumps and nozzles. The search was also on for a better form of scavenging than the Schnürle system. By 1939, two-valve two-strokes but also engines with tubular and rotary slide valves were under development.

The AUTO UNION stand at the German Motor Show (the "IAA") in Berlin, 1935

Exemplary achievements

The AUTO UNION AG of Chemnitz was in existence for sixteen years. Six of these were war years, the liquidation process took another three, leaving only seven years – under half of the company's lifetime – for it to demonstrate its powers of innovation and growth. But what it in fact achieved during these seven

The HORCH 930 S was new at the 1939 German Motor Show (at right in picture)

years was truly astonishing. This was the period in which motoring forged ahead by leaps and bounds in Germany. Demand went up steeply, so that thorough preparations for long-term volume production were needed instead of many companies' prevailing "build to order" policy. New development and testing methods were needed. Not for nothing was the DKW F 7 one of the first cars in Germany for which not only a pre-production run as we would understand it today, but also a genuine pilot-production batch of cars, was authorised.

A systematic approach

In 1936 the Central Development and Design Office run by Oskar Siebler and Werner Strobel began work on the DKW F 9. This was not only intended to continue the success of the company's "Front" model, but also as the AUTO

UNION's answer to the challenge implied by the announcement of the "Volkswagen", or People's Car. The Saxon automobile group was the first and indeed the only manufacturer in Germany to have its own solution to the mass motorisation problem ready to hand. By 1940, it was planned to offer the F 9 for sale with a 30 hp three-cylinder two-stroke engine, front-wheel drive and a wind-tunnel tested body. A new engine plant took shape on the splendidly named Chemnitzer Kauffahrtei, and there were plans to reduce the car's asking price to 1,200 Reichsmarks within five years.

The first crash tests

Also formed in 1936, the Central Experimental Department was organised as three divisions; technical, scientific and road testing. In connection with the department's development and testing work for the last pre-war DKW models, particularly those with a plastic body, it is interesting to note that AUTO UNION was the first German manufacturer to draw up a well-planned, empirical crash test programme, the criteria for which were thoroughly modern, with simulated frontal and sideswipe collisions and a lateral roll-over test. The sheer inventiveness of the Saxon automobile engineers is best documented by the granting of more than 3,000 patents to them at home and abroad. It reaped the deserved rewards: every fourth car newly registered in Germany in 1938 was an AUTO UNION product, and every fifth had been built in Zwickau. Furthermore, every third motorcycle registered for the first time in Germany was a DKW.

Day trips and leisure activities were important stimuli for mass motorisation from the very outset

Dates in the history of
AUTO UNION AG, Chemnitz

1932	Backdated to 1st November 1931, the AUTO UNION AG in Chemnitz was formed by amalgamating the Zschopauer Motorenwerke J. S. Rasmussen AG (DKW), the HORCH Werke AG in Zwickau, the AUDI Werke AG in Zwickau and, by a separate lease and purchasing agreement, the WANDERER Werke in Siegmar near Chemnitz. Share capital: 14.5 million Reichsmarks (RM)
1943	31st May: capital increased to 20.3 million RM
1943	31st October: capital increased to 30 million RM

Eight workers were needed to cover the wooden DKW body by hand with imitation leather

In a single move, the AUTO UNION had become Germany's second-largest automobile manufacturer. It expanded a further four times over during the following six years, its consolidated turnover went up from 65 to 276 million Reichsmarks and the workforce grew from 8,000 to more than 23,000. Annual output of motorcycles increased from just under 12,000 to over 59,000, and automobile production went up from 17,000 to more than 67,000 units.

Compared with the year in which the AUTO UNION was established, output of HORCH cars had more than doubled by 1938, five times more WANDERER cars were being built and the increase in the volume of DKWs was more than tenfold.

The AUTO UNION's share of new motorcycle registrations in 1938 was in the region of 35 percent, and for cars was 23.4 percent. The Group contributed a 27 percent share to Germany's motor-vehicle exports.

In due course, the AUTO UNION became one of the major suppliers to public authorities and the armed forces. By 1937/38, this market had reached a volume greater than civilian sales of AUDI, HORCH and WANDERER taken together.

Orders 124 and 126 dated 30th and 31st October 1945, issued by the Soviet Military Administration in Germany (SMAD) declared the AUTO UNION AG of Chemnitz to be expropriated by the occupying powers; in 1948 its name was expunged from the trade register.

Richard Bruhn

1886	Born on 25th June 1886 in Cismar, Eastern Holstein, where he visited junior school and then became an apprentice electrician, before switching to a commercial career later
1907	Clerk in an engineering office operated by the AEG company in Bremen
1910	Commercial manager of the AEG office in London
1914–1918	Military service
1918	Studied economics in Kiel and received his doctorate in 1921
1921–1926	Commercial director of Neufeldt & Kuhnke in Kiel
1927–1929	Member of the board of management of Junkers in Dessau
1929–1930	Director of the Pöge electricity company in Chemnitz
1930	Employed by the State Bank of Saxony, which appointed him as its director on the board of the Zschopauer Motorenwerke J. S. Rasmussen AG. Preparation for ...
1932	... and establishment of the AUTO UNION AG, of which he became Board Chairman
1945	Left Chemnitz on May 7th
1945–1947	Interned by the British Army of Occupation
1949	First general manager of the re-established AUTO UNION GmbH in Ingolstadt
1952	Awarded an honorary doctorate in engineering by the Rhine-Westphalian College of Advanced Technology in Aachen for his services to the German motor-vehicle industry
1956	On 6th November, retired from the AUTO UNION's board of management, but remained in contact with the company for a further two years as chairman of its Supervisory Board
1964	Died on 8th July 1964

Conveyor-belt production at the AUDI plant, which began to make front-wheel drive cars in 1931

Dr. Richard Bruhn (1886–1964)

Dr. William Werner (1893–1970)

William Werner

1893	Born on 7th November 1893 in New York
1907	Returned to Germany with his parents, who hailed from Oederan in Saxony
1912	Apprentice mechanic, then mechanical fitter in the workshops of the American Multigraph company's branch in Berlin
1914–1918	Attended evening classes and passed the mechanical engineering examinations. As an American citizen, Werner was not called up for military service
1920–1924	Production engineer at leading German machine-tool companies, for instance Bergmann-Borsig, Berliner AG previously Freund and Schuchardt & Schütte
1924	Plant director at the Ludwig Loewe machine-tool company
1925	Technical director of Schiess AG in Düsseldorf
1926	Study tour of the US automobile industry; worked for the Chrysler Corporation in Detroit
1926	Joined the HORCH Werke AG in Zwickau/Berlin
1927	Technical director of the HORCH Werke AG
1929	From 24th May on, full member of the HORCH Werke AG board of directors
1934	Technical director of AUTO UNION AG, Chemnitz
1942	Honorary doctorate from the Dresden College of Advanced Technology for his work on modernising and improving the production efficiency of the German motor-vehicle industry
1945	Obliged to flee to Bad Homburg
1948	Set up a factory for motorcycles and mopeds in Rotterdam for the Plivier company, and became its manager
1956	Joined the management of the new AUTO UNION GmbH with responsibility for technical affairs. Worked initially in Düsseldorf and from 1961 onwards in Ingolstadt
1962	Retired from the AUTO UNION
1970	Died in Sempach, Switzerland, on 20th June 1970

AUDI's new dynamism

Even before the new company group was officially established, AUDI's design office had drawn up plans for a new car. It was to have front-wheel drive and a six-cylinder engine. The most suitable source of power was considered to be the new 40 hp WANDERER engine designed by Ferdinand Porsche, thanks to its low weight of 130 kilograms.

To keep the vehicle as light as possible, it was decided to use a box-section backbone chassis, which led to the adoption of independent suspension all round.

The result was named the AUDI Front, and the AUTO UNION AG exhibited it at the 1933 International Automobile and Motorcycle Show in Berlin. Alongside Stoewer and Brennabor, the marque thus paved the way for front-wheel drive on medium-size automobiles.

AUDI's clientèle at the time was primarily interested in comfort, convenience and ample space rather than sheer performance. But by the mid-thirties a change set in, and was reflected by management decisions concerning AUDI model policy. Dynamism and sporting character were now considered more important: powerful cars, but not large ones. The aim was to communicate AUDI as a progressive source of highly innovative design. Jaray's streamlined body outlines were considered, and pulsating-action automatic transmission. The new car was to be aimed at a specific buyer group, in this case one with greater awareness of automobile engineering principles, which would appreciate the technical merits of a car designed for enthusiastic day-to-day driving – and which of course possessed the necessary financial resources to adopt this approach to driving.

In view of all this, the designers had to find more power from somewhere. The WANDERER engines had already been uprated to 55 hp, and could not be deve-

The principal AUDI models, 1932–1939

Type	Number/layout of cylinders	Bore x stroke in mm	Displacement in cc	Output in hp	Years of manufacture	No
Front UW	6 inline	70 x 85	1949	40	1933–1934	FW
Front 225	6 inline	87 x 92	2255	50 (55)	1934–1938	FV
920	6 inline	87 x 92	3281	75	1939–1941	

AUDI was always among the pioneers of the streamlined body; this is an experimental car based on the AUDI Front, and utilising Jaray's patents

The 1933 AUDI with front-wheel drive and swing axles, here with a Gläser sports convertible body

Only two of these most attractive AUDI Front Roadsters were ever built (1935)

Experts take a close look at the new AUDI 920: they are racing drivers Walfried Winkler and Ewald Kluge (1939)

loped any further. The front-wheel drive shaft joints were rated for a maximum operating life of 30,000 kilometres. Since a top speed of well over 120 km/h was called for, there was no option but to revert to conventional rear-wheel drive.

The new AUDI 920 was the work of AUTO UNION's central development and design office in Chemnitz; since early 1934, AUDI had had no design office of its own. Instead of striking new technical departures and modern design features, and also because of the permanent shortage of raw materials from which the industry was suffering, which had the effect of delaying development schedules, there was no alternative but to be content with modified standard bodies and other well-proven design elements. The new six-cylinder OHC engine developed 75 hp, enough to propel the car up to a top speed of more than 130 km/h.

DKW – the world's largest motorcycle manufacture

The motorcycles

During the era of the Four Rings in Zschopau, technical development concentrated mainly on the adoption of the Schnürle loop scavenging principle, The first DKW motorcycle to use it was the "Block 350", launched in 1932.

In 1934 it was followed by the celebrated SB series, with four engine sizes between 200 and 500 cc, and in some cases with a dynastarter. At the end of 1934 the R T100 was added at the lower end of the model programme; it cost only 345 Reichsmarks. 72,000 were built in all, making it DKW's most successful motorcycle.

In October 1936, DKW modified its engines to run on a 25:1 instead of 20:1 mixture of fuel and oil. Vegetable oils could have been used even more sparingly, but were found to cause resin deposits inside the engine, and therefore mineral oils continued to be specified.

In 1937 DKW produced 55,470 motorcycles, of which 11,500 were exported, making it once again the world's largest motorcycle manufacturer. The NZ series succeeded the SB models in 1938. It consisted of versions with 250, 350 and 500 cc engines. The largest-engined NZ model was the first DKW motorcycle to have rear suspension.

Twenty years after engines had first been produced in Zschopau, in 1939, the RT 125 was introduced; as the culmination of a long phase of development, it set entirely new standards for a popular motorcycle. In a straightforward, practical and entirely logical manner, it embodied two decades of dedication to the Zschopau factory's fundamental concepts: simplicity, practicality, reliability, economy, long life and performance potential – all achieved at minimum expense, com-

The DKW RT 100 was introduced in 1934, and was the start of Zschopau's most successful model line

A contemporary street scene: the DKW motorcycle as family transport

114

The early days of mass production: in 1934 well over 10,000 DKW front-wheel-drive cars were built for the first time

plexity and upkeep cost. This was the declared intention, and by and large it was achieved. When the one-millionth DKW engine left the assembly line in March 1940, it was – how could it have been otherwise – used to power an RT 125.

At this time the Zschopau engineers gave some thought to reviving the motorised bicycle, and developed the "Hummel" ("Bumble-bee") as a rear-wheel hub unit. Like most other projects, this was put aside when war broke out.

Passenger cars

Development of four-cylinder models proceeded in accordance with the strategy laid down by Rasmussen. When it was time for new models to be announced in 1933, a replacement for the "Sonderklasse" known as the 1001 was launched. It was joined later by a cheaper version, the 1002.

The DKW 1001 with rear-wheel drive, swing-axle suspension and a four-door saloon body

In addition to a four-seater cabriolet-sedan, a four-door saloon was offered for the first time.

The "Schwebeklasse" ("Floating (sic!) Class") model was announced in 1934, with a more powerful engine and an entirely new body. The name was derived from the new suspension layout, with wheel location on the axis of the centre of gravity, thus greatly reducing pitch and roll when cornering. A rigid axle with a high-mounted transverse spring was used, and the rather clumsy term "Floating Axle" was protected as a trade mark by the AUTO UNION.

The new engine proved to suffer from various shortcomings: fuel and oil consumption were too high, and there was a tendency for piston seizure to occur. Although the design concept was convincing enough, production units incurred all kinds of problems in the hands of the customers; these had not been foreseen, and had to be eliminated at considerable expense and with a corresponding loss of brand image.

Significant management errors, from the premature introduction of new designs to an inability to master DKW's model integration problems, not to mention hostility on the part of the dealer organisation, did their part to render the technical problems still more severe. For two years, defects had to be put right by recourse to extremely costly after-sales service campaigns.

The next model to be introduced, the "Sonderklasse 37", was a new design. The bodyshell was no longer of the unitary type, but possessed a fully-fledged chassis frame. Apart from ensuring the necessary strength, this enabled a wide selection of bodies to be fitted. Instead of the rigid front axle, a low-slung transverse spring was used in conjunction with triangulated upper wishbones, the shock absorbers being pivoted on the wishbone axes. The "floating" rear axle layout had proved highly successful and was therefore retained, as was the four-speed gearbox with the freewheel so typical of a DKW. On this model it was installed behind the gearbox, the input shaft of which changed its direction when the car was reversed. The freewheel therefore only operated in the forward gears. The same engine was installed, but was given a thorough design revision. The previous DKW body with its plywood surfaces covered with imitation leather was discarded in favour of a sheet steel body which resembled the WANDERER W 24 in appearance. Unfortunately not much could be done to minimise the sheer complexity involved in manufacturing and machining the parts of the charge-pump engine; this was the principal reason why the three-cylinder DKW engine which Carl Hahn had suggested as long ago as the Autumn of 1935 was eventually preferred, since it lacked the other engine's built-in shortcomings.

One of the most attractive DKW models, the F 5 sports roadster (1935–1937)

From "Reichsklasse" to "Meisterklasse"

In the years which followed, the front-wheel-drive cars were gradually perfected, culminating in the F 9. Schnürle's patent loop scavenging system had been adopted at the end of 1932, after which power output went up from 15 to 18 hp. From the Spring of 1933 on, there was a choice between the "Reichsklasse" model with a 600 cc, 18 hp engine and the "Meisterklasse" with a 700 cc engine

developing 20 hp. With a specific power output of about 30 horsepower per litre, the small DKW occupied a position at the top of the list among contemporary German cars. In 1935 the F 5 model appeared with a central box-section frame and the so-called "floating axle" at the rear, a patented design which had already proved its worth on the four-cylinder cars.

This basic design survived until production had to cease, though with certain modifications, notably an entirely new type of frame for the F 8. Unusually, a few Type F 7 cars were built with a four-door saloon body, but these were intended exclusively for export. For countries in the Far East with rainy climates, the DKW Front was also built with a sheet steel body.

Adding new colour

Together with the IG Farben company, development work started on material for a synthetic-resin body using phenolic resins processed at high pressure, with paper as a reinforcement. However, the cost was too high and the decision was taken at an early stage to use a sheet steel body for the F 9. The bodyshell was tested in a wind tunnel in accordance with Jaray's patented methods. The completely new three-cylinder engine was developed for use in this car, which was scheduled to enter production in 1940.

At that time, the DKW front-wheel-drive cars were not only among the world's top-selling small cars, but also worthy proponents of the front-wheel drive principle.

The F 9 body, developed with the aid of wind-tunnel testing, was a thoroughly forward-looking design. The gear lever, however, still emerged at the traditional point on the fascia

The principal DKW motorcycle models, 1932–1939

Type	Number of cylinders	Bore x stroke in mm	Displacement in cc	Output in hp	Years produced
SB 200	1	60 x 68	190	7	1933–1938
SB 500	2	68 x 68	494	15	1934–1939
RT 100	1	50 x 50	98	2.5	1934–1938
KM 200	1	63 x 64	198	6	1934–1936
NZ 250	1	68 x 68	245	9	1938–1941
NZ 350	1	72 x 85	343	11.5	1938–1945
NZ 500	2	64 x 76	489	18	1939–1942
RT 125	1	52 x 58	123	4.75	1939–1944

The SB series, launched in 1934, remained largely typical for the DKW motorcycle until 1939. The de luxe version was available with an electric starter

This sports bike was available over the counter! Between 1934 and 1939, about 200 of these 250 cc bikes with charge-pump engine were built

The sectioned model of the new NZ series, as shown at trade fairs and exhibitions

The motorcycle as the key to seemingly unlimited leisure and pleasure – a phenomenon not restricted to the nineteen-thirties of this century

In September 1938 this DKW SB 500 was delivered to the King of Iraq – the gilded fuel tank was of course not a standard item!

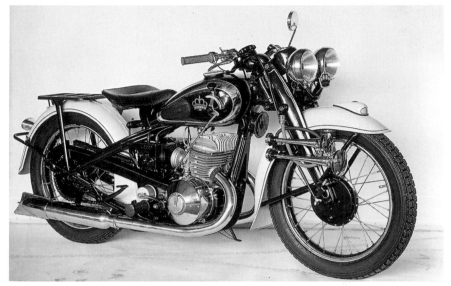

All the large DKW motorcycles were suitable for sidecar use

Historical marque data

In 1938 about two-thirds of world motorcycle production came from Germany. Of the annual total of about 200,000 units, about a third were DKWs. By 1945 the Zschopau plant had built some 660,000 motorcycles. With an annual output of 60,000 units in 1937, DKW once again became the world's largest motorcycle manufacturer. Its share of the German market for new motorcycles, according to registration statistics, was of the order of 35 percent.

It was the end of 1939 before the 500 cc NZ model appeared with the twin-cylinder two-port engine and a new feature for DKW, adjustable rear suspension. The illustration shows the version for the German Post Office, with load-carrying sidecar

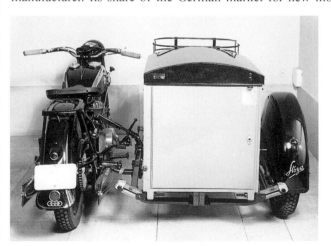

The principal DKW automobile models, 1932–1939

Type	No. of cylinders	Bore x stroke in mm	Displacement in cc	Output in hp	Years of manufacture	Notes
DKW with rear-wheel drive						
Sonderklasse incl. 1001/1002	4 V	68 x 68.5	1000	26	1932–1935	
Schwebeklasse	4 V	70 x 68.5	1100	32	1934–1937	
Sonderklasse 37	4 V	70 x 68.5	1100	32	1937–1940	

From 1932 until production ceased in 1940, some 25,000 of these cars were built.
They were assembled in Berlin-Spandau.

Type	No. of cylinders	Bore x stroke in mm	Displacement in cc	Output in hp	Years of manufacture	Notes
DKW with front-wheel drive						
F 2	2 inline	74 x 68	584	18	1932–1935	
F 4	2 inline	76 x 76	690	20	1934–1935	
F 5	2 inline	76 x 76	584	18	1935–1936	Reichsklasse
	2 inline	76 x 76	690	20	1935–1936	Meisterklasse
F 7	2 inline	76 x 76	690	20	1937–1939	as F 5
F 8	2 inline	76 x 76	690	20	1939–1942	as F 5
F 9	3 inline	70 x 78	900	30	1939	Prototype

At AUDI's plant in Zwickau, a total of approximately 270,000 DKW front-wheel drive cars were produced by an average workforce of 1,350 people.

DKW's share of all new registrations in 1938, for example, was about 19 percent, that is to say almost every fifth new car bought in Germany was a DKW. The cheapest DKW model at this time was the two-seater with 18 hp engine, sold at 1,650 RM (1936). For the de luxe four-seater front-wheel-drive convertible with sheet steel body, 3,400 RM had to be paid.

Also for export only: the four-door F 7 Meisterklasse

DKW's FWD models proved highly satisfactory as expedition vehicles too

wo-seater coupé
on of the DKW
as for export to
Africa only

's front-wheel-
cars were
g German
try's top-selling
t articles

DKW advertising slogans

- *Everyone is delighted at the way the DKW masters the road.*

- *The DKW starts like lightning and gets you there in perfect safety.*

- *Roadholding is always important – the DKW has it.*

- *A DKW fulfils the norm - low consumption, plenty of power.*

- *Finish your journey as fresh as you started – space to spare in the DKW.*

- *Everybody says so – the DKW is the ideal small car.*

- *What fun to ride a motorbike, the heart beats faster, the air is clean.*

   The joy of living cannot be kept down when you thrill to the DKW's engine.

- *Sooner or later you too will drive a DKW.*

- *DKW, the small miracle, goes up hills like the others go down.*

HORCH – setting the tone in the luxury class

Immediately prior to the creation of the AUTO UNION, chief designer Fiedler had completed a new twelve-cylinder car, destined to be the HORCH company's flagship. The V-12 engine had its cylinder banks at a 60-degree included angle and developed 120 horsepower from a swept volume of six litres. The crankshaft ran in seven main bearings and carried twelve balance weights and a torsional vibration damper. The single camshaft was driven by a triple roller chain. Hydraulic valve clearance adjusters ensured supremely low noise levels, together with the special intake air silencer for the twin-choke downdraught carburettor and the ZF "Aphon" gearbox, with synchromesh on all gears from 2nd upwards. Of this elite HORCH model, 80 were built in all. On the day the AUTO UNION was announced, a Type 670 twelve-cylinder convertible drew attention to the new group most effectively: it won the Grand Prix d'Honneur in Lausanne, one of the major international "concours d'élégance" of the type so frequently held in those pre-war years.

The first news item from HORCH following the establishment of the AUTO UNION concerned the 3-litre V 8 engine intended from 1933 on for the forth-coming "small" HORCH. The 830 type code indicated the number of cylinders and the displacement, just as the straight-eight engine in the "large" HORCH, with its displacement of 5 litres, was referred to as the Type 850.

Beauty on the move

One of the finest-looking series of cars that even HORCH had produced was to be seen at the 1935 Berlin Motor Show: a two-door, two-light sports convertible with four to five seats and admittedly monumental but also extremely elegant lines. With the luggage rack extended, the car was almost six metres long and

The "small" HORCH with the typical corrugations on the boot lid (1934)

Interest in HORCH automobiles from Far Eastern visitors to the 1937 Berlin Motor Show

about 1.80 m wide over its expansively styled running boards. The attraction went below the surface too: to match the car's sheer beauty there was an entirely new chassis. The front suspension was of the swing-axle type, with two transverse springs and lateral control arms. At the rear there were double universal-joint halfshafts and a De Dion axle tube. The big car's roadholding was outstandingly good as a result. The smaller HORCHs had already acquired independent front suspension, and were given the new rear-axle layout a short time later. In addition to these running-gear improvements, the Zwickau plant was mainly concerned with increasing engine power output. The luxury and opulent equipment of these bodies took a severe toll in terms of weight, but more powerful engines were still some way from production readiness. Not that it was impossible to boost the output of the existing ones: the 5-litre unit received a camshaft with more agressive valve timing intervals and a higher compression ratio, which boosted its output to 120 horsepower. Similar measures applied to the smaller V-engine proved even more satisfactory: its initial 62 hp output went up to 70 and later to 82 horsepower by 1937; the 1938/39 version surpassed this with a further power hike to 92 hp, an increase of almost 50 percent within a relatively short time. The cars' performance now gave no grounds whatsoever for complaint. Testers from the "Allgemeine Automobil Zeitung", one of Germany's most reputable motoring magazines, took the HORCH 930 V with the 92 hp 3.8-litre engine, for a 529.9 km long "autobahn" run from Berlin to Munich on November 25th, 1938. They arrived after only 3 hours and 53 minutes - an average speed of 136 kilometres an hour! Like all HORCH automobiles from that year on, the test car had the specially high "autobahn" gearing which kept engine speeds low. This device was a synchromesh planetary gear train attached to the main gearbox, with direct drive and a step-up ratio for use on high-speed roads. The effect was precisely the same as the overdrive units or extra-high top gears frequently offered in later years.

HORCH had an abundance of far-reaching ideas and innovations up its sleeve, so to speak, for forthcoming models. One of the most drastic of these new depar-

tures was the streamlined body developed for the 930 S in the wind tunnel according to the patents held by Paul Jaray. This was on display at the 1939 International Motor Show. The body had no B-posts, and featured a full-width front bench seat instead of the customary individual seats. The drag coefficient was an impressive $c_D = 0.43$, far lower than any rival luxury car. Such developments on the part of the AUTO UNION were evidence that it had grasped the path which future developments in automobile technology would take much more clearly than many other manufacturers.

The demand for HORCH cars rose rapidly, and by the Summer of 1939 customers were obliged to wait up to nine months for delivery.

August Horch had declared many years before that he intended, come what may, to build only large, powerful and above all good cars. Nothing had changed at the company which bore his name. In the 1920s and 1930s, HORCH employed the very finest designers. Zoller, Daimler and Fiedler created and formed the various HORCH engines, the refinement of which has remained a byword to this day. Apart from the V-12 units, HORCH built only eight-cylinder engines from 1927 onwards – almost 70,000 of them by the time production ceased. None of its German competitors succeeded in matching this figure.

The HORCH 8 symbolised the ultimate quality expected of a top product from the German automobile industry. Its quiet, smooth running and high-quality workmanship were assured by the Zwickau company's concentrated skills and know-how in the production of large motor-vehicle engines. The "crowned H" emblem was effectively synonymous with the elegant, distinguished automobile of the day, and HORCH stood as a name for the finest manufacturing precision and for a kind of restrained solidity combined with elegance and an impressively high standard of luxury travel.

As the annual registration figures confirm, HORCH gained an increasingly firm grip on the luxury automobile market in Germany (cars with engines larger than 4 litres). In 1938, about 55 percent of

the large cars registered in Germany had the "crowned H" adorning their radiator grille. In the class below, that is to say cars powered by engines of between 3 and 4 litres' displacement, HORCH also maintained a very strong sales position.

Production figures

From the formation of AUTO UNION AG until civilian production had to cease in the Spring of 1940, about 15,000 HORCH 8 cars were built for private customers. The 25,000th HORCH 8 left the Zwickau factory in July 1937. From 1934/35 until 1942, about 45,000 special vehicles were manufactured for the armed forces, and the HORCH workforce totalled more than 3,000 wage-earning and salaried staff.

In the 1938 new car registration statistics, the HORCH marque secured a 21.7 percent share of the German market in the 3-4 litre class, and no less than 55 percent in the over-4 litre class.

DKW F 4 and HORCH 853 in London's Hyde Park (1935)

The last of many HORCH innovations: the streamlined body announced in 1939 on a V8 chassis ($c_D = 0.43$)

The principal HORCH models, 1932–1939

Designation	Number/layout of cylinders	Bore x stroke in mm	Displacement in cc	Output in hp	Years of manufacture	Notes
830	V 8	75 x 85	3004	62	1933–1934	
830 B	V 8	78 x 85	3250	70	1934–1937	
830 BL	V 8	78 x 92	3517	75	1935–1939	
850	Straight 8	87 x 104	4944	100	1934–1939	
853	Straight 8	87 x 104	4944	100	1935–1939	from 1937: 120 hp
855	Straight 8	87 x 104	4944	120	1938–1939	Special roadster
930	V 8	78 x 100	3823	92	1937–1939	
951	Straight 8	87 x104	4944	120	1937–1939	

The "small" V 8 HORCH (surely the most relative of terms) cost 8,500 RM as a saloon and 9,700 RM as a convertible. The "large" straight-eight HORCH in Pullman limousine guise cost 17,500 RM and the Type 853 sports convertible 15,250 RM. The most expensive "standard" HORCH, at 23,550 RM, was the Type 951 open six-seater.

...with every possible device installed!

"Germany's AUTO UNION is exhibiting in Paris for the first time. On its stand close to the Salon's entrance, HORCH has just three cars on show – three magnificent specimens each with a different body: a short, light green sports convertible with 4.5-litre engine, a gleaming silver convertible (5-litre) and a dark brown twelve-cylinder limousine with twin downdraught carburettor, intake air silencer, combined air and hydraulic servo brakes, synchromesh gearbox with overdrive ratio, fresh-air heater, illuminated card table, built-in four-wheel jacks, anti-theft alarm etc. – an astonishing list of equipment. The seemingly extensive HORCH programme, incidentally, is evidence that a large range of models can be assembled from relatively few resources if these are deployed carefully."

Report in the Automobiltechnische Zeitschrift, (ATZ), 1932, No. 20.

*The Pullman bo
always had a div
between chau
and passer*

Ample space for six and luxuriously upholstered seats in the HORCH 951 Pullman Convertible (1938)

Among the HORCH accessories: a special set of valises for the HORCH 930 V.

WANDERER in new guise

WANDERER automobiles went through their radical modernisation process shortly before the AUTO UNION era set in, when the 1.7- and 2.0-litre six-cylinder OHV engines designed by Ferdinand Porsche were introduced. After this the running gear received attention stage by stage, first of all with swing axles at the rear and later with independent suspension at the front as well. Finally, the cars were modernised in appearance, but in such a way as to appeal not only to loyal customers appreciative of lasting quality at the expense of style, but also to less conservative first-time buyers. The improvements were carried

through without undue loss of time, and resulted in a range of WANDERER models that remained on sale for some five years in all. In 1936, a new WANDERER body, the W 51, was shown in Berlin; it was of importance not only to the marque itself but to the entire AUTO UNION group. For the first time a body concept valid for all the Group's upper midsize cars was available, which meant that the four brands were no longer functioning separately but were able to enjoy the economies of scale which true amalgamation implied. A year later, the process of unification was taken a stage further with an entirely new WANDERER model series. This was indeed new: the engine, the chassis and the body had not been seen before. For the first time, the task of standardisation and the use of shared components and assemblies had been tackled seriously, and rationalised produc-

Cockpit of the supercharged WANDERER W 25 K sports car

The AUTO UNION 's plans to modernise its image took on initial shape at the 1936 Berlin Motor Show in the form of the WANDERER W 51 Special

Porsche-designed engine, rear swing axle and modern outfit: the WANDERER W 22 (this is the 1934 Pullman limousine)

tion methods adopted. The effort proved to be justified: WANDERER enjoyed greater sales success than at any time in its previous history.

The W 23 designation for the six-cylinder and W 24 for the four-cylinder model continued the customary WANDERER naming system. The W 25 K was something rather special: a supercharged sports car using the Porsche-designed six-cylinder engine as well, but with the Group's "floating axle" suspension. W 26 referred to a Pullman limousine with the new 2.7-litre side-valve six-cylinder engine, which retained the customary swing axles at front and rear. This was the last code number to be allocated by WANDERER. The W 28 Pullman limousine with double-jointed half-shafts at the rear remained at the planning stage, probably because it would have competed too closely with the HORCH Pullman. The WANDERER cars scheduled for introduction from 1940 onwards would have been called the W 4 and W 6, but the outbreak of war meant that they never saw the light of day.

Production figures

67,000 WANDERER cars in all were built between 1932 and 1939. Their share of total German registrations was in the region of 5 percent, but in the 2- to 3-litre class they often rose above 40 percent (for instance in 1937). The average workforce in Siegmar-Schönau was 3,220.

The prices charged for WANDERER cars were between 4,490 RM und 6,950 RM (1936).

The principal WANDERER models, 1932–1939

Designation	Number/layout of cylinders	Bore x stroke in mm	Displacement in cc	Output in hp	Years of manufacture	Notes
W 21	6 inline	65 x 85	1680	35	1933–1935	
W 22	6 inline	70 x 85	1950	40	1933–1935	
W 240	6 inline	70 x 85	1950	40	1935–1936	
W 250	6 inline	71 x 95	2250	50	1935–1937	
W 40	6 inline	70 x 85	1950	40	1936–1938	
W 50	6 inline	71 x 95	2255	50	1936–1938	
W 51	6 inline	71 x 95	2255	55	1936–1938	
W 52	6 inline	75 x 100	2632	62	1937–1938	
W 23	6 inline	75 x 100	2632	62	1937–1940	
W 24	4 inline	75 x 100	1755	42	1937–1940	
W 25 K	6 inline	70 x 85	1950	85	1936–1938	super-charged

Automatic shift ...

"A gearbox should be developed with three regular synchromesh ratios and a 4th gear as an automatic overdrive, which would cut in by itself at a speed still to be determined. Assuming that the car's top speed is about 120 km/h, it would be

A special taxicab version of the WANDERER W 24 was supplied to Budapest

Developed very rapidly, the WANDERER truck (1941/42) never went into production, but its forward-control cab was extremely advanced for its time

The WANDERER W 24 Cabriolet promised pleasant leisure motoring

best for the overdrive to engage at 80 km/h. However, to permit rapid overtaking, the third gear ratio be restored if the driver depressed the accelerator fully, say at 90 km/h, and the overdrive ratio would not engage again after this until the car had reached 100 km/h. This would avoid any risk of over-revving the engine in any circumstances and would make operation considerably more economical at speeds above 80 km/h."

William Werner's report to the Supervisory Board on 3rd May, 1939 concerning technical development work within the AUTO UNION and the new transmission under development for WANDERER cars.

Motor sport

The four marques which formed the AUTO UNION differed in their motor-sport traditions. AUDI's golden age had been before the first World War, with successes in the 1912, 1913 and 1914 International Austrian Alpine Trials, all of them won by an AUDI team. From these three events, no fewer than eleven first prizes in various classes and the coveted trophy itself had been won. Benz was well behind, with five first prizes, whereas Mercedes and NAG had gained only two. This success is fully comparable with, for example, today's world rally championship.

The most successful of the marques in competition was undoubtedly DKW, with its motorcycles. The Zschopau factory had operated its own racing department since 1927, managed by August Prüssing. Two years later, the company's advertising was able to claim no less than 1,000 race victories! Many great names were associated with DKW at that time: Walfried Winkler, Arthur Geiss, Ewald Kluge and others.

HORCH's greatest sporting successes, like those of AUDI, were gained before the first World War. In 1906 it won the Herkomer Trial, followed by numerous triumphs in reliability trials held in Scandinavia and Russia. Success on the Avus racing circuit in 1922 and 1923 was only moderate, after which the cars from Zwickau maintained a lower sporting profile. In 1929, however, Prince zu Schaumburg-Lippe caused a sensation by competing in the Monte Carlo Rally with an almost standard 350 Pullman limousine, reaching the finishing line as the only German driver not to exceed the time limit and securing a creditable 19th place in the overall results.

Hans Stuck driving the AUTO UNION Type A (16 cylinders, displacement 4.3 litres, 295 hp) in the 1934 German Grand Prix on the Nürburg Ring

Willi Walb, Hans Stuck and Ferdinand Porsche with the AUTO UNION Type A before the Brno Grand Prix (1934)

August Momberger with the long-tailed AUTO UNION Type A at the Avus race meeting in 1934

In the 1935 Avus race, one of the AUTO UNION Type B racing car's drivers was Bernd Rosemeyer

Before long, HORCH automobiles were recording one success after another in a different type of competition, the newly fashionable gymkhanas and "concours d'élégance", where good looks and high quality were the criteria. HORCH models were entered for these events in great numbers, and frequently swept the board.

WANDERER joined the sporting fray in 1922, with an entry in the Targa Florio road race. This brave attempt to reach for the stars remained a one-off occurrence. It was not until the end of the decade that the cars bearing the winged "W" emblem began to notch up victories in major long-distance events of considerable difficulty, for example the 1931 Alpine Rally and Ten Thousand Kilometre Run.

Although this marque was never particularly prominent on the motor-sport scene, it made a specific contribution to the AUTO UNION's subsequent glory: it was the WANDERER company which commissioned Ferdinand Porsche to design a racing car, an order placed with him by Managing Director Klee during the Paris Motor Show in the Autumn of 1931.

A world record as a première

After the establishment of the AUTO UNION, a department set to work in Zwickau on March 7th, 1933 to build the racing cars. The existing motorcycle racing department continued to operate from Zschopau, and in 1934 a new factory sport department was set up in Chemnitz with August Momberger as its manager, to coordinate the entire Group's off-road, reliability trial and long-distance racing activities.

The public's attention was naturally enough focused on the new racing cars bearing the four-ring badge. For the first time, the sixteen-cylinder engine was installed behind the driver; its initial power output was 295 horsepower. The cars were first shown to the public on March 6th, 1934, precisely 365 days after work had started on them, when Hans Stuck took a brand-new car round the Avus circuit in Berlin and immediately shattered the world record. During the

next season Stuck won the German, Swiss and Czechoslowakian Grands Prix. He was victorious in all the most significant hill-climbs and came in second in the Italian Grand Prix and the Eifel race. With this car he gained the German road racing and hill-climbing titles and was European champion. The first members of the AUTO UNION racing team alongside him were Prince Leiningen and August Momberger, with the Italian star driver Achille Varzi joining in the following year. In 1935, Bernd Rosemeyer began to make a name for himself within the team. Other members were Ernst von Delius, Rudolf Hasse and H.P. Müller. In 1937 another top Italian driver, Luigi Faglioli, took the wheel of the sixteen-cylinder AUTO UNION. By the end of that season the company had taken part in 54 races and won 32 of them, setting up 15 world records and 23 class records in the process.

Success from A to D

As one racing season gave way to the next, the cars were steadily improved. The individual development stages were identified by capital letters: A for 1934, B for 1935 and C for 1936/37. At the same time the engine size grew from 4.3 to over 6 litres and the potential maximum power output rose to 520 hp, or even to 560 hp in the case of cars set up for record-breaking. While the 750-kilogram formula was in force, it is interesting to see how the engine speed went up only from 4500 to 5000 rpm, but torque rose from 54 mkg at 2700 rpm to 87 mkg at only 2500 rpm. The power-weight ratio improved from 2.8 to 1.5 kg/hp, in other words by almost half.

When the new three-litre formula was enforced in 1938, AUTO UNION introduced its Type D; following the split with Porsche, this was developed by experimental engineer Eberan-Eberhorst. The engine was a V-12 with supercharger, rated for an initial output of 420 horsepower according to the requirement specification. But by the end of 1939, with no change in the displacement of three lit-

The DKW motorcycle racing team concentrated on the 250 cc class: Ewald Kluge, Arthus Geiss and Walfried Winkler (from left) usually dominated the proceedings

Kahrmann/Eder took their 700 cc DKW through every corner with equal verve, and gained many successes in sidecar racing events

res, it was producing almost 500 hp – nearly as much as had been obtained from twice the swept volume only a few years before.

Following Bernd Rosemeyer's fatal accident during a record-breaking run on January 28th, 1938, the Italian Tazio Nuvolari led the AUTO UNION team, supported by Hans Stuck, Rudolf Hasse, H.P. Müller, and for one season the Swiss driver Christian Kautz. In 1939 the legendary racing motorcyclist "Schorsch" Meier also joined the team. Although victories were not as frequent as under the previous 750-kilogram formula, the Zwickau engineers, mechanics and drivers none the less scored many an impressive triumph.

AUTO UNION's total financial outlay on Grand Prix racing amounted to 14.2 million Reichsmarks. Since 1935, the racing department had maintained a large store of components and assemblies from which cars were assembled for each individual race, so that the actual cars were never the same from one race-meeting to the next. The total numbers of cars built in this way were 5 in 1934, 7 in 1935, 12 in 1936 and 1937, 16 in 1938 and 15 in 1939.

After the war the Soviet occupying powers took possession of 12 Auto Union racing cars and shipped them back to the Soviet Union as reparations, where they were supplied to the local automobile industry for experimental purposes.

DKW dominated the scene in motorcycle road racing. The double-piston engines first developed in the early 1930s, when combined with the charge pump, enabled power outputs to be boosted very significantly. DKW's URE 250 racing bikes, powered by these engines, were developing about 22 hp at 4200 rpm in

1933, rising to 25 hp at 4700 in the final stage of development for the 1937 season. Their potential top speed was in the region of 160 km/h.

In 1937 the ULD was launched, both the climax and conclusion of development work on the successful twin-piston racing engines. The new rotary disc valve boosted power by up to 15 percent, initially to 28.5 hp at 6000 rpm from the 250 cc engine, later to 30 hp at 6500 rpm.

During record attempts in 1937, a top speed of 183 km/h was recorded.

At the end of 1934, engineer Küchen, who was currently in charge of competition matters in Zschopau, was asked to develop a DKW road racer that could be sold to private entrants. It was to be offered at 1,550 Reichmarks. Küchen, a master of simplicity in technical matters, created the most straightforward version of the water-cooled DKW twin-piston engine so far, with the charge pump facing forwards and delivering directly into the crankcase. The two Amal carburettors supplied mixture to inlet ports controlled by the edge of the piston. The engine was lubricated at a fuel:oil ratio of 15 to 1; its nominal power output scarcely increased over the years, and was quoted as the same 20 hp at 5000 rpm in 1939 as it had been in 1935. The top speed was 150 km/h. This was the only racing motorcycle of its day which the public was able to purchase "over the counter", so to speak.

In the 250 cc class, DKW motorcycles seemed to have booked a season ticket to victory and to the championship in every successive season until the outbreak of war. In 1936, the champions in four of the six classes rode DKW: Kluge (250 cc), H.P. Müller (500 cc) and Braun/Badsching and Kahrmann/Eder in the two sidecar classes. A year later Ewald Kluge on the new ULD became the first foreigner to win the Isle of Man Tourist Trophy, an event that had been held since 1907. Sidecar racing ceased in 1938, and DKW concentrated on its solo bikes, with considerable success: the German and European championships were captured in the 350 cc class (Fleischmann) and the 250 cc class (Kluge).

The factory's motor sport department mainly entered for off-road events and reliability trials. Notable among these were the annual Alpine Trial and the international Liège-Rome-Liège long-distance rally. The AUTO UNION in some cases developed entirely new vehicles for these events. The special chassis of the model developed in 1938 for off-road competition was adapted from a DKW off-road vehicle, but powered by a WANDERER engine reduced in size to 1.5 litres. It proved far superior to all its rivals.

The streamlined body developed in the wind tunnel was used in the 1937 Avus Race and for record attempts in October of the same year, installed on a Type C Chassis

*Prof. Robert
Eberan-Eberhorst
(1902–1982)*

Robert Eberan-Eberhorst

1902	Born on 4th April in Vienna
1922	Practical work at Puch in Graz after completing school and studies
1924	Worked for Elite in Brand-Erbisdorf (Saxony)
1927/28	Freelance driving instructor in Vienna
1928–1933	Assistant at the Institute for Motor Transport of Dresden College of Advanced Technology. His tasks included investigating the balancing of rotating bodies, motor-vehicle chassis and body vibration and work on carburettors and brakes
1933	From 1st June, experimental engineer with AUTO UNION AG in Chemnitz
1937	From 1st July, manager of the experimental department operated by the AUTO UNION racing department in Zwickau. Designer of the AUTO UNION Type D 3-litre, 12-cylinder racing engine and racing car
1940	Doctorate on the subject of charge levels in forced-aspiration engines, based on an AUTO UNION experimental report entitled "Gas-exchange processes in high-speed racing engines"
1941	From 1st September, professorship at Dresden CAT, Chair of Motor Transport and Lightweight Engine Design; also Director of its Motor Transport Institute
1947	Worked with Porsche in Gmünd, Austria; shared in the development of the Cisitalia racing car
1949	Chief engineer at ERA in England
1950	Chief engineer at Aston Martin in England
1953–1956	General Manager of the Technical Development Division of AUTO UNION GmbH
1956	Appointed Director of the Batelle Institute's mechanical engineering faculty in Frankfurt on the retirement of Professor Wunibald Kamm
1960	Appointed Director of Vienna Technical University's Institute for Combustion Engines and Motor Transport
1965	Retired from active teaching
1982	Died in Vienna on 14th March

*One last jump for joy:
after winning the
Belgrade City Park
race on September
3rd, 1939, Tazio
Nuvolari is seen in
the act of jumping out
of his car. No-one
could know that it
had just completed
its last race*

AUDI – an overview

AUDI Front, type UW (1933)

AUDI Front 2-litre (1934)

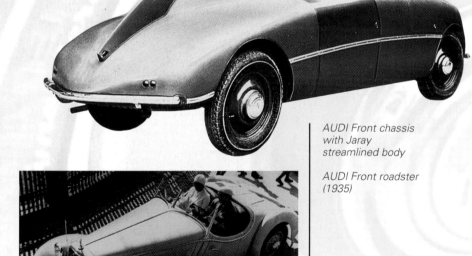

AUDI Front chassis with Jaray streamlined body

AUDI Front roadster (1935)

*AUDI Front
Special Coupé for
the 2,000-km race
(1933)*

AUDI Front 225

*AUDI Front 225
Special Cabriolet
(1937)*

*AUDI 920 Cabriolet
(1939)*

DKW – an overview

DKW Sonderklasse
1001 (1934)

DKW Schwebeklasse
(1935)

DKW Sonderklasse
with pressed-steel
body (1938)

A special version of
the DKW F 4 (1934)

DKW Front deluxe
two-seater (1936)

DKW F 5 delivery van
(1935)

DKW F 7
Meisterklasse with
special four-door
body (1938)

DKW F 7 Front
deluxe four-seater
cabriolet (1938)

DKW F 8 delivery
van (1939)

DKW F 9 (1939)

HORCH – an overview

HORCH 500 B
Pullman cabriolet
(1933)

HORCH 853 Sport
Cabriolet with 5-litre
straight-eight engine
(1936)

HORCH 780 Sport
Cabriolet (1933)

HORCH 830 BL with
ambulance body
(1937)

Special coupé on
HORCH 830 chassis
for the 2,000-km race
(1933)

HORCH 855 Special Roadster (1938)

HORCH 930 V saloon with sliding roof (1937)

HORCH 951 saloon (1937)

HORCH 951 A saloon (1939)

HORCH 930 S (1939)

HORCH 951 A Pullman Cabriolet (1939)

WANDERER – an overview

WANDERER W 22
cabriolet (1933)

WANDERER W 25 K
roadster (1936)

WANDERER W 22
open tourer (1934)

WANDERER W 22
estate-car (1934)

WANDERER W 50
cabriolet (1936)

WANDERER W 26
Pullman limousine
(1938)

WANDERER W 23
cabriolet with six-
cylinder engine
(1937)

WANDERER W 24
cabriolet with four-
cylinder engine
(1937)

WANDERER W 24
two-door saloon
(1939)

AUTO UNION Type B
racing car (1935)

AUTO UNION Type C
racing car (1936/37)
with and without
racing bodywork
(1937)

AUTO UNION Type D
racing car (1938)

AUTO UNION Type D
racing car with
streamlined body
(1938)

AUTO UNION Type D
hill-climb car with
16-cylinder engine
(1939)

*DKW racing engine,
water-cooled, with
charge pump (1935)*

*DKW ULD 250 and
URe 250 racing
motorcycles (1937)*

*DKW URe 250 racing
motorcycle (1937)*

*DKW 600 cc racing
motorcycle with side-
car (1937)*

From a mountain of rubble to an economic miracle

"Give me ten years, and you will not recognise Germany again!" Hitler's prophecy had fulfilled itself in the most gruesome manner possible by 1945. At the end of a merciless war, the world mourned the deaths of fifty million people. Germany was one vast heap of rubble, its cities destroyed, its industry buried in the ruins and its population in dire straits. Six million of them also failed to survive Hitler's policies of genocide. The war took as it chose – the deserving and the undeserving, the women, the children. Only one in every four men in the age-group between 25 and 30 survived the war.

They died at the front lines, they died at home in a hail of bombs, they were murdered by the Nazi terror regime. About half a million Jews lived in Germany in 1933. In 1945, the figure was less than 15,000.

Millions of German refugees wandered over the countryside, driven from the places where their fathers before them had lived, whole regions which Germany had staked against the Allied powers in its obscure claim for more "Lebensraum", only to lose these territories of its own for ever.

But at long last the gunsmoke and dust began to clear, and mental desperation driven by sheer hunger gave way to more sober considerations of how to survive. Life began to stir again in the ruins. Machinery was dug out and cleaned, wheels began to turn on roads and rails, an occasional factory chimney emitted a plume of smoke. Regardless of what was inscribed on the company's nameplate, its remaining employees set to and produced what the people needed: grist mills and handcarts, hoes and cooking pots. The automobile industry was no exception, though its primary task proved to be repairing an assortment of vehicles in order to keep them mobile. The occupying powers encouraged this work: wrecked cars were collected, and a few private customers even brought their vehicles in to be refurbished. At two places in Germany, new cars were being built before the end

The car park at the Solitude race track on September 18th, 1949. Pre-war vehicles dominate the scene

of 1945: at VW in Wolfsburg and at BMW in Eisenach. Mercedes-Benz, Opel and Ford restarted production in the years which followed.

Much of the automobile industry's machinery and equipment had been dismantled and taken away. The Kadett assembly line in Rüsselsheim was lost to Opel, the Munich BMW factories were unable to produce engines. In the East, that is to say in the Soviet Military Zone, whole factories were uprooted and carted away: HORCH and DKW, AUDI and VOMAG, PHÄNOMEN and FRAMO. Everything was taken, right down to the last light switch, door or window-frame. If the buildings still stood, they were now totally naked, stripped bare. As war reparations, the automobile industry in Saxony alone lost 28,000 machine tools.

The AUTO UNION was effectively dealt a death-blow by this scorched-earth policy. To make matters worse, the occupying powers had its name erased from the trade register in 1948. This was surely the end for what had once been Germany's second-largest motor-vehicle manufacturing group.

However, many of its former senior executives had already come together again in South Germany and were negotiating with the banks for loans and with the local authorities about potential factory sites. In 1949, the AUTO UNION celebrated its recall to life in the Bavarian town of Ingolstadt. Its first new vehicles left the assembly line before the year was out. A process quite unique within the automobile industry had taken place: a major company had not only moved its headquarters to a location many hundreds of kilometres away, but had in fact crossed a new national border. This was not merely a management regrouping process. Shop-floor workers and former salaried staff followed the call of the

The "Stachus" in Munich (1950): More than any other mode of transport it was still the bicycle which provided personal mobility

Only a few years later, the car dominated the urban street scene

Four Rings in large numbers from Saxony to Bavaria. Some 5,000 companies in all fled to the Western half of Germany and set themselves up in new surroundings. Not all succeeded. Within the automobile industry, the AUTO UNION was the only manufacturer to be reborn in this way.

Something did remain of the former company at its headquarters in Chemnitz, soon to be renamed Karl-Marx-Stadt, and in Zwickau and Zschopau. Ninety percent of the staff of the so-called IFA Research and Development Plant were former AUTO UNION employees. Basic technical design principles were drawn up here for the German Democratic Republic's automobile industry. This establishment produced that country's first plastic-bodied car, and also the last HORCH. It was indeed fortunate that the three-cylinder two-stroke engine first developed in the nineteen-thirties, and the small car concept with its transversely mounted twin-cylinder engine (also a two-stroke), proved so durable. The hardships of the immediate post-war period were gradually overcome. Scars healed, memories either faded or were suppressed. What remained was the misery of people forced apart by a divided Germany, despite all hopes that this might be of only short duration. Mobility in one area was almost unlimited, in the other a rare, carefully monitored privilege. West of the River Elbe, the car population went up and up; on the Eastern bank, a waiting period of ten or more years for a new car became commonplace.

Condemned to the ageing two-stroke engine and a series of interminable shortages, the GDR plunged into a kind of Dark Age of motoring. The West, on the other hand, tried out every conceivable novelty, from the motor scooter and bubble car to the sub-compact and Mini, as part of an irresistible urge to keep moving – and of course to earn money too. Heaven on wheels had arrived. The industry boomed, and if any wish remained unfulfilled, it was probably only the wish for still more cars.

Travel boomed as the "Economic Miracle" set in, a sign of the unsated demand that had been building up for so long

Cars were built in cramped conditions and by the simplest of methods

Road traffic in Munich (1953)

An end and a new beginning – the Four Rings in Bavaria

The AUTO UNION's board of directors and its most important remaining colleagues held a final meeting in Chemnitz on May 6th, 1945. The next day Dr. Bruhn, Dr. Hahn and Dr. Werner left the town and began to work their way westwards, after having agreed with the newly constituted employees' committee that Dr. Hanns Schüler should take over as chairman of the board.

On July 12th, 1945 Germany was officially split up into four occupied zones. Any attempt to re-enter the town of Chemnitz required a special permit, and would have been a risky and possibly fatal undertaking for the AUTO UNION's executives following their successful flight to the West. As it became obvious that all the AUTO UNION plants in Zwickau and Zschopau would be dismantled and their contents removed, Bruhn and Hahn, together with trustworthy colleagues, met at the Munich branch of the company to discuss how the remnants of the AUTO UNION could be restored to some kind of life. Karl Schittenhelm, the former Service Manager, was there, together with Erhard Burghalter, previously manager of the Stettin subsidiary and Oswald Heckel, general agent for the AUTO UNION in Sofia.

Ingolstadt, a nearby town, offered excellent terms for the setting up of a large parts store and for preparations to be made for restarting production. The Bavarian State Bank agreed to make a loan on the basis of Dr. Hahn's and Dr. Bruhn's personal standing. On December 19th, 1945 a contract was signed for the establishment of the "Zentraldepot für AUTO UNION Ersatzteile Ingolstadt GmbH", with registered offices at No. 3, Schrannenstrasse in Ingolstadt.

Refugees flooded in during 1946 in even greater numbers, particularly after AUDI's works manager Heinrich Schuh and his DKW colleague Arlt were arrested by the Russians and taken away, to be put to death later as it transpired. HORCH company manager Zerbst, experimental department manager Werner Geite and many others all made their way to Ingolstadt. By the end of 1946, the

Ingolstadt depot was the largest spare parts store in Germany, with a turnover in excess of 3 million Marks.

Even this sum, however, was insufficient to administer the still-extensive real estate which the company owned in the West, collect sums due to the previous AUTO UNION and settle suppliers' bills. On March 25th, 1947 therefore, the AUTO UNION GmbH was set up in Ingolstadt as a subsidiary of the AUTO UNION AG in Chemnitz.

Following the currency reform of June 1948 and the liquidation of the parent company in Chemnitz, which took place in August of the same year, it was clearly necessary to clarify the legal and property situation in order to ensure that the new company's status with the banks was not endangered. As a means of maintaining continuity, it was decided to set up an independent company having no links with the previous one. On this assumption the Bavarian State Bank expressed its readiness to provide a six-figure loan.

And so, on September 3rd, 1949, again with its head offices in the Schrannenstrasse, the "new" AUTO UNION GmbH was established, with an initial capital of 3 million Marks. Dr. Bruhn was elected General Manager, with Dr. Carl Hahn as his deputy. Paul Günther, the former commercial director of the HORCH company, Dr. Schüler and Fritz Zerbst were also members of the management team. A seat on the Supervisory Board, which was chaired by Baron Friedrich Karl von Oppenheim, was offered to August Horch, the pioneering engineer, as a gesture of friendship and respect. The AUTO UNION had now been completely transplanted to its new home, and was ready to start afresh in Western Germany.

Production of the F 89 L rapid delivery van commenced in the Autumn of 1949 in Ingolstadt; this is the minibus version. The DKW F 10 can be seen at the left of the picture

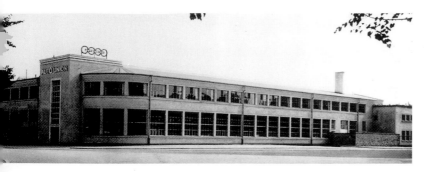

The AUTO UNION's new production facility in Ingolstadt

In June 1957 an estate-car version of the large DKW 3=6 known as the "Universal" became available

Initial successes – and those who helped

Fritz Zerbst had begun to plan the AUTO UNION's very first post-war product while still occupying premises at the central parts depot. It was to be a small delivery van, as this was considered the most suitable conveyance to help tackle post-war transport problems. A very wise assessment of the situation! At the Hanover Spring Fair in 1949, the new DKW rapid delivery van was presented to the public; it had a two-stroke engine and front-wheel drive and broke new ground in having a forward-control cab – the first of its kind. The company's dealers were delighted, placed their orders – and paid their first deposits.

In a sense, the new AUTO UNION's most valuable capital was of the immaterial kind, namely

- a feeling of loyalty among the workforce, which even included working for low pay as the company struggled to survive in the early days;

- the dealership;

As Dr. Hahn was to put it later: "We had loyal dealers throughout the new Federal Republic ... more than 90 percent of our former DKW dealers had waited for us, often making considerable financial sacrifices to do so."

- our customers;

To quote Dr. Hahn again: "... this was our backbone and our strength: the community of former DKW two-stroke owners and enthusiasts, who waited eagerly for everything we produced and never lost their faith in our products."

Marque traditions and the simple nature of the product were bound to lead to the new AUTO UNION being primarily identified with the previous DKW brand. Production commenced in Ingolstadt before the end of 1949, and by 31st December 504 of the new F 89 L rapid delivery vans and 500 motorcycles of Type DKW RT 125 had been despatched. The "W" in the name stood for

"West", to set the new Ingolstadt product clearly apart from the motorcycles of the same type being built in Zschopau.

It was clearly the AUTO UNION's ambition to build passenger cars again. An obvious solution was to start production of the F 9, which had been developed to production readiness by the time war broke out. Drawings were acquired by devious means, and missing parts were recreated. A site formerly occupied by the Rheinmetall company in Derendorf, a suburb of Düsseldorf, was rented on favourable terms with a view to starting production. The first workers for a pre-production run were recruited in April 1950, and the first cars left the line, incredibly, by July. 1,538 of them were produced in the first year.

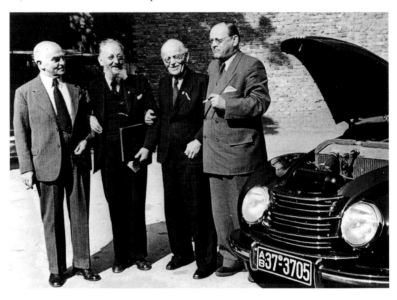

The first post-war DKW passenger car leaves the AUTO UNION's assembly line in Düsseldorf. This picture of the presentation ceremony in 1950 shows (from left): Dr. R. Bruhn, W. Ostwald, Dr. A. Horch and Dr. C. Hahn

Although the AUTO UNION was able to benefit from European reconstruction-fund and other special loans to a considerable extent, it still suffered from a chronic shortage of capital. But help was suddenly at hand from an unexpected source. Ever since the 1930s, there had been close links with the Zürich-based Swiss businessman Ernst Göhner. He had imported DKW and AUDI cars for a time, and later installed his own wooden bodies on the two-stroke chassis. Göhner's company Holzkarosserie AG, or HOLKA for short, built a total of 1,674 such vehicles between 1935 and 1945.

In post-war years, Göhner's fortunes flourished and he had interests in many business areas. As a means of thanking the company for the help which he had received from the AUTO UNION AG in Chemnitz, and of maintaining business links of very long standing, Göhner advanced the princely sum of 2.5 million DM as a contribution to the new company's equity, and joined Bankhaus Oppenheim as one of the principal partners in the Four Rings.

Under a new star

In 1954, Friedrich Flick acquired a financial interest in the Ingolstadt and Düsseldorf automobile manufacturing operations, having been previously obliged by an international court verdict to dispose of his traditional coal and steel investments. The initial commitment was concealed by making purchases through various companies within Flick's vast business empire. As increases in equity were decided on, Flick's holding in the AUTO UNION rose considerably. From November 1956 onwards he was represented on the Supervisory Board by Dr. Odilo Burkart, chief executive of the Maximialianshütte foundry, another Flick possession. In December 1957, having been exposed to more or less gentle persuasion, various of the pioneering members of the company's management – Bruhn, Zerbst, Hensel, Schmolla, Ferber and, soon afterwards, Dr. Hahn – sold their own shares. Göhner and the Flick Group were then the majority shareholders, both with approximately 41 percent. In April 1958, Flick instructed Burkart to offer his holding to the Daimler-Benz Board of Management. The same day, the Stuttgart-based company purchased Göhner's holding as well. This left only Oppenheim's, which saw no reason not to follow suit

From the very moment when they resolved to set up in business again in the West, the managers and senior employees from the former AUTO UNION plants in Chemnitz, Zwickau and Zschopau had been accustomed to making the decisions. After the turbulent initial period, calmer waters were reached in due course, but the time had also come for clear and far-reaching decisions to be taken about the company's future. Dr. Bruhn, still General Manager, had demonstrated his mastery in handling a limited flow of funds. He was a highly correct, not to say almost over-accurate person who treated his colleagues most honourably and would have been described by his contemporaries as a "workaholic" if they had happened to know the term. What he may well have lacked

A motorcycle with a roof over the rider's head – the idea and its practical interpretation in the constant search for a workable compromise

was an element of entrepreneurial vision and willingness to take risks. As a result, essential decisions were constantly postponed or, worse still, cancelled at a later date. With Flick's increasing involvement in the company's affairs, it was obvious that he expected structural and managerial reorganisations to take place. This could only culminate in the replacement of the existing executive team.

On 15th October 1956 Dr. Werner Henze took the place of Dr. Richard Bruhn. Henze had entered the motor-vehicle trade before the war when he joined the Famo Fahrzeug- und Motorenwerke in Breslau. After the war he had worked for Kolbenschmidt in Neckarsulm and later in the central offices of the German Motorcycle Industry Federation in Frankfurt.

Although he soon succeeded in slowing down the negative business trend at AUTO UNION, it was clear that the equity was still not sufficiently high to provide the necessary security. Flick's situation was clear: the capital would have to be increased considerably, and business concentration within the industry could not be disregarded either. At the end of 1957, Ford expressed interest in acquiring AUTO UNION, and talks were held to discuss the project.

Before any deal could be negotiated with Ford, however, Flick (in his capacity as a major Daimler-Benz shareholder with 38 percent of that company's equity) contacted Deutsche Bank spokesman H.J. Abs and offered the Stuttgart-based group an opportunity to purchase AUTO UNION. After hesitating for only a short time the Daimler-Benz board resolved on 6th March 1958 to take up the offer, and by 26th April of that year the sale had been concluded: 88 percent of the holdings in AUTO UNION were now concentrated in the hands of the former rival. Daimler-Benz's board of management spokesman Dr. Könecke summed up the deal as follows: "We have married a nice girl from a good, old-established family!" It should not be forgotten, however, that following Volkswagen, Opel, Daimler-Benz and Ford the AUTO UNION was the fifth-largest German automobile manufacturer in terms of production volume – ahead of Lloyd, Borgward, NSU and BMW.

The DKW 3=6 Coupé with its outstanding visibility all round was one of the most attractive cars of the period (from 1955 on: F 93)

Until 1961 the large DKWs, now renamed AUTO UNION 1000, were built in Düsseldorf

Another sign of luxury: well-upholstered seats in the 1000 cc AUTO UNION Coupé

This dashing convertible had two seats and ample luggage space (1954)

The products

The first DKW post-war passenger cars – if one disregards the IFAs from Zwickau – came from Stuttgart. The Baur coachbuilding company, which had often co-operated closely with the AUTO UNION in the past, developed two pressed-steel bodies for the F 8 and offered them to the company as a replacement for the weatherbeaten wooden ones. Starting in January 1950 the new AUTO UNION supplied F 8 chassis, which unlike the pre-war version had hydraulic brakes and telescopic front shock absorbers, to Stuttgart, had the body installed by Baur and then sold the cars in small numbers as its model F 10.

This was a provisional solution, adopted to keep both dealers and customers happy until the company could set up its own passenger-car production line.

Production of the F 89 L rapid delivery van began in Ingolstadt during 1949. It had front-wheel drive and was powered by a twin-cylinder two-stroke engine. It was Germany's first post-war commercial vehicle to adopt the forward-control cab layout, the advantages of which had first been recognised by the AUTO UNION's engineers back in the early 1940s. The idea was widely copied and soon appeared on all light commercial vehicles of this kind.

The passenger-car assembly line in Düsseldorf started up in 1950, manufacturing the F 89 P, which was given the "Meisterklasse" name as in former times. The type reference signified the combination of a pre-war chassis design with a two-stroke engine, now developing 23 hp (F 8) and the body of the F 9. A saloon, a four-seater convertible (with Karmann coachwork), and a two-seater convertible and coupé (Hebmüller) were listed. An estate car was also announced under the name "Universal"; it had a combined timber and steel body at first, later an all-steel one.

In 1953 the DKW acquired the three-cylinder two-stroke engine originally intended for it (3=6). This was the Type F 91, which was named "Sonderklasse" in
continuation of the pre-war naming policy. Two years later, the "large DKW"
with a lengthened chassis followed. Its engine had an output of 38 hp and the
body had grown by 10 centimetres in width. The model code F 93 applied to all
the two-door bodies, F 94 to the four-door versions and the "Universal" estate
car. In 1957 the engine was uprated to 40 horsepower. The car remained on sale
until 1959, and the total production volume of some 157,000 made it the most
successful of the post-war DKWs up to that time. The Karmann company of
Osnabrück supplied convertible bodies for the DKW 3=6 until 1956.

In 1954, the AUTO UNION secured the Federal German Army's contract for an
all-purpose vehicle with off-road capability, fending off competition from Porsche and Borgward. This vehicle went into production in 1955, and was made
until 1968, when the army contract expired. Its designation, in best officialese,
dated from 1962: "Multi-purpose Universal Off-road Vehicle with All-wheel
Drive", but most people referred to it by
the acronym formed by the German
initials ("Munga"). Although it may have
seemed as if the company clung too long
to the pre-war DKW concept of three-cylinder two-stroke engine and "floating-
axle" running gear with aerodynamically

shaped body, the engineers in Ingolstadt were by no means lacking in new ideas.
At the German Motor Show in 1957, the DKW 3=6 was the first German production car to be offered with a fully-automatic clutch. This was the "Saxomat",
developed jointly by Fichtel & Sachs and the AUTO UNION, and cost an
additional 275 Deutschmarks.

*On a visit to the British Army
of the Rhine, Queen Elizabeth
and Prince Philip reviewed
troops in a DKW Munga*

The motorcycle rolls again

As well as the rapid delivery van, Ingolstadt was able to develop the first post-war DKW motorcycle during 1949; this was the RT 125 W (W for "West"). A simple, light but sturdy and extremely economical means of transport, it was precisely what many buyers had dreamed of in the immediate post-war years. The original design was drafted out in the 1930s in Zschopau by Hermann Weber; in Ingolstadt it was prepared for renewed production by Nikolaus Dörner, a former employee of the Central Experimental Department in Chemnitz, Franz Ischinger, once manager of DKW's off-road sport department in Zschopau and Herbert Kirchberg, another long-serving DKW employee. Within two years, more than 30,000 RT 125 W motorcycles were built and sold. At the end of 1950 it was given telescopic front forks, and in 1952 the more powerful RT 125/2 was introduced. Rear suspension was fitted in 1954.

The motorcycle programme was enlarged in 1951 to include the 8.5 hp RT 200, which was superseded by the RT 200/2 in 1954. This had a short-stroke engine and a four-speed gearbox, features which re-appeared on successive DKW models of the 1950s. The RT 175, RT 250 and the twin-cylinder RT 350 appeared in due course to round off the programme; the RT 175 in particular was highly suc-

Protective clothing or a safety helmet were still unknown, but DKW motorcycles already possessed such modern features as full-width hub brakes, telescopic forks and rear suspension

The first DKW RT 125 W (1949) had rubber suspension at the front, but the rear wheel was unsprung at this time

A DKW RT 200 for driving schools, with duplicated steering, brakes and throttle

cessful. All DKW motorcycles now had telescopic front forks and swinging-fork rear suspension. The cylinder with its "porcupine" finning enabled higher thermal loads to be withstood. The fully enclosed chain was a typical DKW feature from 1954 on, together with the concealed carburettor on all models except the RT 125. In October 1956, all DKW motorcycles except the RT 350 acquired a leading-link front fork, the most modern system then available.

Attempts to develop a powerful motor scooter (up to 200 cc engine size) were not successful for cost reasons. Since there was unsatisfied demand at the lower end of the performance scale, the Ingolstadt engineers instead developed a 3 hp, 75 cc motor scooter which was remarkable for being the first such vehicle to have automatic transmission. It was launched as the "Hobby" on October 1st, 1954 and became popular immediately, particularly among women riders. 45,303 had been built by the time production ceased in 1957.

The DKW "Hummel" moped appeared in 1956. It was the first such model to have a three-speed gearbox. With the engine and rear swinging arm pivoted to the frame and spring struts with rubber-band damping, it was more comfortable to ride than many a competitor. Production up to 1958 totalled 117, 617 units.

Although the AUTO UNION was enjoying very strong demand for its products and was able to sell both cars and motorcycles in large numbers, the management in Ingolstadt and in Düsseldorf were fully aware that the marque was still subsisting largely on the basis of pre-war development work. As early as 1949, the technical experts had appreciated the need for a genuinely new product, which they envisaged as a small car of extremely simple design. Designer Kurt Schwenk, who had already contributed much detail work to the F 89, produced a sketch for its successor, code-named FX. It was again to have front-wheel drive and a two-stroke engine, but the then prevalent small-car craze led the management to believe that an engine of lower displacement would be sufficient. There was also a rival faction within the AUTO UNION which would have preferred to switch from a two-stroke to a four-stroke engine at this stage. Chronic shortages of funds and the inability of the board of management to come to a decision made the situation worse. A second design office was set up for no evident reason, run by Jenschke, who put forward the notion of a "four-wheel motor scooter", in other words an even smaller car. Internal competition was the regrettable result of this ill thought-out move. Neither the FX nor the scooter-mobile reached production, but both of them consumed large amounts of time and money.

This was the situation in 1953, when Dr. Bruhn invited the former head of testing work at the AUTO UNION's racing department, Professor Eberan-Eberhorst, to come to Ingolstadt, hoping that his acknowledged authority and skills would put an end to this process of casting around in the dark. He was given the task of developing a plastic body for a baby car which would be powered by a 200 to 300 cc engine, and achieved the required result by adopting glass-fibre reinforced polyester. Several prototypes of this plastic-bodied vehicle, known internally as the "STM" were developed, as three-seaters with a central steering wheel or as four-seaters; they were subjected to lengthy tests and came very close to production maturity. However, economic production called for giant presses costing about 35 million DM, a sum which the company simply could not raise.

Once again the company resolved to obtain help from outside and to resort to the experience and know-how of former colleagues. Bruhn obtained the services of William Werner, who had been a member of the board in Chemnitz with responsibility for technical matters. In May 1956 he became Technical General Manager in Ingolstadt. Werner brought with him Oskar Siebler, formerly head of

The DKW Hummel ("Bumble-bee") brought the AUTO UNION a share of the profitable moped market (1956)

The Hobby scooter's engine was started by hand, with a pull cable

engine development at the AUTO UNION in Chemnitz. Together with the company's Commercial General Manager Dr. Henze, Werner's first decision was to call a halt to the work being done on the plastic-bodied car. This provoked Eberan-Eberhorst into leaving Ingolstadt, but in itself went no further towards solving the question of the AUTO UNION's future from a technical standpoint.

British racing motorcyclist John Surtees demonstrates the twin-cylinder RT 350 to interested soldiers in Great Britain

Liaison with the three-pointed star (1958–1964)

The company

After having been taken over by Daimler-Benz, the central question for the AUTO UNION remained that of future model policy. This became rapidly more urgent as sales of motorcycles began to drop alarmingly. The motorcycle range had been one of the principal mainstays during the rebirth and build-up of the post-war AUTO UNION. Ever since 1949, the Ingolstadt-based company had earned far more from its two-wheelers than from its passenger cars. It was evident, however, that this situation could not persist for ever: since 1953 buyers had begun to look for a "roof over their heads" to an increasing extent and the motorcycle market had dwindled in volume, including a violent drop of 35 percent from 1955 to 1956. A decision was therefore taken: on October 1st, 1958 the complete motorcycle production facility was sold to Victoria AG in Nuremberg.

The "large" DKW was considered impressive enough in the 1950s for prominent personalities to be seen driving it, for example film star Romy Schneider ...

... Max Schmeling

Before that, on April 28th 1958, the shareholders' general meeting had resolved to start production of a new small car and also to purchase a 350,000 square metre site for a brand-new factory in Ingolstadt, with a view to producing 250 cars every working day initially. The Bavarian State Bank made this decision practicable by granting an investment loan of 25 million DM. The ground-breaking ceremony took place in July 1958, and just over a year later the first DKW Junior left the assembly line. Production of the AUTO UNION 1000, as the existing models had been renamed in 1957, continued in Düsseldorf. Sales boomed: the Junior was enthusiastically received by press and public alike, and dealers could not get hold of as many as they were able to sell. Turnover doubled within three years, and reached more than 800 million DM in 1962, which was the AUTO UNION's best business year since the war. The dyna-

mic effects of the Daimler-Benz take-over were so obvious that the parent company also entertained the idea of taking over the ailing BMW company, in which Herbert Quandt was a majority shareholder. Plans to this effect were well advanced, but violent protests from smaller shareholders in BMW put a stop to the project in 1959 – certainly a welcome development, as events have since proved. On 21st December 1959 Daimler-Benz made an offer for all the AUTO UNION shares not yet in its possession, and thus became the sole owner of the company. A decision to abandon Düsseldorf as a production site and to manufacture all future AUTO UNION vehicles in the new Ingolstadt plant was taken on May 31st, 1961. The plant site in North Rhine-Westphalia's capital city was sold to Daimler-Benz in 1962.

Whereas William Werner and his team of technicians regarded the success of the DKW Junior as evidence that they had found the right formula for future models, their new partners in Stuttgart were calling for further activity on the part of the AUTO UNION; they naturally gave preference to the four-stroke engine, and were able to promise extensive help with the necessary development work. Time was pressing: sales of the larger DKWs were dropping, and despite its popularity the Junior was a small car and unable to generate very high profit levels. Werner was far-sighted enough to accept that the four-stroke offered greater potential for the more distant future, but like Dr. Henze, remained loyal to the two-stroke as a short-term measure. This aroused strong disapproval at the parent company in Stuttgart of what was regarded merely as a delaying tactic. Friction, mutual reproaches and refusal to see the other side's point of view were the outcome. Daimler-Benz's decision, taken at about this time, to concentrate its efforts on the luxury car and commercial vehicle markets in the future, could have only one logical conclusion: AUTO UNION was to be sold off again.

Once again it was Friedrich Flick who paved the way for the necessary negotiations. In 1962 he met Heinrich Nordhoff, then chief executive of VW, and discussed a possible take-over with him. The Wolfsburg company realised that the move would give them an immediate increase in production capacity of

*...or aviation pioneer
Elly Beinhorn*

100,000 cars a year, as well as eliminating one of their more serious competitors from the market. For these two advantages, a purchase price in the region of 300 million Deutschmarks did not seem too high.

From its AUTO UNION excursion, Daimler-Benz retained certain material assets in the form of the IMOSA delivery van plant in Spain and the Düsseldorf production facility, which it had bought in 1962. Of the non-material ones, it chose to keep control of the trade mark, which had once belonged to its more successful pre-war competitor HORCH. On its departure from Ingolstadt, however, the Stuttgart management allowed the company to retain its Technical General Manager Ludwig Kraus, as it was to transpire an innovative "secret weapon" for the years to come.

The product

At the German International Automobile Exhibition in 1957, a design study for the DKW 660, as yet not for sale, was displayed and greatly admired. It was to become the DKW Junior in due course, with a 750 cc engine. The aim was to introduce a model below the existing 3=6, but to rely on tried and tested DKW design elements such as front-wheel drive and the two-stroke, three-cylinder engine. In place of the "floating axle" dating back to the 1930s, Kurt Schwenk produced a new rear suspension layout using a cut-open axle tube with torsion-bar springs. At the same motor show, the existing DKW models were upgraded. They now bore the name "Auto UNION 1000", and came in three versions which differed quite considerably in price. In 1959 the body was modified, and acquired the then highly fashionable wraparound windscreen. Another product dating from 1957 was the two-seater AUTO UNION 1000 Sp coupé. Chief stylist Josef Dienst gave it certain marked American features, as he later recalled: "Technical Director Werner came to see me one day and

This DKW 660 prototype was shown to the public at the 1957 German Motor Show (the "IAA"), and marketed two years later as the DKW Junior

The F 12 roadster was introduced in September 1963

said, with his strong American accent well to the fore: 'Draft me out a sports car. It has to go like a bomb and look the same way!"

The Baur company was commissioned to build the bodies, and the car was assembled in Ingolstadt. In October 1961 it was joined by an extremely pretty roadster, which was also greatly admired by the public for its bold, chic styling. This new model was a highlight of the company's sales program, but of course it was not the high-volume product which it urgently needed. Professor Nallinger from Daimler-Benz declared that in the opinion of his board a successor for the 3=6 ought to be found without delay. He also felt that it should have a four-stroke engine, possibly of horizontally-opposed layout, and should retain the front-wheel-drive principle. Werner played along, and instructed Siebler to start design work on the F 100. For this car, Daimler-Benz suggested that a 1.5-litre flat-four engine rated at 60 bhp be used, and proposed to supply all the necessary drawings.

In the meantime, the current Junior models had to be improved and their sales volume stimulated. The result of this project was known as the F 12. The engine was enlarged to 900 cc, and disc brakes were fitted at the front – an improvement which many a larger and far more expensive rival product was unable to offer at the time.

At long last, in the Summer of 1963, the successor to the AUTO UNION 1000 S was ready for production. Known as the F 102, it was much more modern in design, had been extensively tested by Daimler-Benz (with even the legendary Uhlenhaut taking a hand) and was an altogether better car than its predecessor. It had only one congenital shortcoming, to be frank: it still had a two-stroke engine. This was actually a new three-cylinder design of just under 1.2 litres' capacity, with an output of 60 bhp – the largest DKW three-cylinder unit ever built.

The two-stroke engine had already lost much of the fascination evidently felt by the generation that had adopted it so enthusiastically in the 1930s, and which constituted DKW's loyal clientèle for so long. They did not care if their cars trailed a long plume of exhaust smoke behind them – after all, ageing four-strokes did the same! Nor were they disturbed by the noise: this nervous spluttering was one of the things that set them apart from the common herd. On the positive side, the engines started willingly, developed plenty of low-speed torque and were incredibly simple in construction, so that maintenance and repair costs were low. But after the war and in the 1950s, four-stroke engines reached such a high standard that the younger generation could no longer be wooed with nostalgic recollections of DKW's better days.

Probably the main source of complaint, and the one which sealed the fate of the two-stroke engine, was crankshaft damage, particularly if the cars were frequently used for short journeys only. Corrosion would attack the moving parts in the crankcase and cause the crankshaft to seize. A possible answer would have been to provide a separate lubrication system, and this would also have helped to reduce the proportion of burnt oil in the exhaust. Together with the Bosch company, an automatic oil feed was therefore developed, and installed on all AUTO UNION models from 1961 onwards. Perhaps it was developed with too much haste, or else the problem was more complex than the engineers realised. At all events, the automatic system tended to give up the ghost in cold weather. After a winter with record low temperatures for several weeks in 1962/63, the number of crankshaft failures also reached a new, albeit negative, record.

Sales accordingly took a further sudden turn for the worse. Despite this, AUTO UNION's management clung to its two-stroke engine policy and commissioned the Müller design office in Andernach to develop a six-cylinder two-stroke unit

Another beautiful AUTO UNION product, but one not intended for series production: the 1000 Sp with a Coupé body designed in Italy by Fissore (1959)

with a rated output of 80 bhp. Henze felt this move to be necessary in order not to arouse the hostility of the existing, loyal customers. The project came to an abrupt end when VW took over the reins: chief executive Nordhoff commented sourly that he "did not wish time to be wasted on trivia such as six-cylinder two-strokes",

Even when warmer weather prevailed again and the company improved its automatic oil feed system, the customers stayed away in droves. Another reason for this was undoubtedly the persistent rumours that the next AUTO UNION engine would be a four-stroke.

Tail fins: part of the American Way of Life. The 1000 Sp Coupé was the "dream car" of many a German two-stroke fan

Even beauty queens – here Germany's 1964 winner – loved to ride in the attractive 1000 Sp roadster

AUTO UNION in motor sport

Having told the world that "DKW is back" by recommencing operations in Ingolstadt, the AUTO UNION was naturally obliged to consider its position as a works entrant in motor sport events. The tuners Döring and Erich Wolf in Wiesbaden had developed a very promising 125 cc DKW racing engine with charge-pump. In 1950 the company hired them and took over their design. H. P. Müller, already a well-known rider before the war, was entered for suitable events, and carried off the German championship in the 125 cc class

Ewald Kluge (with start number 170) helped to continue the pre-war tradition of racing success

in 1950. Ewald Kluge rode for the works team in the 250 cc class, and Siegfried Wünsche in the 350 cc class. The motorcycles themselves were largely based on pre-war know-how and experience. The DKW team, despite initial successes, failed to acquire the necessary momentum. 1952 was the first season in twenty years, apart from the war period, in which this renowned marque failed to win a championship title in any motorcycle racing class. Müller had left the AUTO UNION team and was riding privately entered Italian Mondial bikes. Curiously enough, 1952 was precisely the year in which the new "secret weapon" from Ingolstadt, the three-cylinder 350 cc DKW, began to win races. A power output of 38 bhp at 12,500 rpm was enough to terrify the opposition, but a series of piston ring breakages meant that the bikes retired frequently without finishing the race. Kluge and Wünsche did however ride this model to its first double victory on the Eilenriede circuit, after most of the technical shortcomings had been eliminated. The excessively high piston speeds were cut back in favour of a better torque curve. Peak power none the less rose to 45 bhp, but was obtained 1000 rpm lower down the engine-speed scale.

From this time on, all the racing team's efforts were concentrated on this promi-

First post-war champion on a DKW 125 was H. P. Müller, the "Racing Tiger", in 1950

sing design. It was ridden by Wünsche, Hoffmann and Hobl in 1954, the last-named coming in second in the relevant German championship class. 1955 saw even greater success for the team, with Gustav Hobl third in the world championship and German champion in the 350 cc class, with Wünsche and Hoffmann as runners-up. In 1956 Hobl only just failed to become world champion in his class, the title being secured by Bill Lomas. In the German championship, DKW riders again occupied the first three places. Despite all these successes, the decision to withdraw from road racing did not come entirely as a surprise, following similar moves by such companies as NSU. Sporting achievement on its own was simply not enough to resist the collapse of the motorcycle industry.

The prospects of competition success were good for DKW automobiles as well in the post-war years. The first two-stroke cars bearing the AUTO UNION badge were entered for reliability trials in 1951, and performed well. Private entrant Heinz Meier secured the first gold medal for the F 89 at a winter trial in Garmisch-Partenkirchen. The three-cylinder "Sonderklasse" appeared in 1953, and was immediately seized upon by dedicated motor sport practitioners as a promising competition vehicle. Gustav Menz and Heinz Meier from the Ingolstadt experimental department were now joined by Hubert Brand, who achieved many fine results with the "Meisterklasse" during the season, including an overall win in the Austrian International Alpine Rally.

In 1953 the factory's "Sonderklasse" entries gained no less than twelve gold medals, making the car extremely well-known in motor sport circles within a very short time.

In the Autumn 1953, a competition department was set up to enter vehicles on its own account and support private entrants. This far-sighted decision led to an unmatched series of successes in the next few years which naturally contributed to the popularity of DKW cars among the general public as well. Right at the start, Meier won his class in the Monte Carlo Rally, and the first year of participation on this new basis ended with a genuine sensation: the DKW "Sonderklasse" won all the eight heats of the European championship for which it was entered, and carried off the 1954 European Touring Car championship with Walter Schlüter at the wheel, who had been successful with his colleague Polenski for Porsche in the previous season. DKW drivers were also among the runners-up. This made the DKW "Sonderklasse" Europe's most successful touring car racer. Not only was its

roadholding excellent: it was also extremely fast. Careful tuning had raised the engine's power output to more than 50 bhp. The amazing simplicity of the two-stroke principle tempted other leading tuners on to the scene later, and in some cases more than 100 bhp were seen from this engine.

World records were broken in 1956 on the Monza circuit in Italy, using a "Sonderklasse" model with special plastic body. In the up to 1100 cc class it set up new speed limits over 4,000 miles, 48 hours, 5,000 miles, 10,000 km and 72 hours, driven by Ahrens, Meier, Theiler and Barbay. The special body had been commissioned by Günther Ahrens and DKW tuner A. M. Mantzel from, and built by, the Dannenhauser & Stauss company in Stuttgart. The car was shod with Dunlop tubeless tyres. A limited edition of about 230 DKW Monza models was built to cash in on this success; the Heidelberg DKW dealer Fritz Wenk had them built initially by Massholder in that town, and later at Schenk in Stuttgart.

The ten-year period between 1954 and 1964 in which the AUTO UNION maintained an active factory presence in motor sport, and also lent its support to touring car race entrants, yielded a rich harvest: more than 100 championship titles, 150 overall wins and 2,500 class wins for DKW drivers.

Star DKW drivers Walter Schlüter, Gustav Menz und Heinz Meier (from left to right) secured the first three places in the 1954 European touring car championship with their DKW "Sonderklasse" cars

August Hobl at the wheel of the three-cylinder DKW on the Nürburg Ring in 1955, the year in which he was world championship runner-up in his class

AUTO UNION tempts Porsche drivers

A memorandum issued by the AUTO UNION testing department in October 1953 reads as follows:

"The three-cylinder car made an unexpectedly favourable impression on the motor sport people who attended, and some Porsche drivers expressed their intention of switching to the "Sonderklasse" in the future or buying it as a second car. We believe this to be an opportunity for publicity too good to miss ... we shall therefore be organizing a competition department, with a manager and three mechanics. They will be supplied with six standard saloons with specially selected engines which the experimental department in Düsseldorf could also tune slightly. Four of the cars will be placed at the disposal of the DKW works drivers, the other two loaned to dealers or selected customers for specific events."

In December 1956 the drivers Meier, Theiler, Barbay and Ahrens broke a number of world long-distance records in a plastic-bodied DKW at the Monza racing circuit

Figures, facts and types

Dates in the history of
AUTO UNION

1945	Central AUTO UNION depot set up in Ingolstadt on 19th December. Share capital: 50,000 RM. Turnover: 3 million RM p.a.
1947	On 25th March, establishment of the "first" new AUTO UNION GmbH in Ingolstadt by AUTO UNION AG of Chemnitz. Equity: 200,000 RM. This company took over all the AUTO UNION AG's assets in the West. Purpose of the new GmbH: to obtain spare parts sales and consolidate the company's assets in Western Germany
1948	On 17th August, AUTO UNION AG of Chemnitz was deleted from the local trade register
1948	At the end of the year, AUTO UNION GmbH acquired the spare parts depot.
1949	On 3rd September, establishment of the "second" AUTO UNION GmbH in Ingolstadt. Capital: 3 million DM. The main partner was the 1st AUTO UNION GmbH (1,200,000 DM), which contributed its real-estate assets, the spare parts business and a general licence for all patents and similar rights. Bankhaus Oppenheim contributed 900,000 DM and the rest came from the partners, including Dr. Bruhn, who was appointed General Manager, and his deputy, Dr. Hahn
1951	In January the equity was increased to 5,500,000 DM as a result of a 2,500,000 DM deposit from Ernst Göhner
1954	In the following four years the equity was gradually raised to 30 million DM; Göhner's holding increased to 12,300,000 DM = 40.5 %
1958	On 24th April, Daimler-Benz AG acquired 87.8 percent of the capital
1960	Equity raised from 30 to 60 million DM on 6th December
1962	Düsseldorf plant sold; it had produced 483,368 DKW vehicles up to that time
1963	Equity increased to 80 million DM in March
1964	Equity increased to 160 million DM in December; 50.3 % of this was taken up by VW immediately

A DKW 3=6 station wagon as driven by the leading US car magazine "Road & Track"

A 3=6 rapid load-carrier was used to carry personnel while the new plant in Ingolstadt was under construction (1951)

Production figures

The rapid delivery van continued in production until 1957, almost 50,000 being built (an average of some 6,200 per year). At the same time, 187,000 passenger cars and 6,300 Mungas were produced.

The prices asked for the passenger cars fell from about 6,000 DM for the two-door saloon to 5,700 DM in 1957. The van, on the other hand, went up in price from 5,800 to 6,300 DM.

From 1,400 at the end of 1949, the workforce grew to 9,750 by the end of 1957.

Including scooters and mopeds, Ingolstadt produced 518,735 DKW motorcycles from 1949 onwards. The best-selling model was the RT 125, of which 133,945 were made.

In 1949 the RT 125 was the only post-war DKW motorcycle to cost less than 1,000 DM. By 1952, 1,420 DM were being asked for the RT 175, and two years later 1,575 DM for the RT 200. In 1956 the 250 cc model with all-swinging arm suspension was priced at 1,815 DM and the RT 350 at about 2,250 DM. Lower prices were of course charged for the Hobby and Hummel models: the single-seater scooter cost 950 DM, the moped 598 DM.

From 1955 onwards, the Spanish IMOSA company in Vitoria built the DKW rapid delivery van under licence. Its own F 1000 L went into production in July 1963 and was sold by the AUTO UNION. IMOSA later passed into the ownership of Daimler-Benz, but the delivery vans it manufactured were sold as "AUTO

e principal AUTO UNION DKW models, 1949–1958

	Number/lay-out of cyls.	Bore x stroke in mm	Displace-ment in cc	Output in hp	Years of production	Notes
l delivery vans						
	2 inline	76 x 76	684	20	1949–1954	From1952: 22 bhp Transverse engine
	2 inline	78 x 83	792	30	1954–1955	Front-to-rear engine
	3 inline	71 x 76	896	32	1955–1962	
enger cars						
erklasse	2 inline	76 x 76	684	23	1950–1954	From1951, also Universal estate
erklasse	3 inline	71 x 76	896	34	1953–1955	
4, 3=6 e" DKW	3 inline	71 x 76	896	38/40	1955–1959	
UNION1000	3 inline	74 x 76	980	44	1957–1960	
00 S	3 inline	74 x 76	980	50	1959–1963	
00 Sp	3 inline	74 x 76	980	55	1958–1965	
F 91/4	3 inline	71 x 76	896	40	1955–1968	***

om 1958 on, 1000 cc engine; known as "Munga"; also as F 91/6 and F91/8 6- and 8-seaters

UNION DKW" until 1975.

Early in 1962 the last of the rapid delivery vans was produced in Ingolstadt. From 1958 onwards, 9,339 of them came from this plant. For the F 800/3 (3=6), a price of 6,300 DM was charged; the 1000 L was listed at 7,000 DM.

Altogether, Düsseldorf and Ingolstadt made 250,958 DKWs between 1958 and 1965. By the time production ceased in 1958, another 40,400 cars had been completed.

The last passenger car with a two-stroke engine left the assembly line in Ingolstadt on March 24th, 1966; it was a four-door F 102 saloon. The Munga continued in production until 1968. The first listed price for the two-door DKW Junior saloon was 4,950 DM. The F 12 to a similar specification cost 5,375 DM and the F 102 6,850 DM. The marque's share of total registrations was 7.2 percent in 1961, falling to 3.7 percent by 1964.

The principal DKW motorcycle models, 1949–1958

Type	Number of cylinders	Bore x stroke in mm	Displacement in cc	Output in hp	Years of production	Notes
RT 125 W	1	52 x 58	123	4.75	1949–1952	
RT 125/2 H	1	52 x 58	123	5.7	1952–1957	Rear suspens
RT 175	1	62 x 58	174	9.6	1954–1958	
RT 175 VS	1	62 x 58	174	9.6	1957–1958	
RT 200	1	62 x 64	191	8.5	1951–1952	
RT 200 H	1	62 x 64	191	8.5	1952–1956	
RT 200 VS	1	66 x 58	197	11	1957–1958	
RT 250/1	1	70 x 64	244	11.5	1953–1953	
RT 250/2	1	70 x 64	244	14.1	1953–1957	
RT 250 VS	1	70 x 64	244	15	1956–1957	
RT 350	2	62 x 58	348	18.5	1955–1956	
Hobby	1	45 x 47	74	3	1954–1957	Continuousl iable V-belt
Hummel	1	40 x 39	49	1.35	1956–1958	

The DKW F 102, seen here with a four-door body, was the last two-stroke car to be produced in Ingolstadt

DKW F 102 saloon (1964)

principal DKW models, 1959–1964

	Number/layout of cylinders	Bore x stroke in mm	Displacement in cc	Output in hp	Years of production
unior (F 11)	3 R	68 x 68	741	34	1959–1962
11/64	3 R	70.5 x 68	796	34	1963–1965
12	3 R	74.5 x 68	889	40	1963–1965
12 er	3 R	74.5 x 68	889	45	1964
102 elivery van	3 R	81 x 76	1175	60	1964–1966
L	3 R	74 x 76	981	40	1963–1968

The Hobby scooter stood up to the toughest day-to-day treatment

AUTO UNION – an overview

A HORCH as ceremonial transport for guests of the Berlin Senate: welcoming the Federal Chancellor in 1950

DKW F 10 Cabriolet (1950)

F 89 Meisterklasse saloon (1950)

F 89 Cabriolet (1950)

Four-seater F 91 Coupé (1953)

Wooden model of
FX prototype (1951)

Two-seater F 91
Coupé (1953)

Two-seater F 91
Cabriolet (1953)

The AUTO UNION
1000 Sp at the German Motor Show in
Frankfurt (1957)

Special police-force
version of F 91 (1954)

DKW Junior (1959)

DKW Junior with van body (built to special order by the Rometsch company, Berlin)

AUTO UNION 1000 S with wraparound windscreen (1960)

Two-door DKW F 12 saloon (1963)

DKW F 12 Roadster (1964)

DKW 3=6 minibus (1958)

An experiment produced in small numbers: the DKW rapid delivery van with electric motor propulsion (1956)

DKW F 1000 L rapid delivery van (1963)

Ewald Kluge and a DKW racing motorcycle (1950)

World championship runner-up August Hobl with two DKW racing bikes: at left, the 3 50 cc three-cylinder. at right, the 125 cc single-cylinder

NSU

Bicycles instead of knitting machines

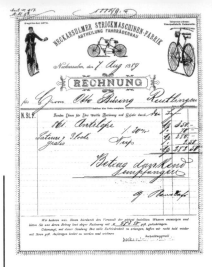

The company

In 1873 two mechanics, Christian Schmidt and Heinrich Stoll of Riedlingen, a town on the upper reaches of the River Danube, set up a workshop to build knitting machines; in 1880 they moved it to Neckarsulm. Four years later the name was changed to Neckarsulmer Strickmaschinenfabrik AG, and after a further two years the company began to produce bicycles; these were of the "ordinary" or "penny-farthing" type and sold as the "Germania". Very soon, conventional bicycles were also produced, since a front wheel 1.47 m in diameter was not to every rider's taste.

NSU knitting machines vanished from the market in 1892 (the three letters are always accepted as an abbreviation for "Neckarsulm"), and five years later the company acknowledged its diversification into bicycles by renaming itself "Neckarsulmer Fahrradwerke AG". From 1901 onwards, the fumes of petrol could be smelt inside the factory, since motorcycle production commenced in that year. In 1903 a 300-metre long testing and demonstration track was laid out on the factory site. The first motorcycles were powered by a Zedel engine obtained from Switzerland, but from 1903 onwards the company installed its own NSU engines, with power outputs from 2 to 3.5 hp. Their advertising stated: 'We have now resolved to build a strong three-horsepower motorcycle for riders with strong nerves. It is extremely fast, but can also be ridden slowly!' NSU bicycles

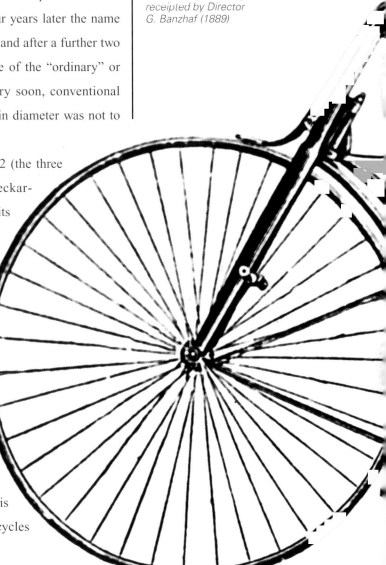

The "Arrow" safety cycle (1888)

and motorcycles were sold through the company's own branches in Düsseldorf, Hamburg, Leipzig, Berlin, Königsberg, Moscow, London, Paris and Zürich. Business flourished, and the company began seriously to consider manufacturing an automobile. By 1905, its plans had borne fruit, and the first car to be produced in Neckarsulm left the factory – a Belgian Pipe built under licence. In parallel with this, the NSU engineers were working on a concept of their own. It proved to be a tricycle, rather similar to the Zyklonette, with a 3.5 hp motorcycle engine located above the front wheel, which it drove by chain. This vehicle was named the "Sulmobil", and went on sale in 1906.

Neither large nor small automobiles of this type appealed particularly to buyers, nor did they evidently satisfy the manufacturer. In the same year, the company launched its "Original Neckarsulm Motor Carriage", versions of which with larger and more powerful engines followed before long. A full range of models was soon built up: they had no separate designations but, like the motorcycles, were simply labelled "NECKARSULM" in large letters. From 1911 onwards the vehicles from Neckarsulm were referred to by the far more convenient three-letter abbreviation: NSU.

Both powerful twin-cylinder bikes and lighter tourers were included in the motorcycle programme. Rear suspension was available from NSU as early as 1911, together with chain (only the 7.5 hp racing machine) or belt drive, a two-speed gearbox and a sprung front fork. The NSU Pony was the smallest bike, rated at 1.5 hp and weighing 48 kilograms. It was none the less capable of reaching 60 km/h! One litre of fuel would take the rider a distance of

45 kilometres. For the heavyweight bikes with 800 cc, 6.5 hp engine, which tipped the scales at 125 kg, lightweight basketwork accommodation for the pillion passenger soon gave way to fully-fledged "phaeton-bodied" ones. The tricycle concept – "runs like a car but is as cheap as a motorcycle" was not entirely defunct; its place had clearly been taken by the sidecar outfit. Before the First World War, NSU was Germany's most active exporter of motorcycles. Most German-made motorcycles abroad proved to have originated in Neckarsulm. They were shipped to Russia, to most European countries, to Turkey and Scandinavia, and even the Citizens' Guard of Sao Paulo in Brazil rode these bikes. When war broke out in 1914, NSU was obliged to modify its product range to suit the needs of the military authorities. The result was the 3.5 hp twin-cylinder "military" model of 1915. The small cars continued in production, and were painted in field grey and stripped of their luxury features before being delivered to the army. Trucks for payloads of 1.25 t and 2.5 t were also built in Neckarsulm, by order of the Imperial government.

Motor sport

No sooner had motorcycle production begun in 1901 than competition successes began to accrue. The public first had its attention drawn to the marque by its victories on indoor tracks. Other gold medals soon followed: Martin Geiger won the Feldberg Trial in 1904 on a Neckarsulm model, completing the course (which was almost 10 km in length with gradients of up to 1 in 8) at an average speed of

A 270 km long auto-mobile race held in the Argentine (1913)

Gertrud Eisemann, one of the first women to take an interest in motor sport, won the Eisenach-Berlin-Eisenach long-distance run in 1905 on a 2 hp NSU motorcycle

38 km/h. Also a source of immense public interest in the same year: Gertrud Eisemann, one of Germany's first and most successful woman motorcyclists. She set up a number of records and recorded a long list of successes in long-distance events. She also drove HORCH cars a number of times in competition events during this phase of her career.

The first time that cars from Neckarsulm took part actively in competition was in the 1909 Prince Henry Trial. The three-car NSU team completed the course without penalty. The cars also tackled other long-distance runs with complete success, for instance the Quality Trial from Moscow to Oryol, where they gained two first prizes. None the less, the NSU marque derived its sporting image primarily from its motorcycles, which were also highly successful abroad. A fine achievement was Karl Gassert's gold medal in the 1911 British Tourist Trophy, followed by a win at the Semmering circuit in Austria. In the 1913/14 season, NSU riders won no fewer than 375 first prizes in Germany alone.

The principal NSU automobile models, 1906-1918

Type	Number of cylinders	Bore x stroke in mm	Displace-ment in cc	Output in hp	Years of production
Sulmobil	1	64 x 70	451	3,5	1905–1906
6/10 PS	4	68 x 90	1308	12	1906–1907
8/15 PS	4	76 x 100	1750	15	1907–1908
10/20 PS	4	85 x 115	2608	20	1907–1910
6/12 PS	4	70 x 100	1540	12	1907–1908
6/18 PS	4	75 x 88	1550	18	1908–1914
5/10 PS	4	60 x 100	1132	10	1909–1911
10/30 PS	4	85 x 115	2608	30	1911–1914
13/35 PS	4	97 x 115	3397	35	1911–1914
8/24 PS	4	80 x 104	2110	24	1912–1925
5/15 PS	4	70 x 78	1232	15	1914–1925
2.5-tonner	4	94 x 130	3606	54	1914–1924

Dates in the history of NSU

1873	Knitting machine factory established by Christian Schmidt and Heinrich Stoll in Riedlingen
1880	Company moved to Neckarsulm
1884	Neckarsulmer Strickmaschinenfabrik AG established on 27th April with an equity of 140,000 Marks
1886	Production of "ordinary" bicycles commenced (the "Germania")
1892	Knitting machine production ceased
1897	24th Sept.: Neckarsulmer Fahrradwerke AG, capital 1 million Marks
1900	Freewheel and brake hub production started
1901	First motorcycles produced
1906	First automobiles produced
1913	Neckarsulmer Fahrzeugwerke AG established on 10th February, capital 3.6 million Marks
1914	In 1913 and 1914 NSU produced more than 12,000 bicycles, 2,500 motorcycles and 400 automobiles. The total workforce in Neckarsulm, with salaried staff, was 1,200.

Some of many NSU winners before the First World War

The "Original Neckar-sulm Motorcycle" with basket for pillion passenger, seen in the East Indies (1904)

The principal NSU motorcycle models, 1901–1918

Type	Number of cylinders	Bore x stroke in mm	Displacement in cc	Ouput in hp	Years produced
Neckarsulm 1.5 PS	1			1.5	1901–1903
Neckarsulm 2.5 PS	1	75 x 75	329	2.5	1903–1905
Neckarsulm 1.25 PS	1	62 x 70	310	1.25	1907
Neckarsulm 4 PS	1	64 x 75	554	4	1909
Neckarsulm 2.5 PS	2	52 x 74	315	2.5	1909
Neckarsulm 6 PS	2	75 x 90	795	6	1909–1911
NSU 2.5 PS	1	73 x 78	326	2.5	1913
NSU 3.5 PS	2	63 x 80	495	3.5	1913–1921
NSU 6.5 PS	2	75 x 94	830	6.5	1913–1921

A. Gikeleiter, cement-track champion on NSU in the class up to 1000 cc (1910)

Crises and triumphs between the wars

NSU – the company

Like most makes at the end of the First World War, NSU survived by using up residual stocks. The first new vehicles, however, were being manufactured by 1920/21: bicycles and motorcycles for the most part, in particular the army bike, which had proved its merits during the war. Demand for accessory items also grew, and so the production of freewheel hubs was built up until one was being completed every thirty seconds.

To commemorate the company's 50th anniversary, which fell on 12th April 1924, the company had increased the size of its factory premises to a most unusual extent, considering that inflation was still rampant in Germany. A separate telephone exchange, laboratories and even a photographic studio were installed. In the same year, work started on a branch factory in nearby Heilbronn; this was not completed until 1927/28. In accordance with a tendency for German motor-vehicle companies to amalgamate at this time, NSU joined forces with Schebera AG, a coachbuilding company in Berlin which belonged to the Schapiro Group.

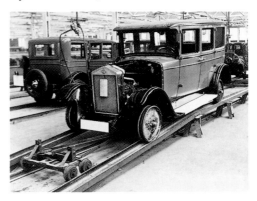

NSU 7/34 hp assembly at the branch factory in Heilbronn, using conveyor-belt methods (1928)

From 26th November 1926 onwards, a new name was adopted: NSU Vereinigte Fahrzeugwerke AG, Neckarsulm. Production continued at the main plant, and the former Schebera company was involved in sales activities, concentrating in particular on the taxi business in Berlin. NSU automobiles were to be seen frequently on the streets of Germany's capital as hire cars. Unfortunately, too many licences were granted, so that the individual taxicab owners suffered a drop in their earnings and were unable to make the agreed instalment payments to the manufacturer. NSU itself got into financial difficulties in 1926 as a result. Urgent reorganisation measures were taken, which lasted until 1928 and led to the giant Italian automobile manufacturer Fiat purchasing the Heilbronn factory

to make its own passenger cars. For a time, Fiat obtained chassis from NSU and installed its own bodies on them. The Neckarsulm plant ceased to manufacture automobiles at all. Until 1932, Fiat continued to build NSU cars in Heilbronn, selling them under the NSU Fiat name. This name was retained even when purely Italian vehicles were built in Heilbronn, for example the Balilla Sport and the Fiat 500, 1000 and 1100 models.

On January 1st 1930 Fritz von Falkenhayn, son of the famous Chief of Military Staff, became sales manager of NSU. Two years later he joined the board of directors, and after a further six years took over as its chairman. He began to build up an effective sales organisation. In the same highly successful way as DKW had done, he arranged for NSU to offer its dealers full-scale training courses for workshop mechanics. A central customer service department was organised, and also a showroom in which the complete range of vehicles was always on display.

Showroom with complete product range (1923)

A joint sales operation was negotiated in 1928 with WANDERER in Chemnitz, but failed to get off the ground because the Saxon company abandoned its

motorcycle division only shortly afterwards. A further project involving the coordination and amalgamation of production and sales with the Deutsche Industriewerke AG in Berlin (makers of the D-Rad) led in 1932 to a short-lived change of name to "NSU D-Rad-Vereinigte Fahrzeugwerke Neckarsulm". In 1936, NSU acquired Opel's complete bicycle production facility. Shortly afterwards, the D-Rad vanished from the market, and so this addition to the NSU company name was deleted once again in 1938.

Motorcycles

When the first new motorcycle after the war was designed and built – it appeared in 1921 – it was clearly a victim of the times: the 350 cc single-cylinder engine developed 3 hp and drove the rear wheel by belt, a cheap but not particularly effective solution.

Three years later, chain drive was adopted once again; it had in fact been featured on NSU motorcycles before the war. There was a new front fork, with parallelogram-action suspension and shock absorbers. Starting in 1927, NSU used a single engine block containing the three-speed gearbox and also the primary, magneto and oil pump drives.

The dimensions were standardised in order to permit the cylinder of either a side-valve tourer or an overhead-valve sports model to be attached. In 1928, when engines of up to 200 cc were exempted from tax, a suitable model was introduced (the NSU 201 R), and a 300 cc bike (the NSU 301 T) was also included in the model programme. In 1931 the first two-stroke, with a 175 cc engine, was introduced.

As tangible evidence that motorcycle sales were booming, a brand-new running-in track was set up behind the factory; opened in 1929 and 1,670 km long and 5 m wide, it was among the most modern in Germany. In the same year, NSU recruited a new chief designer, the Englishman Walter William Moore. He had previously worked for Norton, where he had designed the famous single-cylin-

The "Motosulm", the first motorised bicycle to be mass-produced (1931)

der engine with vertical-shaft drive to the valve gear, a legend in its time. His handwriting could be seen not only on the NSU sports models but also on the OSL series with their 200, 250, 350, 500 and 600 cc engines, which dominated the range right through to the nineteen-thirties. The Neckarsulm company also took a closer interest in the lower-priced end of the motorcycle market at the end of the 1920s, starting with the NSU 201 R and continuing in 1931 with the "Motosulm".

The principal NSU motorcycle models, 1919–1945

Type	Number of cylinders	Bore x stroke in mm	Displace-ment in cc	Output in hp	Years of production
NSU 4 hp	2	63 x 80	495	4	1920–1925
NSU 8 hp	2	80 x 99	995	12	1924–1927
NSU 251 R	1	63 x 80	248	6	1924–1928
NSU 502 T	2	80 x 99	498	10	1924–1927
NSU 251 T/S	1	60 x 80	249	6	1928–1931
NSU 501 S	1	80 x 99	497	20	1928–1930
NSU 201 R/T	1	56.5 x 80	199	4.5	1928–1930
NSU 301 T	1	66 x 88	298	7	1929–1930
NSU 351 TS	1	71 x 88	346	8	1930–1932
NSU 175 Z/ZD	1	59 x 64	174	4.5	1930–1933
NSU 201 Z	1	63 x 64	198	5	1930–1932
NSU 251 Z	1	70 x 64	244	5.5	1930–1933
NSU 501 SS	1	80 x 99	494	30	1930–1935
NSU 601 SS	1	87.5 x 99	592	38	1930–1935
NSU 501 TS	1	80 x 99	494	12.5	1930–1936
NSU 601 TS	1	87.5 x 99	592	16	1930–1939
NSU Motosulm	1	45 x 40	63	1.25	1931–1935
NSU 251 OSL	1	64 x 75	242	10.5	1933–1952
NSU 201 OSL	1	58 x 75	198	8.5	1933–1939
NSU 201 ZDB Pony	1	63 x 64	198	6.5	1934–1940
NSU 351 OSL	1	71 x 88	346	18	1932–1940
NSU 501 OSL	1	80 x 99	494	22	1935–1939
NSU Quick	1	49 x 52	98	3	1936–1953
NSU 351 OT	1	75 x 75	331	12.5	1936–1939
NSU 601 OSL	1	85 x 99	562	24	1937–1940
NSU 125 ZDB	1	52 x 58	123	4.5	1941–1951

This was a motorised bicycle with a 1.2 hp two-stroke engine above the front wheel; it proved capable of reaching a top speed of 35 km/h. In the early Thirties it was followed by the ZDB models, all of them with an easy-to-manufacture two-stroke engine.

On the NSU stand at the 1936 International Automobile and Motorcycle Exhibition in Berlin, a 100 cc motorcycle with bicycle-type cranks and pedals and either a men's or a women's frame was to be seen.

It was named the "Quick" in accordance with a spontaneous suggestion made by a Berlin woman. It cost 290 Reichsmarks and consumed under two litres of fuel per 100 km. It was an immediate and lasting sales success: NSU built and sold more than a quarter of a million.

Automobiles

The Berlin Motor Show in 1921 was a treasure-trove of all the products that could not be exhibited while the war had been in progress.

The most unlikely concepts were to be seen: unconventional bodies, like Edmund Rumpler's "teardrop". New technical departures were on show, for example the adoption of left-hand drive by AUDI. The bulk of the cars, however, retained their pre-war appearance, with pointed radiator grilles. This was

NSU 7/34 PS (1929)

true of the three NSU exhibits too, which had acquired an electric starter and lighting system but were otherwise new versions of pre-war designs: the 5/15 hp, 8/24 hp and 14/40 hp, later replaced by a 5/30 hp model.

All these cars had a four-cylinder engine. A 2.5-ton truck was also displayed, but did not remain in the sales catalogue for long.

The luxury version of the NSU 5/15 hp model was called the "Dove" and had a saloon body with detachable upper section, which could be removed to convert the car into a phaeton. In Neckarsulm, too much attention was evidently devoted to motorcycle development after this, because a successor for this particular car did not appear until 1928! For all the intervening period, the company evidently felt that it could live off its substance, as accumulated before the war. The eventual replacement was a 6/30 hp design with six-cylinder engine and three-speed gearbox. NSU hoped for an entry to the taxicab business with this car. In the same year, the engine was bored out to 1.8 litres, resulting in a new 7/24 hp model. But all these moves came too late: although Fiat continued to build the cars unchanged after acquiring the plant from NSU, the Neckarsulm marque disappeared from the four-wheeler scene for many years from 1928 onwards.

One "intermezzo" deserves special mention, however. In 1933 Dr. h.c. Ferdinand Porsche commissioned NSU to build a prototype "People's Car" to his designs. The result was the Porsche 32, which had a close resemblance already to what was later to be produced as the Volkswagen (the "Beetle"). At the end of 1933,

NSU had completed three prototypes and begun a road testing programme with them. The engine, as hindsight would lead us to expect, was a 1.5-litre flat four, installed at the rear and rated at 30 horsepower. The car's top speed in prototype form proved to be 115 km/h.

W. Glöckler driving a 5/15 hp racing car (1923)

The prototype "People's Car" commissioned by Ferdinand Porsche from NSU (1933)

NSU 5/25 hp (1928)

Motor sport

When motor sport events became possible again at the end of the First World War, many private entrants were naturally keen to try their luck. For NSU, it was the cars rather than the motorcycles which collected the first honours after the war. At the opening race on the Avus circuit in Berlin (1921), an NSU 8/24 hp car won its class. Drivers Klöble and Kist, already well known for their prowess on motorcycles, also recorded the day's second-best lap time. Their two-seater was only slightly modified in relation to the production car, but two years later the NSU management decided to pull out all the stops.

In 1923, on the same racing circuit, they entered a 1.3-litre, 50 hp car derived from the standard 5/15 hp model, but using a compressor to extract additional power. These cars came first, second and third in the small-car class. Later, the man in the street could buy an unsupercharged 30 hp version, for which demand was exceptionally high. The Neckarsulm team, incidentally, repeated their victory the following year. The designers, however, were already hard at work drafting out a new vehicle. Intended initially for competition and later for series production, it was to have a six-cylinder engine, which would be supercharged for track racing and would then develop 60 horsepower. At the very first German Sports Car Grand Prix meeting, the prototype was entrusted to a driver who later achieved considerable fame at the wheel of WANDERER and AUTO UNION sports cars: August Momberger.

The Wartberg race (1914)

Momberger, at the time a student completing a practical course with NSU, won the race - a sensational achievement! NSU had taken on the entire elite, with such resounding names as Mercedes and Bugatti, and left them behind. In the following year the company carried off the first four places in the 1.5-litre class, the drivers being Georg Klöble, Josef Müller, Ernst Islinger and Jakob Scholl. By this time, top speeds were reaching 175 km/h. This car too later went into series production, and in this guise set up an impressive endurance record. At the end of 1928 it was driven continuously for 18 days and nights on the Nürburg Ring, covering 20,000 kilometres without breakdown. Two years later, on the ADAC long-distance run, the NSU team entered the same car and won the principal gold medal.

Automobile production then ceased, and such victories passed into history. NSU did not begin to take an official interest in motorcycle racing again either until William Moore engaged one of Great Britain's best riders, Tom Bullus, for its team. Moore had developed a brand-new 500 cc supersport bike for his countryman to ride. On June 29th, 1930 he justified the faith shown in him and the bike by winning the Motorcycle Grand Prix on the Nürburg Ring. This broke the spell, so to speak, and NSU now began to demonstrate its true prowess in this cubic-capacity class – and, or so it seemed at least to competitors, to attain almost unbeatable status. Bullus went on to repeat this triumph on the Solitude circuit and also to win the Eifel event, the Klausen Pass hill-climb, the German Hill-climb Grand Prix, the Gaisberg race near Salzburg and the International Grand Prix in Monza.

Klöble and Kist won their class in an 8/24 hp racing car at the inaugural race on the Avus circuit (1921)

The principal NSU automobile models, 1919–1945

Type	Number of cylinders	Bore x stroke in mm	Displacement in cc	Output in hp	Years produced
14/40 hp	4	94 x 130	3606	54	1921–1925
5/25 hp	4	68 x 90	1307	25	1924–1928
6/30 hp	6	60.8 x 99	1567	30	1928–1930
7/34 hp	6	62 x 99	1781	34	1928–1931

This made him one of the most successful racing riders of all time. As for the motorcycle, when suitably modified it proved to be just as successful in reliability and off-road trials. The vertical-shaft drive to the valve gear and the well-chosen centre of gravity, which made for excellent roadholding, were just two of the features that predestined the SS 500 to be a winner wherever it was entered. The first major design revision took place in 1937, whereupon Heiner Fleischmann, riding a 350 cc version with an output of 36 hp, carried off the German championship title in his class. A year later, when Moore had left the company, it fell to the new chief designer Albert Roder to produce a supercharged version to be entered for sidecar races. The project came to nothing, unfortunately, because the authorities banned sidecar racing that year after various severe accidents had occurred. Roder therefore changed his plans and built a supercharged 350 cc twin with double overhead camshafts. Straight from the drawing board, it developed 44 horse-power! This time it was the outbreak of war which put paid to further development work.

The NSU supercharged six-cylinder racing car of 1925, overall winner of the first German Grand Prix; it also took places 1 - 4 in the 1,500 cc class on the Avus a year later

*Scholl, Islinger, Klöble
and Müller
(from left), 1926*

Chain reaction

During the war years, the NSU name was closely linked with the remarkable half-tracked motorcycle which it manufactured for a variety of heavy load handling duties from 1940 onwards, though of course primarily for use by the German armed forces. It was driven by the 36 hp, 1.5-litre Opel Olympia engine and was quite amazingly manoeuvrable, with a turning circle of only 3 metres. This was because the crawler-track brakes could be used to aid steering movements. Without a trailer, the maximum gradient was quoted as 45 degrees, and the fording depth was 440 mm. Yet on a flat road, the half-tracked motor-cycle could be ridden at up to 80 km/h! Furthermore, it was only 100 cm wide, and could therefore pass through narrow gaps. NSU manufactured almost 8,000 of this unusual multi-purpose vehicle.

Data from company history: NSU, 1918–1945

1927	NSU Vereinigte Fahrzeugwerke AG established on 16th March, with a capital of 12.5 million Reichsmarks (RM)
1928	Automobile production abandoned
1932	NSU D-Rad Vereinigte Fahrzeugwerke AG established on 3rd Sept.
1938	NSU Werke AG registered on 8th June, with a capital of 3,600,000 RM. In the late 1920s, both bicycle and motorcycle production were running at about 20,000 units p.a. The NSU workforce averaged about 4,000 at that time
1938	A production staff of about 3,000 produced 63,000 motorcycles and 136,000 bicycles

From two-stroke motorcycle to Wankel-engined car

The company

The years following the Second World War were no different for NSU than for most of Germany's industrial companies: the first step was to clear away the dust and rubble, then to get production going again at a low level, using pre-war designs. Later came the German currency reform, and a boom set in, giving the manufacturers a chance to satisfy pent-up demand. This demand focussed on anything connected with personal mobility that could be had at a reasonable price in those arduous post-war years: bicycles, motorcycles, scooters and cars, particularly small cars.

NSU started production up again in peacetime with its Quick motorised bicycle, the 125 ZDB and the 251 OSL. Production figures quickly soared. Walter Niegtsch had taken over as the company's board chairman on July 1st, 1946. He not only insisted on a rapid build-up of motorcycle production, but also approved the intentions of his chief designer, Albert Roder, to follow up with new models. Niegtsch began exporting again at a very early date, and can truly be said to have laid the foundation stone for NSU's growth after the war.

Following his death in 1951, Gerd Stieler von Heydekamp took over. He maintained the existing expansive approach. Production figures for 1954 in Neckarsulm were 250 bicycles, 350 scooters and motorcycles and 1000 Quickly mopeds per day. A year later the company reached its absolute peak output of some 50,000 bicycles and 300,000 motorised two-wheelers. NSU was at that point in time the largest motorcycle manufacturer in the world. Despite this fame and the associated rewards, the Neckarsulm management none the less had to face the fact that the long boom in motorcycles was coming to a close, and that urgent measures would be needed to keep turnover at its present high level. A logical solution was to recommence production of NSU passenger cars. Before this

could be undertaken, however, a degree of obstinacy on the part of the Fiat company had to be overcome. Back in 1929 NSU undertook by contract never again to manufacture cars bearing the NSU name, in order not to damage the sales prospects of cars produced by the Italians at the former NSU plant in Heilbronn. These cars still bore the name NSU/FIAT or Neckar. It was 1966, after a lengthy legal dispute, before Fiat was ready to abandon these names. After that date only the Neckar name was used for a while, and from 1968 on the cars were badged as Fiat.

NSU re-entered the automobile market in 1957. The same year, an event occurred which was also destined to have a promising future: on February 1st, 1957 the first Wankel rotary piston engine ran on the test bench.

Together with its inventor Felix Wankel, the rotary piston engine concept had been actively explored since 1953. A year after work started, Wankel made a decisive breakthrough by developing the three-lobe principle, which enabled his engine to dispense with valves. In 1958, NSU's engineers came up with a more effective unit, in which the piston itself described an epitrochoidal path. But although the intensity, extent and of course cost of the development work increased all the time, tangible results were still a long way off.

The company had changed its name in 1960 to NSU Motorenwerke AG Neckarsulm. In 1963, the sensation was complete. The NSU/Wankel Spider was shown at the International Automobile Exhibition – the first production car ever to have a rotary piston engine. In 1966 the last NSU two-wheeled vehicle, a Quick 50, left the assembly line; since the establishment of the company, about one and three-quarter million bicycles and 2,300,000 motorised two-wheelers had been built. Now motorcycle production was ceasing; the bicycle production plant had been sold previously, in 1963.

Poster dating from 1952

RO 80

Excitement was rife in Neckarsulm during the Spring of 1969. First there were rumours, then headlines in the popular press, then at last the facts: the giant VW Group was about to take over the dwarf NSU company. Equally stimulating: 590 cars were being built a day, still not enough to cut the waiting lists. Turnover was up by 23 percent on the previous year, the pioneering Ro 80 was selling well and the Wankel engine concept was attracting an increasing number of licensees. Of course, there were dark clouds too: the NSU Prinz models needed to be complemented by a larger family car (this was the later K 70), the Ro had had a bad press recently and still needed intensive detail work, and for other new models the necessary capital was lacking. In 1965 the Dresdner Bank, as the main NSU shareholder, had urged the chairman of the board to look for a larger partner. Feelers were extended in the direction of Ford and Fiat, but it was VW that eventually showed interest. NSU's capital was increased by the Wolfsburg company from 87 to 215 million DM, and it was decided to amalgamate it with VW's other wholly-owned subsidiary, the AUTO UNION GmbH in Ingolstadt. A new company was set up with head offices in Neckarsulm and a tongue-twister of a name: AUDI NSU AUTO UNION AG. Not a moment too soon, as it transpired: the Ro 80 was selling badly on account of unsolved technical problems, there was worldwide disappointment with the rotary piston concept, and the K 70's only chance of seeing the light of day was for it to be launched as a VW product.

Max and Maxi (1956)

Final assembly of the NSU Prima scooter (1957)

The products: motorcycles

NSU launched its first post-war design in 1949, the NSU Fox. It had a 100 cc OHV four-stroke engine which developed an impressive 5.2 hp. In 1950, at the Frankfurt Trade Fair, the Lambretta scooter was first displayed with an NSU engine. It was built under license from Italy, but improved somewhat in Neckarsulm and rendered easier to operate. The power unit was a 125 cc NSU two-stroke rated at 4.5 hp, which drove the rear wheel by shaft. This was one of the very first motor scooters on the German market. It was repeatedly improved and developed, until by 1956 almost 120,000 had been built and it was superseded by the NSU Prima.

In 1951 the 200 cc NSU Lux appeared with a two-stroke engine, and the type and model range was extended with two versions of a larger motorcycle, the Konsul I with a 350 cc and the Konsul II with a 500 cc four-stroke engine. The last pre-war design, the NSU 251 OSL, went out of production in 1952. This was the year in which the Max appeared, a historic motorcycle in more than the narrow sense of the word. It was a four-stroke with overhead valves, but designer Albert Roder had abandoned the expensive vertical shaft and bevel gears used to operate the valve gear in favour of a most unusual rod and crank system, referred to as "Ultramax" valve gear. Before the intake air was enriched with fuel to form the combustion mixture, incidentally, it had a lengthy path to follow on the Max, the aim being to reduce turbulence.

The Lambretta motor scooter at the 1950 Frankfurt Trade Fair

This air settling system was not new, although unusual on a motorcycle. NSU used it to set new noise suppression standards. In 1953, a successor to the Quick appeared: the Quickly, a smaller (only 50 cc) engined version with pedals, weighing only 33 kg and authorised for use without road tax or a driving licence.

"Why walk, let the Quickly take you" was the slogan that revealed NSU's intention of finding new customers among pedestrians who had never owned a motorised two-wheeler before. In the mid-1950s, the NSU motorcycle programme was boosted in both performance and comfort, and had the word "Super" placed before the individual model names: Super Fox, Super Lux, Super Max. Two-colour paintwork had been available since 1954 on many NSU models. Yet the great days of motorcycle sales were clearly over, despite such encouraging news items as the production of the one-millionth Quickly – Germany's number one moped. The last new NSU two-wheeler design appeared in 1962: the NSU Quick 50, a 50 cc light motorcycle with 4.3 hp two-stroke engine. It ceased production when the motorcycle era ended in Neckarsulm four years later.

Quickly exports for all parts of the world (1955)

Quickly – symbolic of Germany's economic miracle (1953)

The principal NSU motorcycle models, 1945–1969

Type	Number of cylinders	Bore x stroke in mm	Displacement in cc	Output in hp	Years of manufacture
NSU Fox 4-stroke	1	50 x 50	98	5.2	1949–1954
NSU Fox 2-stroke	1	52 x 58	123	5.4	1951–1954
NSU Lambretta	1	52 x 58	123	4.5	1950–1956
NSU Lux/Super Lux	1	62 x 66	198	8.6	1951–1956
NSU Konsul I	1	75 x 79	349	18	1951–1953
NSU Konsul II	1	80 x 99	498	22	1951–1954
NSU Max/Super Max	1	69 x 66	247	17	1952–1963
NSU Quickly	1	40 x 39	49	1.4	1953–1966
NSU Super Fox	1	52 x 58	123	8.8	1955–1957
NSU Prima	1	57 x 58	146	6.2	1956–1960
NSU Maxi	1	62 x 58	174	12.5	1957–1964
NSU Quick 50	1	40 x 39.5	50	4.3	1962–1966

Automobiles

The "roof over your head" movement did not embrace the NSU company until a relatively late stage, undoubtedly because it was achieving excellent results with its motorcycles. The automobile plans initially envisaged a vehicle with much of the character of a motorcycle: a three-wheeler cabin scooter with pivoted engine and rear swinging arm, such as would appeal to the more comfort-conscious motorcyclist. However, the commonsense view that a proper car should stand on four wheels soon prevailed. It was to be driven by a rear-mounted 600 cc four-stroke engine rated at 20 hp, based on the new Max engine with its eccentric crank valve gear. The car was light in weight, and proved capable of reaching a top speed of 105 km/h without difficulty. The then fashionable rear engine meant that luggage space had to be provided at the front.

Named the Prinz, the new car was launched in three equipment and engine versions. The climax of its career, so to speak, came in 1936, when it appeared at the German Motor Show in Frankfurt as the world's first production car with a rotary piston engine: the NSU/Wankel Spider. Externally, this version resembled the Sport Prinz introduced some years previously, but was driven by a 50 horse-power Wankel engine and had a top speed of 150 km/h. The original Prinz 4 dated back to 1961, and was given a new body which appealed to the modern customer much more than the previously more rounded styling had done. The air-cooled overhead-valve engine was still at the rear, and developed 30 hp. The Prinz 4 was popular: about 74,000 had been sold by 1963. A year later, when the NSU Prinz 1000 L was shown to dealers, they and the engineers were extremely optimistic about its prospects. Its performance and vitality were aimed at the more demanding driver. The new 43 bhp engine was located horizontally across the rear of the car, but retained its air cooling. At the 1965 Frankfurt Motor Show, it was once again NSU's turn to capture public interest with two

The NSU/Wankel Spider, the world's first production car with a rotary piston engine

NSU Prinz 4 car-carrier train to Italy (1968)

new models: the "Typ 110" with 1100 cc engine and enlarged body was the more spacious and the more expensive of these. The other was the NSU Prinz 1000 TT, a sports variant of the Prinz 1000, with the engine uprated to 55 bhp.

In 1967, a successor was introduced: the NSU TT, with 1200 cc engine and 65 bhp at the driver's disposal. The last new model in this series was the NSU TTS (1967), the 1000 cc engine of which developed 70 bhp. 1967 was the year, however, in which everyone's attention was riveted on just one car on the NSU stand: the Ro 80, with its 115 bhp rotary piston (Wankel) engine. The whole car bristled with new features, and its elegant body with excellent aerodynamics bore this out visually to perfection. With superb suspension and front-wheel drive, this totally new car marked NSU's departure from the rear-engined layout with all its minor disadvantages.

In 1968 the Ro 80 was awarded the "Car of the Year" title. This was indeed a major triumph for NSU's engineering team. With this car they rewrote motoring history – certainly not for the first, but unfortunately for the last time.

NSU 1000 C
(1967-1972)

Motor sport

In the Summer of 1947, when the first racing motorcycles returned to their historic circuits, the NSU marque was among them. Wilhelm Herz had built himself a 350 cc supercharged bike and rode it to victory in the 1948 German 350 cc championship class. At the end of that year, NSU's directors resolved to go racing again with a factory-entered team. This was made up of Wilhelm Herz in the 350 cc class, Heiner Fleischmann on a 500 cc bike and Böhm/Fuchs with their 600 cc sidecar outfit.

1950 was the last season in which superchargers were permitted, and resulted in renewed triumphs for NSU. Böhm/ Fuchs became German cham-

The NSU Ro 80 was futuristic in its styling

World speed-record contenders: Baumm II, and Delphin III, with H. P. Müller and Wilhelm Herz (1956)

pions in the sidecar class and Heiner Fleischmann took the title in the 350 cc category.

On April 12th, 1951 NSU machines began their first record-breaking attempts since the war. On a streamlined 500 cc bike, Wilhelm Herz reached 290 km/h, seizing back the 14-year-old record set up by Henne (279.5 km/h). Böhm also broke the existing record, and eight new records in all were set up. Encouraged by the sales success of the much smaller Fox, it was decided to go racing in this category too. The OHC engine revved up to an amazing 11,000 rpm, and had a peak power output of 11 bhp.

On 20th July 1952, a notable first-time victory was scored. The first world championship race to be granted to Germany since the war was held on the Solitude circuit, and Werner Haas was on the starting line with the new 125 cc NSU Rennfox, also making its debut. He outdistanced the world's elite riders and brought the NSU home to an impressive, well-earned victory.

The Rennmax, a competition bike developed from the production version, appeared in 1952. Its inline twin-cylinder engine had double overhead camshafts driven by two vertical bevel-gear shafts. It also achieved immediate and lasting success. On the Grenzland Ring in 1952, Haas not only won his class but started again with the 250 cc NSU Rennmax in the 350 cc class and outdistanced these riders too. NSU resolved to take part in world championship events in the 1953 season. Werner Haas excelled himself, and ended the year as twofold world champion, in both the 125 and 250 cc classes. He also captured the German championship titles in the same two engine-size categories.

New riders joined the NSU works team in 1954. The best-known newcomer was H. P. Müller, known to enthusiasts as the "Racing Tiger", who had previously ridden for DKW and then for a short time as a private entrant. Hans Baltisberger and Rupert Hollaus completed the team, which was still headed by Werner Haas. The Fox and Max bikes were given a new fairing which earned them the nickname "The Dolphins". The smaller engine's output was now almost 18 bhp, the Rennmax had 39 bhp at the rider's command. The greatest success of the season was in the British Tourist Trophy (the famous "TT"). Hollaus came in first in the 125 cc class, ahead of the Italian Ubbiali, and in the 250 cc class the first four places, no less, were taken by the bikes from Neckarsulm, ridden by Haas, Hollaus, Armstrong and Müller.

From July 1954 on, the appearance of the NSU racing bikes once again underwent certain modifications. The fairing had now lost its dolphin's beak, and had a wider front opening. The brake cooling apertures now suggested a quite different aquatic mammal: the fans began to call them "The Blue Whales" instead. Once again, NSU carried off the championship trophies in the 125 and 250 cc classes, but the Neckarsulm team had to contend with one tragic blow: top rider Rupert Hollaus crashed in Monza and suffered fatal injuries. The season's results were if anything even more impressive than usual: 24 starts had yielded precisely the same number of victories! For two years running, NSU had won the manufacturers' world championship in the two smallest-engined classes, provided bikes for the corresponding world champion riders and also won the German championships. Perhaps it was not surprising that a change was now imminent.

Hockenheim Ring, 1949: the supercharged 500 cc sidecar outfit crewed by Böhm/Fuchs

H.P. Müller, world champion on NSU Sportmax (1955)

The Black Forest Trial, with Kolmar/ Gebert (1953)

Withdrawal first, then new records

At the end of the year the company made an announcement that exploded like a bomb in the midst of the racing motorcycle world: NSU would not be competing in any more races. Its official works team would be wound up and from now on it would only provide support for promising private entrants. However, if people thought that the marque's run of success would dry up as a result, they were mistaken.

In 1955 "Racing Tiger" H. P. Müller pulled off a master-stroke, becoming the first private rider ever to capture the 250 cc world champion's title! And as if this were not enough, NSU itself had now turned its attention back to the breaking of world records.

Gustav Adolf Baumm was a graphic artist by profession. With the help of NSU's engineers he had sketched out and built his own very unusual and highly aerodynamic vehicle, powered by a 3.4 hp Quickly engine installed at the rear. Another version had a 7 hp, 100 cc Fox engine. With this unlikely contrivance, Baumm captured eleven world records in 1954. A year later, after the New Zealander Wright on a 1000 cc Vincent had surpassed Herz's world speed record, NSU resolved to develop a truly invincible, fully streamlined record-breaking machine. In July and August 1956, on the Bonneville salt flats in the US state of Utah, Wilhelm Herz rode this 500 cc motorcycle down the measured course at a speed of 339 km/h. H.P. Müller, in turn, took the Baumm "Flying Deckchair" up to 196 km/h with a 50 cc engine and 242 km/h with a 125 cc engine installed.

NSU thus held all the world records which it was possible for a two-wheeled vehicle to set up. A five-year period of abstinence then set in, until in 1960 the NSU board of management decided that motor sport should once again be given more attention. Although no new works team was set up, the intention was to provide private entrants in touring-car events with more effective support.

An NSU Trophy was therefore presented to the most successful competitor driving one of the company's cars. The compact rear-engined models really came into their own when entered for hill-climbs. In 1962, for example, Karl-Heinz

Panowitz was German champion in every hill-climbing category, outperforming many a much larger-engined rival.

In the following season, Behra and Behra scored a class win in the Monte Carlo Rally and Siegfried Spiess again won the German Touring Car Hillclimb Championship in his NSU Prinz II. Later still, incidentally, the Wankel-engined cars demonstrated that they were no mean performers in competition. In 1966 Karl-Heinz Panowitz was German GT Rally champion in an NSU/Wankel Spider, and in 1967 Siegfried Spiess drove a similar car to become all-classes German Automobile Hillclimb champion.

The NSU TTS goes racing (1968)

The principal NSU automobile models, 1945–1969

Type	Number of cylinders	Bore x stroke in mm	Displacement in cc	Output in hp	Years of manufacture
Prinz I/II/III	2	75 x 66	583	20/30	1958–1962
Sportprinz	2	75 x 66	583	30	1959–1967
Prinz 4	2	76 x 66	598	30	1961–1973
Wankel Spider	Rotary piston	1 x 497	497	50	1964–1967
Prinz 1000	4	69 x 66.6	996	43	1964–1972
Prinz 1000 TT	4	72 x 66.6	1085	55	1965–1967
Typ 110/S/SC	4	75 x 66.6	1085	53	1965–1967
NSU TTS	4	69 x 66.6	996	70	1967–1971
NSU TT	4	75 x 66.6	1177	65	1967–1972
NSU 1200 C	4	75 x 66.6	1177	55	1967–1973
NSU Ro 80	Rotary piston	2 x 497	995	115	1967–1977

Dates in the history of NSU, 1945–1968

1960	NSU Motorenwerke AG established on August 5th, capital 27 million DM
1969	AUDI NSU AUTO UNION AG established on 21st August From the end of the war until production ceased in 1963, 1,034,277 NSU bicycles were made. Annual motorcycle output passed the 100,000 mark in 1953 and reached an absolute peak in 1956 at 236,132 units. From 1957 to the end of 1968, NSU manufactured about 760,000 cars. The workforce rose from more than 5,000 in the 1950s to more than 7,000 in the 1960s
1969	In this year, NSU had 11,504 employees.

NSU Prinz 1000 bodyshell (1965)

Georg Schwarz

1862	Born on 20th December in Bolheim an der Brenz
1879	Began work in the large generating machinery industry
1901–1904	Employed by the Daimler-Motoren-Gesellschaft in Cannstatt and Untertürkheim; a close technical associate of Wilhelm Maybach
1904–1912	Technical director of Fahrzeugwerke Eisenach
1912	Technical director of NSU until December 1927
1924	Honorary doctorate from Stuttgart College of Advanced Technology
1925	Designer of the successful supercharged NSU racing cars
1929	Died on 5th August 1929 in Heilbronn

Georg Schwarz (1862 -1929)

Fritz von Falkenhayn

1890	Born on 27th September in Oldenburg
1896–1900	Went to school in Tsingtau, China Attended the Lyceum in Metz
1910	Professional soldier
1914	Promoted to flying officer in January.
1914–1918	Officer on the staff of the GOC, air attack forces
1919–1921	Commercial posts in the automobile industry
1921–1923	Managed the Daimler-Motoren-Gesellschaft's first branch in New York
1923	Manager of an American export company
1924–1925	Sales manager of the Karl Klein automobile distributorship
1926	Commercial director of the Mannesmann Automobil-Gesellschaft in Remscheid
1927–1928	Mannesmann Brothers' representative in Spain and Morocco
1930	From January on, head of sales and deputy director of NSU Vereinigte Fahrzeugwerke AG
1933	Appointed a full member of the board in May
1937–1945	Chairman of the board
1948–1958	General manager of Opel distributor Auto-Staiger GmbH
1953–1961	On the supervisory board of the NSU Werke AG
1959	Retired; residence in Ronco (Ascona)
1973	Died on March 3rd in Italy

Fritz von Falkenhayn (1890 -1973)

Albert Roder

1896	Born on 20th January in Nuremberg
1910	Apprentice mechanic
1912	Built his own 25 cc two-stroke engine
1914	First of more than 100 patents and registered designs
1916	Military service until 1918
1919	Plant and equipment designer
1920	Together with the mechanic Karl Zirkel, established Ziro-Motoren GmbH in Forchheim, which produced up to 5 motorcycles a week
1923	Company liquidated; in the same year Zirkel, Roder and another partner from Erlangen set up the Erlanger Motoren AG (ERMAG). First products: two-stroke motorcycles
1924	ERMAG 250 cc OHV four-stroke single-cylinder, 12 hp
1928	Zirkel and Roder left the company. Zirkel opened a driving school in Fürth, Roder went to Zündapp
1930	Richard Küchen became Zündapp's chief designer, and Roder prepared many of his designs for production
1936	Moved to NSU, as chief designer and deputy to the Briton Walter William Moore Roder was responsible for the single-cylinder engine with vertical-shaft valve gear, and the twin-cylinder supercharged racing bikes
1939	Moved to Victoria as chief designer
1947	Chief designer at NSU
1949	Designed the FOX ...
1951	... the LUX ...
1952	... and the MAX, together with their sports racing versions
1958	Created the NSU Prima scooter
1961	Retirement
1970	Died on September 3rd in Neckarsulm

Albert Roder (1896 -1970)

Panowitz/Strunz on NSU/Wankel Spider were German GT Rally champions in 1966

NSU – an overview: bicycles

NSU "Germania"
ordinary (1886)

Conventional NSU
bicycle (1896)

NSU bicycle (1893)

NSU bicycle
production (1907)

The NSU "Arrow"
(1912)

NECKARSULMER FAHRRADWERKE A.-G., KÖNIGLICHE HOFLIEFERANTEN, NECK

Hourlier, the "French champion rider" celebrated his greatest triumphs in 1911 on the NSU "Arrow"

NSU "Arrow" (1924)

NSU sports cycle (1939)

NSU tourer (1956)

NSU motorcycles

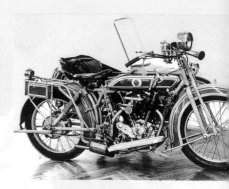

NSU 1.75 hp (1903)

NSU 1.25 hp (1907)

NSU 8 hp twin (1914)

NSU Motosulm (1931)

NSU Fox 4-stroke

NSU Super Lux

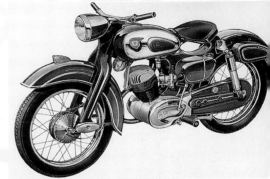

NSU Super Max | NSU Maxi

NSU Max (1954)

NSU Quickly S with
footguards

NSU motorcycle
competing off-road
(1953)

NSU automobiles

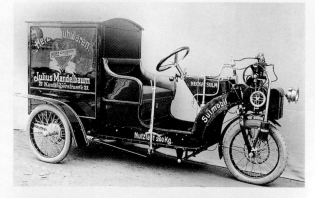

The Sulmobil, NSU's
first passenger car
(1906)

The Enesu-Mobil
(1913)

10/20 hp
"Neckarsulmer
Motorwagen" (1910)

NSU 5/15 hp (1914)

NSU 2 1/2 t truck
(1921)

NSU 7/34 hp
delivery van (1929)

NSU Prinz III

NSU Ro 80

NSU/Wankel Spider

NSU TT

NSU 1200 C (1967)

A new profile for the Four Rings

In the nineteen-sixties, work started on building the Berlin Wall – a further escalation of the Cold War and one from which the Germans suffered most. It was clearly time for new strategies if the balance of force was to be maintained. In the West, economic growth began to slow down and stop; resignation of the government headed by Ludwig Erhard, the "father of the economic miracle", was another significant event. He had appealed for moderation, but his pleas had gone unheard. After defying all the warning signs, the automobile industry found its turnover slumping particularly severely, by 40 percent or more, though before long unsurpassed growth rates took over again, and lasted until 1973/74.

Tackling the crisis with energy

In October 1973 the so-called OPEC nations imposed an oil embargo on all countries considered to be allies of Israel. Within six months, oil prices had quadrupled. This situation, later apostrophised as the "energy crisis", was also felt by the motor-vehicle industry. The spectre of recession reared its head. Manufacturers not only had to face economic difficulties, but also contend with a swing in public opinion against the automobile. The main allegations were wasteful use of energy, environmental burden and inadequate safety. Buyers began to hesitate, thus rendering the financial situation still more precarious, but the challenge implied in the accusations was taken up by the automobile industry, which began to work actively towards the "car of the future" in a variety of areas. The demand for mobility remained quite unaffected by all these political moves: the renewed craze for bicycles told its own story, as did the boom in the tourist industry.

Automobile manufacturers began by concentrating their efforts on reducing fuel consumption, minimising pollutant emissions and enhancing both active and passive safety. These were the areas in which worthwhile progress was made in

The last VW "Beetle" to be assembled in Ingolstadt left the line on July 4th, 1969

the years that followed. Within fewer than fifteen years, pollutant emissions were reduced by two-thirds, road behaviour and ride comfort reached standards previously held to be unattainable, noise and aerodynamic drag were forced down to amazingly low levels. This incredible pace of activity was maintained in the face of falling sales in the 1970s, massive competition from Japanese makes in particular on the German market and more stringent legal requirements both in Germany and the USA. The transfer of authority that had been taking place since

VW, NSU and "elective affinities"

1965 at the AUTO UNION was only a gradual one in terms of finance, but far more radical in the structural and technical areas. At the end of 1964 the Wolfsburg company had acquired 50.3 percent of the AUTO UNION shares, and was thus able to introduce its own industrial management procedures in Ingolstadt.

During the next two years, the remaining 49.7 percent of the shares were purchased, and by the end of 1966 the Four Rings had become the symbol for a wholly-owned VW subsidiary.

The 12,000-strong workforce in Ingolstadt and the 1,200 AUTO UNION dealers expected the change to give rise to models capable of generating higher sales volume. The two-stroke's reputation had never been so low. Some 30,000 cars with this type of engine were still in stock, unsold – and production continued! Work went ahead frenziedly on completing the F 103: this was the existing F 102 powered by a new four-stroke "medium-pressure" engine. The problem was that help was needed immediately. It materialised in the guise of the VW "Beetle", of which between 300 and 500 were assembled every working day in Ingolstadt from May 1965 until July 4th, 1969. This was an effective means of maintaining full employment.

Utilisation of production capacity was one of VW chief executive Nordhoff's problems; the other was the gradual rejuvenation of the entire AUTO UNION management team. Within a matter of weeks, they were all pensioned off or persuaded to relinquish their posts. Nordhoff seconded his best available man to head the newly-acquired company: Rudolf Leiding. "In my opinion there is only one man anywhere in our organisation who can tackle this task: the manager of our Kassel plant, Herr Leiding." The new appointee's task was not merely to sell off the cars in stock, but to reorganise the entire organisation from the ground up, as it were. He summed up the situation as he found it as follows: "The workforce has lost its spirit ...cost awareness is a totally unknown concept in most areas of the entire company. Hard work will be needed before an understanding of the need to save has penetrated through to every department." Nordhoff's declared objective was to "keep Ingolstadt on just as tight a rein as the VW plants in Hanover, Braunschweig and Kassel", and part of Leiding's task was therefore to lower the flag with the Four Rings which still flew bravely in Ingolstadt.

Presentation of the new Audi, with Rudolf Leiding and Ludwig Kraus standing to the left of the car

The marriage

The 1.7-litre "medium pressure" engine developed by Daimler-Benz for the AUTO UNION was now ready for production; it was installed in the F 102 model and presented to the public in September 1965 as the first four-stroke car to emerge from Ingolstadt: it now bore the Audi badge.

Although public response was most encouraging, the company suffered at this stage, like all its rivals in the automobile industry, from the first major post-war recession. This necessitated a cutback in production volume averaging some 20 percent. Clever manipulation of the available model range, however, enabled Ingolstadt to keep the losses to a minimum.

Then, on 12th April 1968, Heinrich Nordhoff died. His place was taken by Kurt Lotz, who lost no time in pressing ahead with the purchase of NSU AG in Neckarsulm. His predecessor had already hatched plans to take over the traditional

The new Audi at the Geneva Motor Show (1966)

Swabian company and to bring its sales programme into line with that of the AUTO UNION. The new regime in Wolfsburg under Lotz, like the old one, had little time for the Wankel engine. A much more potent argument in favour of taking a share in NSU was the need to eliminate unwanted competition. In Neckarsulm it had been obvious for some time that the company's equity was far from sufficient to enable it to survive alone. Problems standing in the way of an amalgamation were on the one hand speculation in NSU shares, which had driven their price up, and on the other the immense number of small shareholders. After lengthy negotiations, both management teams drafted out the unification procedure which they planned to adopt, and after hours of heated discussion, the shareholders' general meeting finally gave its approval. The contract uniting AUTO UNION GmbH and NSU Motorenwerke AG was signed on March 10th, 1969. The establishment of the new joint company, AUDI NSU AUTO UNION GmbH, was backdated to January 1st, 1969.

Audi Super 90 as a cabriolet. Only a few of these fresh-air conversions were made by the Welsch company in Mayen and by Deutsch in Cologne

The new company

From the very outset, AUDI NSU AUTO UNION AG opted for a policy of growth; this called not only for the investment of many thousands of millions of Marks but also for structural reorganisation within the company. Before long, the Volkswagen Group had purchased many of the smaller NSU shareholdings and in this way become almost the sole proprietor of the new share-issuing company, with its premises in Neckarsulm and Ingolstadt. It appointed Gerd Stieler von Heydekamp as chairman of the board of management; in 1971 he was followed again for a brief period by Rudolf Leiding.

The chief executives in later years – Leiding was followed by Dr. Prinz, Dr. Werner Schmidt, Gottlieb Strobl and Dr. Wolfgang Habbel – completed the restructuring process, set up the sales organisation which was to operate in conjunction with VW's own, and above all saw to it that new models were developed and existing ones updated, so that an attractive sales programme could be offered.

The long-term strategic objective has remained the gaining of step-by-step access to the luxury segment of the market. The most important factor in upgrading the AUDI marque was the car's advanced technology which put it among the pioneers in contemporary automobile engineering. After NSU and AUDI had joined forces, an introductory advertisement showing the emblems of both marques appeared, with details of their contributions to motor-vehicle technology. For the student of this list it was hardly surprising when, in January 1971, the first double-page advertisement appeared containing the slogan which has since been so closely associated with the Four Rings: "Vorsprung durch Technik" ("The Technological Edge").

The importance attached to technical research and development was confirmed in August 1969, when Audi began to build its own complex of buildings in Ingolstadt for its technical development staff. The initiator of this project was Technical Director Dr. Ludwig Kraus, who succeeded with great skill in convincing his oposite numbers in Wolfsburg that an independent AUDI development facility was in fact needed. Subsequent events have proved him right. Much of the creative work produced in Ingolstadt proved to be also suitable for a VW model. The resulting cooperation in the research, development and production areas has always been very close. The sales area was also subjected to a restructuring process. By the mid-1970s, a joint VW/AUDI dealer organisation had been built up and AUDI had acquired a more independent marque profile, the outlines of which became even clearer as the end of the 1970s was reached.

The products

In 1965, when the new four-stroke Audi had reached the market, the direction of future development was obvious. The car's engine was described as a "medium-pressure" unit, to imply that its compression ratio was midway between that of a

The 1971 AUDI NSU product programme

72 hp Audi (1965) und Audi 75 Variant (1971)

conventional spark-ignition engine and a diesel. Put more simply, the high compression ratio simply indicated a more efficient engine design. The attractive range of models varied in equipment and trim, but primarily according to the chosen engine power output.

Pilot projects

The first of the new Audis had no precise model designation at first, but was later called the Audi 72 in accordance with its power output. In September 1966 it was joined by the Audi 80 (with 80 bhp engine) and three months later by the extremely well-equipped Audi Super 90. Finally, in January 1968, the Audi 60 (with 55 bhp engine) joined the programme, and at the end of the year both the 72 and 80 models were replaced by a new Audi 75. The smallest-engined model, the Audi 60, was in fact the most successful. There were two- and four-door saloon bodies, with the option of a de luxe specification, and in due course a "Variant" estate car was also offered.

The development department was still a hive of activity, pushed and prodded by the determined Ludwig Kraus. The successful relaunch of the marque was an incentive for him to develop a "real" Audi. He himself usually referred to the first model, with its old DKW body and Mercedes engine, as the "bastard". His task, however, as laid down by the parent company from its Wolfsburg headquarters, was merely to supervise the current series of models: new development was regarded as a VW prerogative. Kraus, on the other hand, already had a clear picture of how he felt a new Audi 100 should look – a distinctly larger car than the existing ones, with a powerful but economical engine, lighter in weight than all its rivals and thus capable of accelerating faster for a given power output, aided by improved aerodynamics.

For the moment, Kraus's only chance was to develop this car in secret, without his new colleagues in Wolfsburg getting wind of it. The Audi 100 slowly took shape in this clandestine fashion. The first person to discover the clay model in

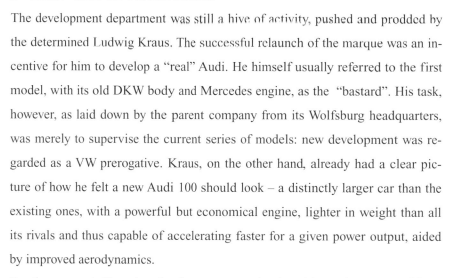

the Ingolstadt plant's styling studio was Rudolf Leiding himself – who was absolutely delighted: "Let's build it – we'll sell at least three hundred thousand!" Of course, Nordhoff's approval was essential, but obtaining it called for a veritable tactical masterstroke. Leiding asked permission from Wolfsburg to undertake "body modifications", then suggested that the Group board of management might care to come down and inspect the results. These were of course so impressive that the Wolfsburg executives, with Nordhoff well to the fore, expressed their admiration and granted permission for production to go ahead.

Audi 80 (1972)

From zero to 100

Audi 100 development went ahead with the project designated Type 104. The new, larger model was announced to the public in the Autumn of 1968. Its concept and styling showed it to be a fully-fledged upper midsize-class model, available with either two or four doors. There was no estate-car version, but in 1970 a most attractive coupé was introduced.

The Audi 100's 1.8-litre engine was derived from the precious Audi 90 model, and offered with power outputs of 80, 90 or 100 bhp. The original "medium-pressure" engine was no longer much in evidence; although this had long since had its compression ratio lowered to a more normal figure, it remained a distinctly rough runner.

By 1976, when the first-generation Audi 100 was discontinued, more than 800,000 had been built, by far surpassing any of the forecasts made on the new car's behalf.

The Audi 100 was a vitally important car for the Ingolstadt manufacturer, because it enabled it to regain a personality of its own. The stopgap assembly of Beetles became unnecessary, and the company moved into the upper midsize class with the declared aim of raising its brand positioning still further.

The next entirely new Audi appeared in the Summer of 1972. With a view to establishing a modular-element design family, Ludwig Kraus had developed a four-cylinder OHC engine (which the Volkswagen Group incidentally used later for its own Passat); this engine later achieved the biggest production volume anywhere within the VW Group. The new car's running gear also incorporated some extremely advanced ideas which were to set new standards in automobile construction: the principle of negative steering scrub radius, for instance, which helps to prevent the car from departing its chosen course unexpectedly if the road surface is poor or a tyre or brake problem occurs. This was not a new or unknown theory, but AUDI was the first company to put it into effect on high-volume production cars. One of the most dedicated exponents of this new wheel

Audi 100 S (1970)

location principle was the Ingolstadt engineer Detlef Banholzer, who in 1977 was awarded the Vienna Technical University's Porsche Prize for "exceptional scientific achievements in the field of motor-vehicle running-gear development".

The Audi 80 was the company's first model to be corrosion-proofed with zinc powder paint in certain areas. It also had PVC underseal. The new car was an immediate sales hit: in the next six years, more than a million AUDI 80s were built and sold. Kraus's idea of a modular-element system took its next step forward with the Audi 50. This was the smallest Audi ever to be built. Its designer felt that every automobile marque should have an entry-level model. In any case, the company had well and truly neglected the small car in recent years. The nightmare of reverting to the primitive vehicles of the 1950s and 1960s evidently haunted the German buyer and caused him to put his trust only in large, powerful cars.

Anti-crisis concepts

When the energy crisis provoked a change in attitudes, Kraus was ready and waiting with a suitable offer. It had a 50 bhp four-cylinder inline engine – hence the designation Audi 50 – and was only 3.5 metres long in its initial form. However, space allocation was excellent with impact-absorbing zones at front and rear and a large tailgate which enabled customers to treat it as a kind of compact estate car. The public took a keen interest in the new car, and orders were not slow in coming in after its launch in 1974, despite the crisis mood which prevailed. The Audi 50 was built in Wolfsburg, where it was also introduced a short time later with a stripped-down specification and a 40 bhp engine as the VW Polo. This survived the small Audi, production of which was halted in 1978 after more than 180,000 had been made.

In the mid-seventies, there was a good selection of small and medium-sized models bearing the four-ring badge: Audi 50, 80 and 100. The second Audi 100 generation was introduced in 1976 and took this model a step farther towards the luxury end of the midsize class. The top model of the new series (from April 1977 onwards) was powered by a 2.2-litre, five-cylinder inline engine with an output of 100 kW (136 bhp). This unusual design, which called for the solution of complex inertial balancing problems, was considered ideal for the mechanical layout adopted by AUDI NSU AUTO UNION, namely front-wheel drive with the engine located ahead of the gearbox and differential. As well as these technical innovations, the programme included a new model version from August 1977 onwards, the Audi 100 Avant with fast-back styling and a tailgate.

The Audi 100 appeared in 1973 with a slightly modified body

Moving up-market

The Audi 200 was first announced in September 1979, and marketed in two versions from the Spring of 1980 onwards: the Audi 200 5 E with 100 kW (136 bhp) five cylinder engine and the Audi 200 5 T, the turbocharged five-cylinder engine of which developed 125 kW (170 bhp). This engine, revised on more than one occasion, supplied Audi's exceptionally sporty models with the necessary urge for some years. The Audi 200 was also the model which enabled AUDI NSU AUTO UNION to set foot in the top automobile category.

The real best-seller from Ingolstadt, the Audi 80, appeared in completely redesigned form in the Autumn of 1978 and proved to be in greater demand than ever before. Up to 800 cars of this type were built every working day. Starting in the Autumn of 1981, customers were able to order the Audi 80 with an 85 kW (115 bhp) five-cylinder engine. This model was renamed Audi 90 in 1984.

Ten years after the Munga had ceased production, Ingolstadt found itself manufacturing an off-road vehicle again. In November 1978 the German Army took delivery of the first examples of the all-wheel-drive VW Iltis, which despite its badging had been developed in Ingolstadt and was only built there.

The highlight of the Audi stand at the Geneva Motor Show in the Spring of 1980 was the adoption of all-wheel drive in a very different form, for a sporty passenger car. This was the Audi quattro, which struck a new note in automobile construction worldwide. In the Autumn of the same year the Audi Coupé began to reach the showrooms, with a body that strongly echoed that of the Audi quattro in its styling.

The crisis caused by the oil price increases in the 1970s and the associated rise in the cost of fuel had a lasting effect on sales of midsize cars. AUDI NSU AUTO UNION reacted to this by exhibiting a research vehicle at the 1981

The second-generation Audi 80 was launched in the Autumn of 1979, with a body which clearly recalled the styling of the larger Audi 100

The Audi 200 was a step towards the upper end of the automobile scale

With a sensationally low drag coefficient of 0.30, the Audi 100 had the best aerodynamics of any standard saloon car when it appeared in 1982

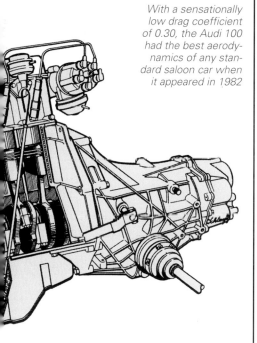

Apart from the 100 kW (136 bhp) five-cylinder fuel-injection engine, a carburettor version (pictured here) developing 85 kW (115 bhp) was offered

German Motor Show in Frankfurt, aided by funds provided by the Federal German Ministry for Research and Technology. This design study demonstrated the significant improvements that were possible in energy and raw material consumption, environmental acceptability, safety, operating economy and practical value. Many of these aspects materialised again a year later in the guise of the new Audi 100. The results were most impressive. The team working under Technical Director Ferdinand Piech had succeeded in combining all the latest technical knowledge and research findings in the new product. Its drag coefficient was only $c_D = 0.30$, giving the new Audi 100 the best aerodynamics of any production saloon car in the world. Numerous international awards confirmed that with this car AUDI NSU had found the right answer to current challenges.

Successful premières

A new Avant model joined the Audi 100 saloon in 1983. Its blend of elegance and practicality appealed strongly to customers, and ensured this body style a firm place in the Audi programme. As expected, the Audi 200 version of the new body was announced in the Autumn of the same year. In 200 Turbo guise, it now developed 134 kW (182 bhp).

Once it became known that the Federal German government was planning to make exhaust emission control by catalytic converter mandatory for automobiles from 1986 onwards, the engineers in Ingolstadt began to make the necessary preparations. In 1983 AUDI NSU became the first German automobile manufacturer to be granted a general operating permit for vehicles using this pollution control technique. Permanent all-wheel drive, too, was gradually offered on more and more models in the Audi range. The breakthrough to large-scale production of this system came in 1982, when the Audi 80 quattro was introduced. By 1984 customers could obtain every Audi model with all four wheels driven.

Within only a few years, the company had succeeded in creating an attractive, technically advanced programme with something for all customers.

quattro – four wheels good

The search for the moment when this concept, which now seems so familiar to anyone who takes an interest in automobile engineering, first saw the light of day takes us back to the winter of 1976/77. Jörg Bensinger, a member of AUDI's technical staff, can claim to be the originator of the idea. He was on a proving run with the all-wheel-drive Iltis (the successor to the Munga off-road vehicle) in Scandinavia. With its generous ground clearance it performed well in snow and ice, despite a far from powerful engine. But how would a high-performance car with four-wheel drive behave on dry roads?

Back in Ingolstadt, Chief Engineer Ferdinand Piech decided that an experimental car should be built. He wanted a genuinely powerful and attractive model, and the engineers resolved to oblige him. To save time and make full use of the fine selection at their disposal, they borrowed the turbo-charged five-cylinder engine from the Audi 200, the floor pan and much of the running gear from the Audi 80 and the body from the Audi 80 Coupé.

Experimental work started in March 1977, using the Iltis all-wheel-drive layout transplanted into a standard Audi 80 saloon. From the very start, everyone concerned was so committed to the all-wheel-drive concept that it was decided to leave it permanently in engagement. Once quattro, always quattro: the goal was a permanent all-wheel-drive system capable of handling high performance in every situation, and no departures from this ambitious objective were tolerated. The main design work centred on the inter-axle differential, which was planned to take the place of the customary heavy transfer box. The necessary weight-saving and simplicity were found by adopting a hollow-shaft principle which combined both functions – speed compensation and power distribution. Experts were unanimous: an "elegant" engineering solution. Test results proved to be extremely positive, and in 1977 the project was allocated an official development

The Audi quattro: when it appeared in the Spring of 1980, not only the international rallying scene was revolutionised

For more than ten years the "original" Audi quattro, with successive design revisions, remained the top sports model in the range

Audi 80 quattro (1983)

number in Ingolstadt. Road trials began in November of that year, and encouraged the Board of Management to include a road version of the car in its forthcoming model programme.

In January 1978 the engineers held a convincing demonstration for the benefit of the VW Sales Director, Dr. Schmidt, on the Turracher Höhe in Austria. This is Europe's steepest mountain pass, with gradients up to 23 percent (1 in 4.4). With summer tyres fitted, and without the aid of snow chains, the quattro prototype stormed up the steep gradient without the slightest traction problems. In April 1978 the 160 bhp quattro was taken to the Hockenheim Ring racing circuit and demonstrated that it had nothing to fear in the way of competition from, say, the average Porsche. In May, on the basis of this overwhelming evidence, VW's head of development Professor Fiala gave the go-ahead for production cars to be built. The power output had in the meantime gone up considerably, not least because of the charge-air intercooler now used for the first time on the Audi quattro: this had 13 aluminium fins which lowered the temperature of the previously compressed intake air from the turbocharger by 50 to 60 degrees. The five-cylinder quattro accordingly had a power output of 177 bhp at 4500 rpm and reached its peak figure of 200 bhp at 5500 rpm.

The Geneva Salon in March 1980 was taken as the opportunity to show the Audi quattro to an international public; it created a genuine sensation, since until then the all-wheel-drive principle had been restricted to relatively clumsy off-road vehicles. Ferdinand Porsche had adopted a similar principle immediately after the war for the Cisitalia racing car, but this had never been able to demonstrate its efficacy in practice. The 1980 Audi quattro was a genuine high-performance car, and began immediately to show its paces on the international rallying scene. In 1982 the Audi 80 quattro was introduced as an all-wheel-drive model for more everyday use, and two years later quattro versions of the 200 and the 100 became available. With its "quattro idea", AUDI had set a great deal in motion. From that time on, most manufacturers were obliged to include at least one all-wheel-drive model in their programmes. The quattro was up and running.

A new AUDI sport tradition

No sooner had the AUDI marque been reborn than it was making a name for itself in motor sport. Private entrants tuned the Audi Super 90 and later the Audi 80 GTE, the car which carried off the European touring car title on

the Zolder circuit in 1980. The factory supported these privateers in various ways. Starting in 1973, an annual trophy was awarded to the best driver of a front-wheel-drive AUDI. As the Audi 80 notched up more and more successes, a competition department was formed once again in Ingolstadt, to maintain close contact with drivers and provide them with every possible form of practical assistance. Leading drivers contributed their knowledge and experience to the development of successful Audi cars for rallying. The main precondition for the quattro principle to be able to prove its worth in serious rallying was approval from the FIA (Fédération Internationale de l'Automobile), which was forthcoming on 1st January 1981.

The Audi quattro was first seen at a major European championship event in Portugal in the Autumn of 1980, though only as a service car. However, the Finnish driver Hannu Mikkola drove it with such gusto that he reached the finishing line unofficially with almost a half-hour lead over the eventual winner!

AUDI then began to enter the new quattro in rallies, and its first season in 1981 was victorious in the Scandinavian Rally, the San Remo Rally and the British RAC Rally. In addition to Mikkola, the team included the Frenchwoman Michèle Mouton. The Finn was accompanied by Arne Hertz, and Fabrizia Pons navigated

The Audi 80 was a difficult car to beat on the racetrack

Hannu Mikkola and Arne Hertz in the Audi quattro during the 1983 New Zealand Rally

*Mikkola and Hertz
during the
Akropolis Rally (1984)*

*AUDI's 1-2-3 win
in the 1984
Monte Carlo Rally*

for Michèle Mouton. The two women were always good for a sensational result, becoming for instance the first ladies' team ever to win a World Rally Championship event, the 1981 San Remo Rally.

1982 was the year in which the cars with the four-ring emblem swept off with the manufacturers' world championship trophy and Michèle Mouton was runner-up in the drivers' championship. An even greater triumph was celebrated the following year, with the driver's title for Hannu Mikkola and the runner's-up title for AUDI. In the years following 1983, the marque won thirteen national championships in Europe and overseas. 1984 was the finest season: AUDI was manufacturers' world champion and the recently recruited star Swedish driver Stig Blomqvist took the driver's title. AUDI's pioneering work on the quattro driveline was acknowledged with the "Motor Sport Car of the Year" trophy in 1984, the year in which AUDI's triple victory in the Monte Carlo Rally, with Walter Röhrl at the wheel of the winning car, was the ultimate climax.

Dates in the history of AUDI, 1965-1985

1965	On January 1st, Volkswagen AG acquired 50.3 % of the AUTO UNION's shares
	In September, the AUTO UNION began production of its Audi model with 72 bhp "medium-pressure" engine
1966	The last DKW passenger car with two-stroke engine, an F 102, left the assembly line on March 11th
	At the end of the year, the AUTO UNION became a wholly-owned subsidiary of VW. In Ingolstadt, a workforce of 12,000 produced an average of about 110,000 automobiles a year
1969	On 10th March, first steps to amalgamate AUTO UNION GmbH and NSU AG
1969	AUDI NSU AUTO UNION AG set up on August 21st in Neckarsulm
1977	The final NSU Ro 80 manufactured in March, marking the end of NSU as a product name
1985	AUDI NSU AUTO UNION AG renamed AUDI AG on January 1st, with registered offices now in Ingolstadt

Ludwig Kraus

1911	Born on 26th December in Hettenhausen (Pfaffenhofen)
1931	School-leaving certificate in Ingolstadt
1933–1937	Studied mechanical engineering in Munich, Stuttgart, Hanover
1937	Joined Daimler-Benz AG on September 1st as designer for airship and high-speed boat engines
1939–1940	Military service
In 1941	Returned to engine design at Daimler-Benz
1951	Head of the racing-car design department
1954	Honorary title of Senior Engineer
1956	Head of hydrodynamic machinery design
1958	Head of advance passenger-car development
1963	From October 1st, Development Director at AUTO UNION GmbH in Ingolstadt
1965	Member of the AUTO UNION GmbH Board of Management
1969	From September 1st, on the board of AUDI NSU AUTO UNION AG with responsibility for development
1973	Retired on 31st December
1974	Honorary doctorate from Hanover College of Advanced Technology for services to automobile manufacturing
1976–1985	On the AUDI NSU AUTO UNION AG Supervisory Board

Dr. Ludwig Kraus

Ludwig Kraus recalls the origins of the Audi 100, which ensured the future of this marque and was the first Audi to be developed from scratch after the Second World War:

"The day arrived when the Board was due to visit us and inspect what we had declared as "body modifications". We put the new car in one of the development shops, still covered up by a cloth, of course. I knew what Nordhoff was like. That morning I said to my wife: "If I come back to lunch with you today, you'll know that I've been thrown out! But if I don't come, then I shall still be the chief executive of the AUTO UNION."

When we entered the room where the car was standing, I still had my coat on and was holding my hat. Everyone else had taken their overcoats off. We pulled the cloth cover off the new car and started it rotating on its turntable. Nordhoff then walked around it a couple of times; all I could see was his bright red neck!

Dr. Rudolf Leiding

Since I knew him well, it looked as if alarm situation number one was about to set in. Suddenly he put on a much more friendly expression. This was the point at which I decided it was safe to take off my coat! Then Nordhoff uttered the words "Herr Leiding, you have my go-ahead for this car." At last, I was off the hook!

Rudolf Leiding

1914	Born on 4th September in Busch (Altmark), son of a dealer in agricultural machinery
1928–1932	After leaving school, four years of apprenticeship as a motor-vehicle mechanic
1932–1935	Attended the mechanical engineering college in Magdeburg
1935–1945	Labour service, civil defence and military service
1945	Joined Volkswagen as a plant engineer
1949	Head of Customer Service department
1958	Director of the VW plant in Kassel
1964	Senior manager of Volkswagen AG
1965	Appointed General Manager of AUTO UNION GmbH in Ingolstadt on 29th July
1968	Appointed Chairman of the Board of VW do Brasil on July 1st
1971	Appointed Chairman of the Board of AUDI NSU AUTO UNION AG on 1st April
1971	Became Chairman of the Board of Management of Volkswagen AG on 1st October
1975	Retired
1976	Honorary doctorate from Berlin Technical University for work on improved production efficiency in the automobile industry

Ludwig Kraus at the "Car of the Year" award for the Audi 80 in 1972

Wolfgang R. Habbel

1924	Born on March 25th in Dillenburg
1942–1946	School-leaving certificate in Koblenz, followed by military service and a period as a prisoner of war
1946–1950	Studied law in Bonn and Cologne
1951–1957	Assistant to the board of management and interim Export Manager at AUTO UNION GmbH in Ingolstadt / Düsseldorf
1957	Doctorate in law at the University of Cologne
1957–1967	Head of Human Resources at the Ford company in Cologne
1967–1969	European Coordinator for Industrial Law and Social Affairs at Ford of Europe in Warley, England
1970–1971	Managing Partner for Human Resources at the pharmaceutical company C.H. Böhringer and Son in Ingelheim am Rhein
1971	On 18th October, appointed to the Board of AUDI NSU AUTO UNION AG with responsibility for Personnel and Social Affairs
1979–1987	Chairman of the Board of Management of AUDI NSU AUTO UNION AG and, from 1st January 1985 onwards, of AUDI AG
1988	Retired on Jauary 1st
1988–1993	Member of the AUDI AG Supervisory Board

Dr. Wolfgang R. Habbel

The principal Audi models, 1965–1984

Type	Number/layout of cylinders	Bore x stroke in mm	Displacement in cc	kW/bhp	Years of production
Audi (72)	4 inline	80 x 84.4	1696	53/72	1965–1968
60	4 inline	80 x 74.4	1496	40/55	1968–1972
Super 90	4 inline	81.5 x 84.4	1770	66/90	1966–1971
100	4 inline	81.5 x 84.4	1760	74/100	1968–1971
100 Coupé S	4 inline	84 x 84.4	1871	84/115	1970–1971
80	4 inline	75 x 73.5	1297	40/55	1972–1978
80 GTE	4 inline	79.5 x 80	1588	81/110	1975–1978
50	4 inline	69.5 x 72	1093	37/50	1974–1978
100	4 inline	86.5 x 84.4	1984	85/115	1976–1978
100	5 inline	79.5 x 86.4	2144	100/136	1976–1982
80	4 inline	75 x 72	1272	40/55	1978–1981
80 GLS	4 inline	79.5 x 80	1588	63/85	1978–1981
Audi quattro	5 inline	79.5 x 96.4	2144	147/200	1980–1987
80 quattro	5 inline	81 x 77.4	1944	85/115	1983–1984
90 quattro	5 inline	81 x 86.4	2226	100/136	1984–1986
Sport quattro	5 inline	79.3 x 86.4	2133	255/306	1983–1984
200 5 T	5 inline	79.5 x 86.4	2144	125/170	1979–1982
100	4 inline	81 x 86.4	1781	55/75	1982–1986
100	5 inline	81 x 77.4	1994	85/115	1984–1990
Coupé GT	5 inline	79.5 x 77.4	1921	85/115	1980–1983

Audi 100 Coupé S (1971)

Gerd Stieler von Heydekampf

Dr. Gerd Stieler von Heydekampf (1905–1983)

1905	Born on 5th January in Berlin
1927	Graduate's diploma in mechanical engineering at Braunschweig College of Advanced Technology, then assistant to the Chair of Strength and Vibration Studies
1929	24th February: Doctorate in Engineering Sciences
1930–1933	Spent in the USA, including work for the Babcock & Wilcox Corp.
1933	Joined Adam Opel AG in Rüsselsheim
1936	Appointed to the board of managers with responsibility for purchasing
1938	Manager of the Opel truck plant in Brandenburg / Havel
1942	Appointed Managing Director of Henschel & Sohn GmbH in Kassel, later deputy chairman of the Henschel Group board until April 1945
1948	Joined NSU Werke AG in Neckarsulm as regional manager in the field sales organisation
1950	Appointed to the board of management with responsibility for sales
1953–1969	Chairman of the board of management of NSU Werke AG
1969–1971	Chairman of the board of AUDI NSU AUTO UNION AG
1971	Retired on 31st March
1983	Dr. Ing. Gerd Stieler von Heydekamp died on 25th January

Audi – an overview

Audi 60 L (1971)

Audi Super 90 (1969)

Audi 100 GL (1972)

Audi 80 GL (1973)

Audi 100 Coupé S
(1971)

Audi 80 GTE (1976)

Audi 50 (1974)

Audi – an overview

*Audi 100 GL 5E
(1980)*

*Audi 80 CL Turbo-
diesel (1983)*

Audi 80 (1978)

*Audi Coupé GT
(1980)*

*Audi 100 Avant GLS
(1978)*

*Audi 200 5T
(1979)*

*Audi Sport quattro
(1983)*

Audi 100 CS (1983)

*Audi 200 Turbo
(1985)*

Audi quattro (1984)

Soon to be the most attractive European on the world market

Although motor-vehicle technology made giant strides during the nineteen-eighties – in the opinion of some experts, more than at any other time in its history – it was none the less obvious that markets were becoming increasingly saturated. As the 1980s drew to a close, the boom began to lose its impetus. Then the wall dividing the two Germanies was swept away, the Eastern bloc collapsed and suddenly there was access to a market on which the demand for private motoring had gone largely unsatisfied for many years. The automobile industry and

Dismantling the Lenin memorial in Berlin-Friedrichshain

its dealers were confronted with an unparalleled flood of potential customers. As a result of growth rates of 40 percent or more per year, the ageing, unreliable infrastructure in the new states that joined Federal Germany on 3rd October 1989 created a fresh series of almost insoluble problems.

After euphoric emotional outbursts from the population and understandable miscalculations by the politicians, a certain sober awareness of the situation took over as Germany faced up to the most demanding political and economic programme it had ever undertaken. Integrated into a Europe which itself is growing in extent and affinity all the time, "what belongs together will grow together".

Tackling new dimensions

In March 1977, when the last NSU RO 80 marked the end of a long product tradition, it was planned to combine marque and company into a single concept. This took place in 1985, when AUDI NSU AUTO UNION AG was transformed into AUDI AG. To ensure that the traditional names remained legally protected, two subsidiaries were set up at the same time: AUTO UNION GmbH and NSU GmbH. Since then, they have been largely concerned with maintaining the marque heritage.

When the company was renamed, its head offices were transferred from Neckarsulm to Ingolstadt.

Competition on world markets showed every sign of becoming increasingly tough, and therefore no less than 943 million Deutschmarks were allocated to new investment in 1985, the largest sum in the company's history. Product progress depends on progress in production technology, and therefore measures related to the products themselves and to restructuring measures were given priority. This related above all to the new Audi 80, which was launched in the Autumn of 1986. Its fully galvanised body, for which the company granted a ten-year warranty against rusting through, set new standards in its class. Like the Audi 100/200 models from the end of 1985 onwards, full galvanising offered optimum protection against corrosion and helped to maintain the car's value to a pre-

Fully galvanised bodyshells called for the adoption of new welding techniques

viously unattained level. However, welding, painting and sheet metal forming techniques all had to be improved before this technological innovation could be introduced.

In parallel with the new production methods which resulted from this, restructuring measures were introduced in the production logistics area. This was when the magic formula "Just in Time" was first heard: AUDI AG approached its outside suppliers with the request for them to

deliver their components and assemblies directly to the assembly lines, at the precise moment when they were needed for installation. More and more companies moved to the regions immediately surrounding the company's plants, so that they could deliver on call in this modern manner. In-house production depth was steadily reduced. At the end of 1995, a Freight Center (the "GVZ") began to operate just outside the factory gates in Ingolstadt. Apart from even closer co-operation with outside suppliers, the "GVZ" enables up to 80 percent of the company's freight to be handled by rail, so that the burden on the roads is reduced. A similar project went into operation in Neckarsulm in October 1996.

Enlargement and extension

In addition to modern production processes and sequences, increasing demands for quality were taken into account. The new Quality Center at the Ingolstadt plant was opened in December 1986, and housed all the specialist quality assurance departments under one roof.

High quality, of course, depends primarily on a skilled workforce. Audi therefore devotes great attention to initial and follow-up training of its employees. In 1987 an extension to the Training Center in Ingolstadt was opened, followed in the Spring of 1989 by a brand-new Training Center for the Neckarsulm plant. At the end of 1995 there were 1,467 trainees, including 144 young women pursuing a commercial career.

As visible evidence of Audi's slogan "Vorsprung durch Technik" ("The Technological Edge"), the Technical Development (TE) facilities in Ingolstadt were extended. In December 1988, Building T 22, a modern glass and steel structure, was completed. It enabled most technical development departments to be concentrated within a short distance of one another. In 1990 Audi started to construct

The key technical development area in Ingolstadt: Building T 22

The Audi Center
in Ingolstadt

a proving ground and vehicle testing facility of its own near Neustadt (Danube), and by the mid-1990s various sections of this had been commissioned or were in operation.

The company's objectives were to extend its product programme, enhance its positioning, adopt modern production methods and improve quality wherever possible. All these activities had of course only one fundamental purpose: to achieve maximum customer satisfaction and in consequence to gain access and appeal to new customer groups. Since then an extensive package of improvements in the sales and marketing areas has been introduced with the aim of strengthening and extending Audi's market position. When the Audi V8 first appeared in October 1988, the delivery centre in Neckarsulm offered customers an opportunity of collecting their new cars personally. Since May 1992 the same facility was offered for cars produced in Ingolstadt, when a new Audi Center opened there as well. Up to 280 people now visit it daily to collect their new Audi cars directly from the factory. Many of them combine this with a tour of the production plant or a visit to the AUTO UNION or NSU historic vehicle collections in Ingolstadt or Neckarsulm, thus adding to the excitement and interest of taking delivery of their new car.

Inside the
AUDI Center

The historic vehicle
collection maintained
by AUTO UNION
GmbH in Ingolstadt

New self-awareness

Well beyond the walls of these two towns, Audi has now established its claim to an elevated position on the automobile market. It is in the process of setting up

Audi Centers at selected points both within Germany and abroad, as a means of satisfying increasingly high customer standards. The same objective is being pursued by the plans for restructuring the dealer organisation which have been implemented step by step since 1995. One of the image-promoting measures which are intended to establish Audi as a force to be reckoned with in the premium automobile class and give the marque an individual profile is its future separation from the other makes within the VW Group. In April 1991, an independent marketing department was set up in Ingolstadt, to perform the product marketing tasks which had previously been undertaken jointly for VW and Audi in Wolfsburg. On January 1st, 1993 AUDI AG also took over responsibility for sales, which had been in the hands of the Wolfsburg colleagues (VW AG) since 1974. The aim of these changes is to implement an exclusive sales strategy: Separate dealer contracts are being negotiated with Audi and Volkswagen dealers in Germany, and the resulting Audi dealership will adopt Audi standards and customer orientation principles worthy of the marque.

A fresh approach to corporate identity matters has also been adopted. The oval Audi logo was abandoned in October 1994, and the emphasis transferred to the four rings, as the emblem which, according to the results of an international survey, best symbolise the Audi marque. With the Audi name in dynamic red, company and product are boldly presented in a manner which will inspire new awareness.

AUDI's wide, wide world

In the early nineteen-nineties, as international business links were forged and Europe began to grow together both politically and economically, Germany's industry and commerce were faced with widespread changes. For Audi, "global sourcing", that is to say the worldwide purchasing of components and services from outside suppliers, was not the only important new trend. Development and production also explored fresh paths. Design centers in Spain and California, and the Audi engine plant in Györ (Hungary), opened in October 1994, were just a few of the projects undertaken to ensure that Audi remains internationally competitive in the long term. Other activities with the same global objectives in mind include the assembly of CKD ("completely knocked down") cars in South

The four rings that symbolise AUDI

Automobile manufacturing in the "Middle Kingdom": Audi 100 production in China

Africa and Malaysia. Preparations for a further CKD project in Indonesia were proceeding on schedule in 1996. Back in October 1988, a cooperation agreement was concluded with the First Automobile Works (FAW) in Changchun, People's Republic of China, which in due course resulted in the Audi 100 being manufactured in that country. In November 1995, it was agreed that AUDI AG should join the existing joint venture between FAW and VW AG. Specific measures are also in hand at sales level for new markets to be opened up, particularly in Eastern Europe, the Asian-Pacific region and South America.

A setback and a recovery

Sometimes trouble rears its head unexpectedly, and an entirely new situation arises. In 1986 a TV consumers' programme in the United States reported on cases when cars were alleged to have accelerated by themselves – usually Audis with the automatic transmission preferred by the US customer. As a consequence of this programme, sales collapsed on the North American market. This trend was made even more severe by vigorous competition from Asian manufacturers and a generally weak US economy. Whereas Audi had sold 74,000 cars in 1985, the total had slumped to 12,000 by 1991. The company conducted a hitherto unparalleled series of tests and investigations in order to demonstrate that the alleged cases of sudden, unexpected acceleration were not due to any technical malfunction. Investigations were also undertaken by numerous road traffic authorities and consumer organisations, and came to precisely the same conclusions.

In 1994, Audi began a "comeback" on the US market, the results of which were already evident a year later. About 18,000 cars were delivered in 1995, a 44 percent improvement on the previous year's figure.

Sales on other markets developed in a most encouraging way. In 1987, Audi achieved record results. Despite unsettled international stock and currency markets, the company was able to pass the 400,000-unit mark for the first time, with total sales of 418,998 cars. The new Audi 80/90 models played a major part in this market success. Total production in 1987 was 443,067 cars, including 25,833 Porsche 944 sports cars assembled on behalf of Porsche AG at the Neckarsulm plant.

At the end of 1987 Dr. Wolfgang R. Habbel retired from the chairmanship of the board of management. During his period of office, Audi had made the step into the upper midsize market segment. His place was taken by Dr. Ferdinand Piëch, who continued the extension of the AUDI AG product range towards the upper end of the market and also devoted his efforts to improving the company's trading results. This culminated in the "1988 Company Concept", negotiated by the management and the general employees' committee headed by Erhard Kuballa, who had succeeded to the position held for many years by Fritz Böhm. A series of measures aimed at improving the cost and results situation was agreed. They included lean production and lean management measures, but also a socially acceptable reduction in the overall workforce. In the same year the number of employees fell from 39,319 to 36,657. Yield on turnover before tax improved as a result of the cost-cutting and restructuring measures from 1.8 to 3.6 percent, and turnover itself rose by 1.5 percent to 11.5 billion Deutschmarks (DM). A year later the total turnover was more than twelve billion DM, and the percentage yield 5.2 percent, even higher than the result which had been anticipated.

Recession and its consequences

When the wall dividing the two parts of Germany fell in November 1989, followed by a currency union on July 2nd, 1990 and German re-unification shortly afterwards, the way was clear for a domestic-market revival, despite the fact that the first signs of an international economic crisis were already evident on markets elsewhere. 1991 was accordingly a record year, as confirmed not only by

The third AUDI 80 model generation appeared in 1986

Many customers choose to collect their new cars direct from the factory

the output figures (451, 265 Audi cars produced) but also by the introduction of various new models. Within a single year, almost the entire product programme was renewed. The high level of market demand which resulted was reflected in the record turnover of 14.8 billion DM. In the following year, vehicle output was increased again, to 492,085 cars – not far short of the magic half a million. By now, however, the international recession was putting a brake on sales, and the unusually high level of domestic business triggered off by German reunification

The very latest techniques and procedures are evident in the production area

was also losing its initial impetus. Unsold stocks and the need to limit production by introducing short-time working were less welcome aspects of 1993, a year in which total vehicle output failed to reach more than a relatively modest 340,956 units.

In May 1992, Franz-Josef Kortüm came to Ingolstadt to run the newly created Marketing Division. On January 1st, 1993 he took over as Chief Executive from Dr. Ferdinand Piëch , who became Chairman of the Volkswagen Group Board of Management and also of the AUDI AG Supervisory Board.

Kortüm left the company in February 1994, his place being taken initially as spokesman of the AUDI AG Board of Management by Dr. Herbert Demel. Demel had joined the company in 1990 as Head of Development, Mechanical Assemblies, and had been appointed to the Board in March 1993 with responsibility for the Technical Development Division. He was nominated Chairman of the Board of Management in March 1994.

The employees' committee was involved in considerable activity as a result of the extensive internal structural changes which were in progress. In July 1993, Adolf Hochrein was chosen as its Chairman, a post which he held until January 1995, when Xaver Meier took over. With regard to representing the employees' interests, a rethinking process was necessary in view of new working procedures and more flexible working hours. The workforce's elected representatives currently have a more challenging part to play than ever before: the work previously performed in certain production areas is now being allocated to outside suppliers, development contracts are being placed with independent companies, production is being moved abroad in some cases and an element of competition is also present between the individual plants and companies of the VW Group. One of the major tests to be performed by the employees' committee will therefore be to ensure that restructuring processes are carried out in a socially acceptable manner but without placing the company's business success at risk. Retention of Ingolstadt and Neckarsulm as plant sites is clearly the top long-term priority. In May 1996, company management and the general employees' committee took an important step towards achieving this by signing the "Audi Plant and Employment Guarantee", which is intended to secure the Audi workforce's jobs and promote further employment until well beyond the year 2000.

Higher positioning, broader scope: the product programme

Hopes ran high in 1994 when it was time for a successor to the Audi 80 to be announced. This was the Audi A4, which made use of the company's new model designation system and was unveiled in Berlin at the end of October. The Audi A4 was received with great enthusiasm; its immediate success exceeded anything that had been anticipated. It was launched and entered volume production at a more rapid rate than any previous model in the company's history, and qualified within a very short time as one of AUDI's greatest successes. Together with the A6 and A8 models and the sporting S versions, it contributed towards a significant increase in total vehicle output in 1995, to 446,808 units.

Audi quattro models, 1985

"Audi in the Fast Lane": the press headlines were not sparing in their praise. The management's task was now to ensure that this comment remained valid for the future, by transforming AUDI AG into a genuinely global enterprise with additional production sites abroad and an extensive worldwide sales network. This task was tackled without delay, and at the same time plans are well advanced to expand the model range still further in the remaining years of this century.

The products

From 1985 onwards, the population has taken an increasingly close interest in ecological matters. AUDI AG not only responded to this trend, but was in fact one of the pioneers in many areas. In the Autumn of 1985, when the 1986 model year began to leave the assembly lines, the Audi 100 and Audi 200 were supplied with a fully galvanised bodyshell. This highly effective means of safeguarding against corrosion meant in practice a considerable gain in long-term quality and retention of value. At about the same time, the German International Automobile Exhibition (the "IAA") opened its doors in Frankfurt, with a full range of cars with low-pollution engines on the AUDI stand.

The third-generation Audi 80 (internal code B3) appeared in September 1986, accompanied in May 1987 by the more powerful Audi 90 with five-cylinder engine and revised body styling. Once again, both cars had a fully galvanised bodyshell. At the British Motor Show in Birmingham, held in 1988, Audi enlarged the midsize model range with the sporty Audi Coupé. At the same time the Ingolstadt engineers were working intensively on an open car: the Audi Cabriolet was shown at the "IAA" in 1989, initially as a design study.

Audi 80/90 (B3)

The true highlight of the model programme, however, was the Audi V8, with which the company took its first step into the premium model category. Powered at first by a 3.6-litre, 184 kW (250 bhp) light-alloy engine, the Audi V8 made its debut in October 1988 and impressed potential buyers immediately with a series of innovative technical details, such as permanent four-wheel drive, four valves per cylinder or electronic control for the four-speed automatic transmission. This new flagship of the Audi fleet, like the Audi 100 and 200 models, was produced in Neckarsulm. The five-cylinder engines also became available with four valves per cylinder at this juncture. From the Autumn of 1988 onwards the Audi 90 and also the new Audi Coupé, with quattro driveline in each case, were also offered with a 123 kW (170 bhp) 20-valve engine. They were followed in the Spring of 1989 by the Audi 200 quattro 20V (saloon and Avant), which obtained 162 kW (220 bhp) from the same engine thanks to a turbocharger. In the Summer of the same year the Audi quattro – now usually given the proud accolade "The Original" – also acquired the 20-valve turbocharged engine.

In 1990, a sports version of the Audi 80 with a 16-valve, four-cylinder engine was introduced.

The exclusive 4.2-litre Audi V8, 206 kW/280 bhp

Less can be more

Not that Audi's engineers were entirely occupied with high power outputs. The public was beginning to demand tangible evidence that industry was capable of working towards the "three-litre car" (by which the fuel consumption per 100 kilometres was meant, not the engine size). Environmental pollution, dying forests, sparing use of the earth's natural resources – such factors began to matter. Audi had already been working on the answer. It was the TDI: the turbocharged, direct-injection diesel engine. The first engine of this kind, a 2.5-litre five-cylinder unit, was shown in the Autumn of 1989 at the Frankfurt Motor Show, powering an Audi 100. After no less than thirteen years of research and development, Audi's engineers had succeeded in adapting a fuel injection principle previously only used for trucks in a manner which made it suitable for passenger cars as well. Until then almost all passenger-car diesels had been of the pre-combustion chamber type, with indirect fuel injection. In Audi's TDI engines, however, fuel was injected at very high pressure into the bowl-in-piston combustion chamber, metered with great accuracy by a sensitive electronic control system. The com-

Sectioned view of Audi TDI engine (1.9-litre four- or 2.5-litre five-cylinder)

A step up to the premium price segment: the Audi V8 (1988)

bustion air, compressed by the turbocharger and with its temperature reduced again by a charge-air intercooler, flowed through a specially formed inlet port which imparted the correct degree of swirl to it. This controlled turbulence ensured full atomisation of the fuel particles and a good combustion pattern. After the Audi technicians had succeeded in reducing the violent sound associated with the direct-injection combustion principle, there was no holding back the TDI engine. Audi direct injection was a low-loss, efficient process, resulting in the low fuel consumption that cars with TDI engines subsequently demonstrated

Audi 80 TDI with 1.9–litre, 66 kW (90 bhp) engine

in a series of impressive low-consumption runs:

- the European record of a modified Audi 100 TDI, which covered more than 4,818 kilometres on a single tank of fuel, equal to 1.76 litres per 100 km, at an average speed of 60.2 km/h (1989)

- once round the world in a standard Audi 80 TDI, distance 40,273 km, average speed 85.8 km/h, consumption 3.78 l/100 km (1992)

- a run organised by the German motoring club ADAC: 2,021 km at an average fuel consumption of 3.4 l/100 km (1993)

- the 1,079 km Vienna – Geneva economy run performed by an Audi 80 1.9 TDI, total consumption 29.9 litres, equivalent to 2.77 l/100 km at an average speed of 70 km/h (1994)

Audi was thus one of the first German automobile manufacturers to succeed in "taming" the direct-injection diesel engine sufficiently for use in upper midsize passsenger cars with no significant loss of refinement.

Alternative concepts

Audi took quite a different approach to environmental acceptability with the Audi duo, seen for the first time at the Geneva Motor Show. This is a standard Audi 100 Avant quattro

with a conventional front engine, but with an electric motor integrated into the quattro driveline at the rear differential. Either one or the other power unit can be engaged as required. This form of hybrid is primarily intended for special fields of operation, for instance as a public-authority vehicle. But it is more than an experimental design study: the "duo" is a practical means of testing alternative propulsion concepts as to their suitability for day-to-day traffic conditions. The most modern version so far, the Audi duo III, based on the A4 Avant, was completed in September 1996.

The early 1990s

1990 was a year in which several Audi anniversaries were celebrated. It was for instance twenty-five years since the re-introduction of the Audi brand name in 1965. The seven-millionth Audi since 1965 was also a notable landmark: it left the line on 9th January. The Audi quattro reached its tenth production year. It had originally been intended to produce only a small batch of 400 cars, but this "father of the all-wheel-drive passenger car" proved to be such a success among enthusiastic drivers that it remained Audi's top sports model for many years. The "Original quattro" was still being built, largely by hand, in Ingolstadt, away from the main assembly lines, and had lost none of initial fascination. Finally, on May 17th 1991, the 11,452nd and last quattro of the original series was produced, and immediately reserved for the AUDI AG's historic vehicle collection. The very first quattro had proved to be the most long-lived Audi model of all. Before production ceased, a potential successor had appeared on the scene; this was the Audi Coupé quattro S2, announced in October 1990.

The Audi duo was shown at the Geneva Motor Show in 1990

The seven-millionth Audi since 1965 left the assembly line on Jan. 9th, 1990

Audi Coupé quattro S2

1991 was also a significant year for Audi. Almost the complete product range appeared in revised form. Shortly before the end of the year the latest Audi 100 (known internally as the C4) was launched, including a six-cylinder version for the first time. The compact V6 engine of 2.8 litres' displacement, developing 128 kW (174 bhp), was shorter and lighter than any other engine in its class. It had a novel form of variable air intake system which ensured ample pulling power at low engine speeds without sacrificing peak power in the higher speed range.

At the Geneva Automobile Salon, held in the Spring of 1991, the long-awaited Audi Cabriolet was the centre of public interest. In the Summer, the Audi S4 was announced as the top model in the new Audi 100 line, powered by the well-proven five-cylinder, 20-valve turbocharged engine. Then came the German Motor Show in the Autumn, where the new Audi 80 (the B4 for internal purposes) and the Avant version of the Audi 100 were on display. The limelight, however, was stolen by a low-built sports coupé with V6 mid-engine and a sensational aluminium body: the Audi quattro Spyder. When the rumour began to spread that a small production run was perhaps envisaged, Audi dealers submitted hundreds of purchase options. But it was not to be: the target price of less

Audi Cabriolet with power-operated soft top

than 100,000 Deutschmarks proved impossible to achieve, and only the two prototypes were ever built.

Before the furore had died down, Audi amazed the motoring world yet again, this time at the Tokyo Motor Show a month later. A futuristic sports car design study in polished aluminium with a twelve-cylinder mid-engine of "W" layout was the centre of attention; the Audi Avus quattro. Although the engine installed in this potent, lightweight vehicle was only a dummy, keen observers of the motoring scene found the whole project highly significant. For some years Audi had been cooperating with the Aluminum Company of America (ALCOA) on the development of a lightweight all-aluminium production car. The aim was clear: for a worthwhile reduction in fuel consumption to be achieved without sacrificing either comfort, convenience or performance, cars would have to be made very much lighter. Compared with the equivalent steel structure, an aluminium body could well be 30 to 40 percent lighter. Furthermore, aluminium is a material that can be reprocessed an almost unlimited number of times without sacrificing its quality. The recycling situation is therefore very favourable: of the energy consumed by the foundry when producing aluminium, only about 20 percent is required to melt it down again, whereas the figure for steel scrap is in the region of 50 percent. All in all, aluminium exhibits an outstandingly good "energy balance sheet".

Start of a new era

The result of many years of research work in this field were presented to the public at the Frankfurt Motor Show in the Autumn of 1993. The design study

*Audi
Space Frame*

entitled "Audi Space Frame" (ASF) attracted a constant crowd of visitors, but not merely because of the remarkable new all-aluminium body. Under the bonnet was an equally innovating engine: a turbocharged V8 diesel with direct injection. Such a magnificent diesel engine, worthy of a large luxury car, was an entirely new departure. The body used convincing new structural principles which went far beyond the mere substitution of aluminium for steel. Together with ALCOA, AUDI had developed a framework in which every panel surface contributed to the load-bearing effect. Extruded aluminium sections were connected together by pressure-cast joint elements, and large-area sheet aluminium panels integrated into the resulting cellular structure.

New design principles naturally call for new production technologies. Improved aluminium alloys and process techniques resulted from the research work. In addition to welding and adhesive bonding, self-piercing rivets were used for the first time as connecting elements in the automobile industry. More than 40 patents either granted or applied for are ample evidence of the innovative thought that went into the development of the Audi Space Frame.

The "Aluminium Audi" celebrated its world première as the successor to the Audi V8 at the Geneva Motor Show in March 1994. The new model designation "A8" introduced a general renaming process within the Audi model programme. The new Audi 80, when launched in November 1994, continued this process, and was called the Audi A4. It also proved to be a trump card in an already successful hand. The saloon version was introduced first, and broke all market acceptance records. In Germany alone, almost 120,000 were sold by the end of 1995. In addition to the 1.6-litre four-cylinder, 74 kW (101 bhp) version, the A4 is also available with a new 1.8-litre four-cylinder engine. This comes in two power outputs: 92 kW (125 bhp) and in turbocharged form, rated at 110 kW

*Audi Space Frame
ASF Concept Car*

Audi A8

(150 bhp). The new engine's most remarkable feature is that it has five valves per cylinder. It is the forerunner of a new generation of Audi spark-ignition engines, and is manufactured in Györ, Hungary. In February 1996, the Avant version of the new A4 began to reach the market.

Audi A4 saloon

Power with feeling

Now that competition on international markets has become so severe, a modern automobile manufacturer cannot survive and prosper merely on the basis of outstanding quality, maximum safety and convincing technical design, however important these aspects

The TTS Roadster and its cockpit

may be. Emotional factors also play a decisive rôle in determining the marque's image. More often than not, the customer does not reach a decision on purely rational grounds. It was precisely with a view to arousing the onlooker's emotions that Audi presented two further design studies in the Autumn of 1995: the Audi TT Coupé at the German "IAA" and the Audi TTS Roadster at the Tokyo Motor Show. Both of these cars represent a successful visual blend of historic automobile design elements and modern styling. backed of course by well-proven modern technology: the four-cylinder turbo-charged engine with five valves per cylinder from the Audi A4, rated at 110 kW (150 bhp), in the TT Coupé, a sporting version of the same engine rated at 154 kW (210 bhp) in the TTS Roadster. Common to both these design studies: permanent four-wheel drive and a five-speed manual-shift gearbox. To ensure a compact mechanical layout (both the Coupé and the Roadster are only just over four metres long), the engine is transversely mounted at the front. The classically rounded body outlines give these sports-car design studies a most unusual persona. Enthusiasm was rife among the public, with one question of course being asked constantly: "Does Audi intend to build them?" In December 1995 the Audi Board of Management decided to do just that. This will add two models to the product range that offer one element of Audi driving in its purest form: pleasure!

Audi TT Coupé

An attractive range of models is essential for market success. The new "small" Audi, the A3, appeared in September 1996 and immediately won the hearts of new customer-groups in the compact automobile class.

An Audi model in the compact class: the Audi A3

Categories and generations

From the late nineteen-sixties onwards, Audi had retained the Audi 100 and Audi 80 names systematically for several model generations. The first Audi 100 was introduced in 1968, the second in 1976, the third in 1982 and the fourth in 1990.

In the case of the Audi 80, the first generation dating from 1972 was superseded by the second in 1978, followed by the third and fourth in 1986 and 1991.

In 1994, however, the entire model range was renamed according to a scheme which it was felt would be more easily understood and accepted by the public:

A4 is used for the model range equivalent to the previous Audi 80, in most cases with a four-cylinder engine. The first five-valve engines have now been introduced, as a means of complying with even more stringent exhaust emission limits in the near future. These engines are built at the factory in Györ, Hungary, opened in 1994.

A6 represents the previous Audi 100 model group, most of which are powered by the V6 engines that have been in producton since 1992.

A8 is the name for the successor to the previous Audi V8, with an engine that has in the meantime been increased in size to 4.2 litres and develops 220 kW (300 bhp). The A8 is also available with a 3.7-litre V8 or a 2.8-litre six-cylinder engine.

A3 was the name given to the newcomer to the Audi range in September 1996: the "small" Audi in the compact motoring class. The 1.8 l four-cylinder engine develops 92 kW (125 bhp), and a 1.9 l turbocharged direct injection diesel, also with four cylinders and rated at 66 kW (90 bhp) is also available. At the beginning of 1997, an entry-level model with 1.6 l, 74 kW (101 bhp) engine is scheduled to appear, and also a more sporting version with a 1.8 l five-valve turbocharged engine developing 110 kW (150 bhp).

Audi has adopted the designation "S" (standing for 'supreme', 'safe' and 'sporting') as a means of identifying the high-performance models with standard quattro driveline in its range.

Whereas the S1 sport quattro evolution model dating from 1985 was still a pure rally vehicle, the 1990 Audi Coupé quattro S2 was conceived as a pure road-

Four generations of the Audi 100, seen when the three-millionth car bearing this name was produced in March 1992

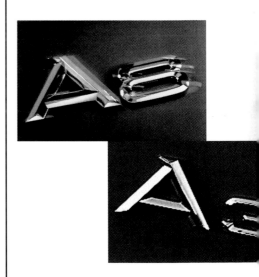

The new-generation model designations

going car and a successor to the original quattro model. From 1993 onwards, it was joined by the Avant S2 and the S2 saloon, in each case using the Audi 80 bodyshell. In May 1991 the Audi S4 was announced, a sports saloon based on the Audi 100; the Avant version was available from September onwards. "S" were originally powered by the five-cylinder 20-valve turbocharged engine, but from the end of 1992 the S4 Avant was also available with 4.2-litre eight cylinder power.

The S4 4.2 l saloon followed in March of the following year.

When the Audi A6 was launched in June 1994, S6 sports models (saloon and Avant) were also available with the five- or the eight-cylinder engine.

The Audi Avant RS2, developed in cooperation with Porsche, occupies a special position. This exclusive high-performance sports estate car, of which 2,891 were built between Autumn 1993 and July 1995, was based on the Audi 80 Avant.

The ultimate models in this group are currently the Audi S8 (based on the A8) and the Audi S6 plus (based on the A6 saloon and Avant). They both have an uprated 4.2-litre V8 engine, and were introduced in the Spring of 1996 at the Geneva Motor Show.

The Audi 100 became the A6 under the new naming system

Audi Cabriolet, 1995 model year

Ferdinand Piëch

1937	Born on April 17th in Vienna, son of lawyer Dr. Anton Piëch and his wife Louise, née Porsche
1962	Graduate diploma from the Cantonal Technical High School in Zürich, Switzerland
1963	Joined the Dr.-Ing. h.c. F. Porsche KG company in Stuttgart-Zuffenhausen in the engine testing department
1966	Head of experimental work at Porsche KG
1968	Head of technical development for Porsche KG
1971	General technical manager of Porsche KG
1972	Joined AUDI NSU AUTO UNION AG as head of the technical development section with special duties
1973	In charge of the entire experimental division
1974	Head of technical development
1975	Appointed to the board of management of AUDI NSU AUTO UNION AG with responsibility for the complete technical development division
1984	In recognition of his achievements in the field of automobile construction, Ferdinand Piëch was granted an honorary doctorate in Technical Sciences by Vienna Technical University
1988	Chairman of the Board of Management, AUDI AG
1993	Chairman of the Board of Management, Volkswagen AG

Dr. Ferdinand Piëch

"Developments heralded in by a roll of drums have to be appropriately timed, and at the moment, evolution is the order of the day instead. In 1982, when we introduced the C3, people were waiting for something like it to appear; they responded very sensitively to every movement from within the technical world. The car with the world's best aerodynamics was just what was needed at the time. Today, things are rather different: most people, above all the classic customers for this class of car, are looking for careful attention to detail, a well-balanced car as a whole and a better general ambience inside it."

Dr. Ferdinand Piëch talking to "Industriemagazin" about the Audi 100 C4 at the end of 1990.

The principal Audi models

Type	Number/layout of cylinders	Bore x s in mm
100	5 inline	81 x 77.
100 TDI	5 inline	81 x 95.
200 quattro 20V	5 inline	81 x 86.
80	4 inline	81 x 86.
80 Turbo Diesel	4 inline	76.5 x 8
90 20V	5 inline	82.5 x 8
V8	V8	81 x 86.
Coupé	5 inline	82.5 x 8
100/2.3 E	5 inline	82.5 x 8
100/2.8 E	V6	82.5 x 8
S4	5 inline	81 x 96.
80	4 inline	82.5 x 9
Cabriolet	5 inline	82.5 x 8
80 TDI	4 inline	79.5 x 8
S2	5 inline	81 x 86.
RS2	5 inline	81 x 86.
A8	V8	84.5 x 9
S8	V8	84.5 x 9
A6	V6	82.5 x 8
A6 TDI	5 inline	81 x 95.
S6	5 inline	81 x 96.
A4	4 inline	81 x 86.
A3	4 inline	81 x 86.

Dr. Herbert Demel

gine size cc	kW/bhp	Years of manufacture
94	84/115	1984–1987
60	88/120	1989–1990
26	162/220	1989–1991
81	55/75	1986–1989
00	50/80	1988–1991
09	123/167	1987–1991
62	184/250	1988–1994
09	98/133	1988–1994
09	98/133	1990–1994
71	128/174	1990–1994
26	169/230	1991–1994
84	85/115	1991–1994
09	98/133	1991–1994
96	66/90	1991–1994
26	169/230	1991–1996
26	232/315	1994–1995
72	220/300	Since 1994
72	250/340	Since 1996
71	128/174	Since 1994
61	103/140	Since 1994
26	169/230	Since 1994
81	92/125	Since 1994
81	92/125	Since 1996

1985–1996

Herbert Demel

1953	Born on 14th October in Vienna
1971	Studied mechanical engineering at Vienna Technical University; graduate engineer's diploma
1978	Technical and scientific assistant at the Institute for Combustion Engines and Motor Vehicle Construction
1981	Doctorate in Technical Sciences
1984	Joined Robert Bosch GmbH in Stuttgart with responsibility for coordination of anti-lock braking system applications
1985	Head of ABS/ASR applications
1988	Head of main ABS/ASR department and quality assurance
1989	Also assumed responsibility for transmission control development department
1990	Joined AUDI AG in Ingolstadt as head of development, mechanical assemblies
1993	On March 1st. appointed to the Board of Management with responsibility for the Technical Development division
1994	On February 4th, appointed AUDI AG Board spokesman with additional responsibility for Technical Development and Marketing/Sales
1995	From March 22nd onwards, Chief Executive of AUDI AG

"People have become far more aware of ecological matters and no longer value excessive status symbols quite as highly. They have also taken a liking to greater individuality. These are all things that harmonise with our new car: it is made of aluminium that can be fully recycled, it is not an exaggerated status symbol and for this reason it is ideal for the individualist. The Audi A8 is a very intelligent alternative. In view of the outstanding qualities of the Audi A8 and its understated character, potential customers will ask themselves whether they still need the status that other brands allegedly offered them."

Dr. Herbert Demel in an interview on the new Audi A8 in May 1994.

Motor sport successes as the century draws to a close

1982 was a year that ushered in a series of magnificent rally successes; it was the year in which Audi first won the manufacturers' world rally championship. In 1983, Hannu Mikkola secured the first driver's world championship title at the wheel of the Audi. After further outstanding successes in 1984 and success in both categories of the world championship, Audi was runner-up in the manufacturers' category in 1985, with Blomqvist/Cederberg second and Röhrl/Geistdörfer third among the works teams. With 23 victories in only five years, the Audi quattro was one of the most successful cars ever entered for world

The Monte Carlo Rally, 1986; Walter Röhrl and Christian Geistdörfer in the Audi Sport quattro S1

rally championship events. Even in the Far East it fascinated hundreds of thousands of spectators: Hannu Mikkola and Arne Hertz won the Hong Kong - Peking Rally on the first occasion it was staged.

The 1986 season was overshadowed by a tragic accident during the Portugal Rally, when the local driver Joaquim Santos lost control of his Ford Sierra Cosworth and careered into a group of spectators. Since the organisers of the various world championship events were unable to agree on measures capable of guaranteeing the safety of spectators lining the routes and of the drivers themselves, Audi decided to withdraw from Group B rallying.

Mountain-climbers, sprinters and marathon runners

In 1987, after the potent Group B cars had been banished to museums and only Group A events were to be held, Audi returned to the world rally championship. Driving the Audi 200 quattro, Hannu Mikkola pulled off his first victory in the notorious Safari Rally in Kenya.

In 1989 AUDI entered the Audi 90 quattro in the US IMSA-GTO series

The 1987 Pikes Peak race in Colorado, USA: Walter Röhrl storms to the top

At the Pikes Peak hillclimb in Colorado, USA, his team colleague Walter Röhrl caused an outright sensation. Driving a 598 bhp Audi Sport quattro S1, he reached the top in record time. This was the third time in succession that an Audi driver had stood on the podium in first place: in 1985 Michèle Mouton and a year later Bobby Unser had also hurled the Audi Sport quattro S1 up the Pikes Peak track in record times. 1978 was also a good year for private Audi entrants Armin Schwarz and H.J. Hösch. They carried off both the drivers' and the manufacturers' categories in the German Rally championship.

The Audi quattro driveline principle does not only perform outstandingly well on loose stones, mud, snow or ice. To prove this, Audi entered for the American Trans-Am series in 1988. The Audi team, with drivers Hurley Haywood, Walter Röhrl and Hans-Joachim Stuck, tackled the 13 circuit races making up this American production-car championship in modified Audi 200 quattros. Despite the anticipated strong competition from American drivers and the imposition of unexpected restrictions such as an increase in the cars' minimum weight, Audi had the title in its pocket by the time the tenth race had been run. Hurley Haywood carried off the drivers' championship title. Back in Germany, Armin Schwarz successfully defended his previous year's German Rally title at the wheel of an Audi 200 quattro.

Audi 200 quattro Trans Am (1989)

Audi 90 quattro IMSA-GTO (1989)

The Audi team spent another successful season in the USA in 1989. This time the challenge was the IMSA-GTO series. For this demanding production sports

car series, the Audi Motor Sport Department had prepared a car based on the Audi 90 quattro, with a five-cylinder 20-valve turbocharged engine from which no fewer than 620 horsepower had been coaxed. This was enough to propel the car, which weighed about 1,200 kg, to a top speed of more than 310 km/h. With a total of seven victories, including five with Audi in first and second place, second place was secured at the end of the season, Stuck and Audi failing to capture the championship title only because the cars were not entered for the long-distance events in Sebring and Daytona.

Motor sport successes with the V8

In 1990, Audi returned to Germany triumphant. For the first time now, the Audi V8 quattro was prepared for racing. The results far surpassed what had initially seemed possible with a car not originally intended for motor sport, and in particular confounded the critics who were wont to refer to this car as the "chauffeur-driven racer". After a dramatic season, Hans-Joachim Stuck won a sensational final race at the Hockenheim Ring to secure the German Touring Car Championship (GTC) title.

Audi drivers:
H.J. Stuck, F. Jelinski,
F. Biela, W. Röhrl
(from left)

The following year, four Audi V8s were on the starting grid. Biela, Jelinski and Haupt joined Stuck in the team. The final, unbelievably dramatic race on the Hockenheim Ring was the decisive one: Biela won both heats, and the title was Audi's! It had become the first automobile manufacturer in the history of the German touring car championship to defend its title successfully.

After the two GTC wins (Hans-Joachim Stuck in 1990, Frank Biela in 1991), Audi regarded the 1992 season as something of a transitional period, without the specific objective of defending the championship title again. The competition department in Ingolstadt was already looking ahead to 1993, when new rules would apply to entrants' cars. In any case, the Supreme National Motor Sport Authority (the "ONS") issued a verdict in mid-season that the crankshaft used in the Audi V8 quattro did not conform

For the 1992 GTC season, the Audi V8 quattro appeared in new red-and-silver livery

with its rules, so that it became impossible for Audi to continue to participate in GTC events. This was despite the fact that the ONS had accepted the Audi crankshaft not once but twice before the season began.

For the rest of the season Hans-Joachim Stuck and Frank Biela took part most successfully in Touring Car Championship events in South Africa and France.

France, as one of Audi's most important export markets, was where Audi's racing activities were concentrated in 1993. Frank Biela drove a 272 bhp Audi 80 quattro in the French "Supertourisme" championship, and was victorious at the end of the season. Together with team colleague Marc Sourd, he also won the

The "Audi 80 competition" was entered for D1 ADAC Touring Car Cup events held according to the internationally valid two-litre formula

266

manufacturer's title for Audi, in a series of races that was strongly contested from start to finish.

New drivers, fresh victories

From this time onwards, Audi's motor sport activities switched to the 2-litre class. The D1 ADAC Touring Car Cup, held for the first time in 1994, enabled the Ingolstadt company to run its Audi 80 "competition" in front of a German public once again. Frank Biela demonstrated a strong claim to the title with a series of convincing wins in the early part of the season. When the results were added up at the end, however, he had failed to maintain his lead by one solitary point, and had to surrender the trophy to BMW driver Johnny Cecotto. Team-mate Emanuele Pirro, also driving the Audi 80 "competition", had rather better luck in the Italian Touring Car Championship, held at the same time. Both the drivers' and the manufacturers' titles fell to the cars with the four-ring badge in that country.

Ten years after the retirement of Audi's highly successful woman rally driver Michèle Mouton, another woman driver took charge of a competition Audi: Tamara Vidali from Italy. She joined the team which was entered to drive the Audi A4 Supertouring in the German D1 ADAC Super-touring Cup events and also in Italian touring car championship races. Also new to the team: Altfried Heger from Essen, who drove in the German races together with Biela, Stuck and Vidali. In Italy Emanuele Pirro was joined by Rinaldo Capello, as in the previous season. Once again, Audi started the season with a flourish and was in commanding position by the time half the Supertouring Cup events had been run. Then luck deserted the team again, and after the final race Biela, Stuck and Heger found themselves only in places three to five. In Italy, on the other hand,

Michèle Mouton and Tamara Vidali

the team's efforts were crowned with the deserved success. Emanuele Pirro won eleven of his 20 races – a new record for the event. He had no difficulty in defending his championship title, and in helping to capture the manufacturers' trophy once again for Audi. Runner-up was his team-mate Rinaldo Capello. Frank Biela too was able to celebrate a truly outstanding win as the season drew to a close. He triumphed in the FIA Touring World Cup final, becoming Supertouring World Champion for the first time, followed by Emanuele Pirro, who came in second overall. Audi had no cause to regret its switch from the GTC to the two-litre near-production touring car race series. Apart from its works entries, it supported importers' entries in the national 2-litre championships held in Belgium, Australia and South Africa. Other importers are taking a keen interest in similar series in their own countries, in view of the powerful image boost for the marque which success clearly brings in its train.

For the 1996 racing season, Audi's head of motor sport Dr. Wolfgang Ullrich decided to enter his cars for the British touring car championship as well as for the events in Germany and Italy. In addition, the Audi A4 Supertouring competed in national touring car championship series in Belgium, Spain, Australia and South Africa, backed by the local importers in each case. This stronger Audi motorsport presence was rewarded in the most convincing possible way: with no less than seven national championship titles.

In 1995 as in the previous season, Emanuele Pirro captured the Italian Touring Car Championship title, this time at the wheel of the Audi A4 Superturismo

*Audi drivers:
S. Blomqvist,
H. J. Stuck,
R. Capello, E. Pirro,
F. Biela, P. Peter,
K. Wendlinger*

AUDI – an overview

Audi 80 (1986)

Audi 100 (face-lift, 1988 model year) saloon and Avant

Audi 90 (1987)

Audi 200 quattro 20V (1989)

Audi quattro
(the "original
quattro",1991)

Audi Coupé (1988)

Audi V8 (1988)

Audi V8 LWB (1988)

AUDI – an overview

Audi Coupé S2 (1990)

Audi 100 (1990)

Audi 100 Avant (1991)

Audi Cabriolet (1991)

Audi 80 (1991)

Audi quattro Spyder
(1991)

Audi Avus quattro
(1991)

Audi 80 Avant (1992)

Audi Avant RS 2
(1993)

Audi A8 (1994)

Audi A4 (1994)

Audi A6 (1994)   *Audi A6 Avant (1994)*

*Audi TTS design
study (1995)*

Audi A4 Avant (1995)

Audi TT design study (1995)

Audi A3 (1996)

Audi A4 Avant duo (1996)

Publisher's data

Published by:

AUDI AG, Public Relations,
85045 Ingolstadt, Germany; Tel. (++) 841-89-3888

Archives and sources:

Prussian Cultural Heritage archives, Berlin; Volkswagen AG archives, Wolfsburg;
authors' archives; August-Horch Museum, Zwickau; AUTO UNION archives,
Ingolstadt; Ullstein Picture Archive, Berlin; Federal German Archives, Koblenz;
NSU GmbH company archives; Saxon State Library/Deutsche Fotothek, Dresden;
Süddeutscher Verlag, Munich; Wolff & Tritschler, Offenburg.

Text:

Prof. Peter Kirchberg, Thomas Erdmann, Ralph Plagmann

Translation:

Colin Brazier, Munich

Artwork, design, layout and DTP:

Queen Advertising Agency, Munich, Stefanie Wagner

Blockmaking:

Network Casdorff, Munich

Printing:

Passavia Druckerei, Hutthurm

Print run: 40,000. Available from Audi Info Service,
Tel. (++) 8458-329521, Fax (++) 8458-329519   © Status: 9/96

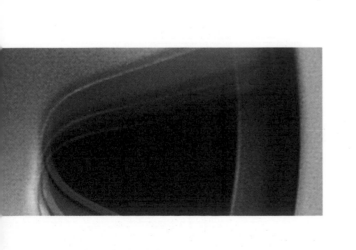